NEW TESTAMENT
THEOLOGY

NEW
TESTAMENT
THEOLOGY

Basic Issues
in the Current Debate

by
GERHARD F. HASEL

WILLIAM B. EERDMANS PUBLISHING COMPANY

Grand Rapids, Michigan

Copyright © 1978 by Wm. B. Eerdmans Publishing Co.
255 Jefferson Ave. S.E., Grand Rapids, Mich. 49503

All rights reserved

Printed in the United States of America

Library of Congress Cataloging in Publication Data

Hasel, Gerhard F.
  New Testament Theology.

  Bibliography: p. 221.
  Includes indexes.
  1. Bible. N.T.—Theology.   2. Theology—Methodology
I. Title.
BS2397.H34   230   78-4830
ISBN 0-8028-1733-5

Contents

Abbreviations

AUSS	Andrews University Seminary Studies
BTB	Biblical Theology Bulletin
CBQ	Catholic Biblical Quarterly
EOTH	*Essays on Old Testament Hermeneutics,* ed. Claus Westermann (Richmond, Va., 1963)
ET	Expository Times
EvTh	Evangelische Theologie
IDB	*Interpreter's Dictionary of the Bible,* 4 vols. (Nashville, 1962)
IDB Sup.	*Interpreter's Dictionary of the Bible. Supplementary Volume* (Nashville, 1976)
JBL	Journal of Biblical Literature
JBR	Journal of Bible and Religion
NNTT	R. Morgan, *The Nature of New Testament Theology* (SBT II/25; London, 1973)
NTS	New Testament Studies
OTCF	*The Old Testament and Christian Faith,* ed. B. W. Anderson (New York, 1963)

PTNT	*Das Problem der Theologie des Neuen Testaments,* ed. G. Strecker (Darmstadt, 1975)
SBT	Studies in Biblical Theology
ThQ	Theologische Quartalschrift
ThLZ	Theologische Literaturzeitung
ZAW	Zeitschrift für alttestamentliche Wissenschaft
ZNW	Zeitschrift für neutestamentliche Wissenschaft
ZThK	Zeitschrift für Theologie und Kirche

Introduction

New Testament theology today is undeniably in crisis. This does not mean that there is no interest in the academic study of the theology of the NT or that there is a lack of monographs that carry the title Theology of the New Testament or the like. As a matter or fact, although in the roughly two hundred years of the existence of the discipline of NT theology there has never been a decade in which more than ten different NT theologies were published, this unlikely event did occur between 1967 and 1976.[1] It is a surprising fact

[1]The first NT theology of this decade was published by H. Conzelmann, *Grundriss der Theologie des Neuen Testaments* (Munich, 1967), Eng. trans. *An Outline of the Theology of the New Testament* (New York, 1969); K. H. Schelkle, *Theologie des Neuen Testaments*, 4 vols. (Düsseldorf, 1968-74), Eng. trans. *Theology of the New Testament*, 4 vols. (Collegeville, Minn., 1971-77); W. G. Kümmel, *Die Theologie des Neuen Testaments nach seinen Hauptzeugen: Jesus-Paulus-Johannes* (Göttingen, 1969), Eng. trans. *The Theology of the New Testament According to Its Major Witnesses: Jesus-Paul-John* (Nashville, 1973); J. Jeremias, *Neutestamentliche Theologie. Erster Teil: Die Verkündigung Jesu* (Gütersloh, 1971), Eng. trans. *New Testament Theology: The Proclamation of Jesus* (New York, 1971); M. G. Cordero, *Teología de la Biblia II et III: Nuevo Testamento*, 2 vols. (Madrid, 1972); G. E. Ladd, *A Theology of the New Testament* (Grand Rapids, Mich., 1974); C. R. Lehmann, *Biblical Theology, 2: New Testament* (Scottdale, Pa., 1974); E. Lohse, *Grundriss der neutestamentlichen Theologie* (Stuttgart, 1974); L. Goppelt, *Theologie des Neuen Testaments*, 2 vols. (Göttingen, 1975-76); S. Neill, *Jesus Through Many Eyes. Introduction to the Theology of the New Testament* (Nashville, 1976); A. T. Nikolainen, *Uuden Testamentin Tulkinta ja tutkimus* (Porvoo-Helsinki, 1971).

that no two scholars who produced works agree on the nature, function, method, and scope of NT theology. Norman Perrin of the University of Chicago began a recent position paper on NT theology with the categorical statement, "The academic study of the theology of the New Testament is today in a state of disarray."[2] The German post-Bultmannian scholar E. Käsemann has come back time and again to essential aspects of NT theology. In a recent essay on the subject he reflects on William Wrede's programmatic essay written in 1897[3] and concludes that in this "unrivalled penetration, radical reflection and brilliantly concise concentration on essentials, the author [Wrede] revealed the cul-de-sac in which we still are today—or to which we have once again returned."[4] This assessment is not unrelated to the views of James A. Robinson.[5] R. Morgan of the University of Lancaster is certainly correct in stating that "New Testament theology is a nodal point in contemporary theological debate."[6] This debate goes on at full force and is at times heated.

Many basic issues in the contemporary debate on NT theology are not unrelated to those in OT theology.[7] In both instances the debate is concerned with fundamental problems and not with peripheral aspects. This may be illustrated by means of the question of the place of Jesus in NT theology. R. Bultmann begins his famous NT theology with this sentence: "The message of Jesus

[2]N. Perrin, "Jesus and the Theology of the New Testament," read at the Catholic Biblical Association, Denver, Colo., Aug. 18-21, 1975.

[3]W. Wrede, "Über Aufgabe und Methode der sogenannten Neutestamentlichen Theologie," Das Problem der Theologie des Neuen Testaments, ed. G. Strecker (Darmstadt, 1975), pp. 81-154, Eng. trans. "The Task and Methods of 'New Testament Theology,'" by R. Morgan, The Nature of New Testament Theology (SBT 2/25; London, 1973), pp. 68-116.

[4]E. Käsemann, "The Problem of a New Testament Theology," New Testament Studies 19 (1973), 237.

[5]J. A. Robinson, "The Future of New Testament Theology," Religious Study Review 2 (1976), 17-23.

[6]R. Morgan, The Nature of New Testament Theology, p. 1.

[7]See Gerhard F. Hasel, Old Testament Theology:Basic Issues in the Current Debate (2nd ed.; Grand Rapids, Mich., 1975).

is a presupposition for the theology of the NT rather than a part of that theology itself."[8] He believes that NT theology proper begins with the theology of Paul. After long reflection Perrin has come to accept Bultmann's dictum. Perrin now believes that the proclamation of Jesus is "the presupposition of the New Testament."[9] As such it is not a proper part of NT theology. While Bultmann includes the "message of Jesus" as a part of his history-of-religion introduction to NT theology,[10] E. Käsemann and G. Strecker begin their lectures on NT theology with the theology of Paul.[11] H. Conzelmann has omitted a section on the message of Jesus in his NT theology. W. G. Kümmel[12] and E. Lohse[13] are on the other side of the spectrum. Both start with the proclamation of Jesus. J. Jeremias is a senior member of this debate and treats the message of Jesus in a whole first volume on NT theology.[14] The British scholar S. Neill states unhesitatingly in his latest work on NT theology, "Every theology of the New Testament must be a theology of Jesus—or it is nothing at all."[15]

Deep historical, theological, philosophical, and methodological problems are hidden behind these disparate positions. The issues underlying these positions can be best appreciated and understood on the basis of the historical development of NT studies in general and NT theology in particular. This is the reason for beginning our discussion of the basic issues in the contemporary debate on NT theology with a historical survey of the beginnings and development of NT theology

[8]R. Bultmann, *Theology of the New Testament* (London, 1965), I, 3.

[9]N. Perrin, *The New Testament: An Introduction* (New York, 1974). See the title of the twelfth and last chapter.

[10]Bultmann, *Theology of the NT*, I, 3-32.

[11]G. Strecker, "Das Problem der Theologie des Neuen Testaments," *Das Problem der Theologie des NT*, pp. 1-31, esp. 30; Käsemann, "The Problem of a NT Theology," p. 243.

[12]Kümmel, *The Theology of the NT*, pp. 22-135.

[13]Lohse, *Grundriss der ntl. Theologie*, pp. 18-50.

[14]Jeremias, *NT Theology: The Proclamation of Jesus* (1971).

[15]Neill, *Jesus Through Many Eyes*, p. 10.

(Chapter I). It is a truism that the present has its roots
in the past and cannot be adequately understood without
a knowledge of it. The selection of issues in the current
debate in terms of the question of methodology (Chapter II), the various problems associated with the center
of the NT (Chapter III), and a variety of aspects related to NT theology and the OT, i.e., the relationship
between the Testaments (Chapter IV), do not aim to be
exhaustive or complete. They seek to touch on those
factors and issues that seem to exercise contemporary
scholars of various schools of thought and are major
unresolved problems. On the basis of our discussion we
attempt to provide some preliminary suggestions for
doing NT theology (Chapter V). A fairly comprehensive
bibliography seeks to serve as a resource tool for further
study and personal research. It is hoped that the reader
will be stimulated to engage in informed and creative
thinking as he acquaints himself with basic issues in
the current debate on NT theology.

I. Beginnings and Development of NT Theology

This chapter provides a historical survey of major trends from the beginnings of Biblical theology. Special emphasis is placed upon the development of NT theology[1] from the early part of the nineteenth century[2] to the beginning decades of this century. The current debate about the scope, purpose, nature, and function of NT theology, and even the fundamental question whether NT theology is possible,[3] have their roots in the past, and often the distant past. New Testament theology is an offshoot from Biblical theology, and thus they must be studied together.

[1]Among leading histories of NT theology are the following: R. Schnackenburg, *Neutestamentliche Theologie. Stand der Forschung* (2nd ed.; Munich, 1965), Eng. trans. made from 1st ed. of 1963: *New Testament Theology Today* (London, 1963); H.-J. Kraus, *Die Biblische Theologie. Ihre Geschichte und Problematik* (Neukirchen-Vluyn, 1970); O. Merk, *Biblische Theologie des Neuen Testaments in ihrer Anfangszeit* (Marburg, 1972); W. Harrington, *The Path of Biblical Theology* (Dublin, 1973); L. Goppelt, *Theologie des Neuen Testaments* (Göttingen, 1975), pp. 19-51; G. Strecker, "Das Problem der Theologie des Neuen Testaments," in *Das Problem der Theologie des Neuen Testaments* (Darmstadt, 1975), pp. 1-31.

[2]The first NT theology of the century was published by G. L. Bauer, *Biblische Theologie des Neuen Testaments* (Leipzig, 1800-1802).

[3]This has been again radically questioned by J. M. Robinson, "Die Zukunft der neutestamentlichen Theologie," *Neues Testament und christliche Existenz. Festschrift für H. Braun zum 70. Geburtstag am 4. Mai 1973,* ed. H. D. Betz (Tübingen, 1973), pp. 387-400; Eng. trans. "The Future of New Testament Theology," *Religious Studies Review* 2 (1976), 17-23.

A. From the Reformation to the Enlightenment

The post-NT church of the early Christian centuries developed neither a Biblical theology nor a NT theology. The reason was the dictum that the content of the canonical writings, if rightly understood, was identical with the dogma of the church, which was believed to be of universal validity.[4] During the Middle Ages the Roman Catholic Church regarded the NT, like the OT, as a part of the ecclesiastical tradition.[5] The NT was not read apart from or over against that tradition, but more or less interpreted by that tradition or brought into harmony with it.

The Reformation freed itself from ecclesiastical tradition and scholastic theology[6] and employed as her battle cry the Protestant principle of "sola scriptura."[7] With this principle Scripture was no longer interpreted by tradition. An authority superior to tradition was recognized in Scripture, which resulted in the self-interpretation of Scripture (*sui ipsius interpres*),[8] and became the sources for the subsequent development of Biblical theology.

Among the Reformers Martin Luther's contribution was particularly significant.[9] He ultimately rejected the

---

[4]O. Kuss, "Zur Hermeneutik Tertullians," *Schriftauslegung, Beiträge zur Hermeneutik des NT und im NT,* ed. J. Ernst (Munich, 1972), pp. 55-87.

[5]W. G. Kümmel, *The New Testament: The History of the Investigation of Its Problems* (Nashville, 1972), pp. 13-19.

[6]Decisive impulses toward this are found in humanism, particularly through Erasmus (cf. E. W. Kohls, *Die Theologie des Erasmus* [Basel, 1966], I, 126ff.; H. Schlingensiepen, "Erasmus als Exeget," *Zeitschrift für Kirchengeschichte* II [1929], 16-57), Laurentius Valla (cf. E. Mühlenberg, "Laurentius Valla als Renaissancetheologe," *ZThK* 66 [1969], 466-480), and Cajetan (G. Hennig, *Cajetan und Luther* [Stuttgart, 1967]). These humanists considered that Scripture and tradition stood next to each other but ecclesiastical authority remained supreme.

[7]The function of "sola scriptura" in the pre-Reformation period is summarized by H. Oberman, *The Harvest of Medieval Theology* (2nd ed.; Grand Rapids, Mich., 1967), pp. 201. 361-363, 377, 380-390.

[8]G. Ebeling, "The Meaning of 'Biblical Theology,' " *Word and Faith* (London, 1963), pp. 81-86.

[9]See K. Holl, "Luthers Bedeutung für den Fortschritt der Auslegungskunst," *Gesammelte Aufsätze zur Kirchengeschichte* (6th ed.;

fourfold sense of Scripture[10] and developed his "new" hermeneutic between 1516 and 1519. The emphasis on the contrast between "letter and spirit" (*littera et spiritus*),[11] the determining distinction of "law and gospel" (*lex et evangelium*),[12] and the christological principle "what manifests Christ" ("was Christum treibet")[13] mark the essence of Luther's "new" hermeneutic of "sola scriptura." The principle of "sola scriptura" functions for Luther in a twofold sense: (1) the distinction between Christ and Scripture, i.e., true Scripture is "what manifests Christ," and (2) the resulting distinction between law and gospel.[14] With these distinctions Luther has cast a long shadow reaching into our own time in the form of the questions concerning the unity of the Bible (and the NT)[15] as well as the issue of "the canon within the canon."[16]

Tübingen, 1932), I, 544-582; F. Hahn, "Luthers Auslegungsgrundsätze und ihre theologischen Voraussetzungen," *Zeitschrift für system. Theologie* 12 (1934), 165-218; G. Ebeling, "Die Anfänge von Luthers Hermeneutik," *ZThK* 48 (1951), 172-230.

[10]See his lectures on Galatians (*WA* 57, pp. 95f.) and Romans (*WA* 56, pp. 175-439) and also *WA* 2, pp. 249ff.; *WA* 5, pp. 644ff.

[11]See, for example, *WA* 3, pp. 11-17, 254-257, 456f.

[12]For example, *WA* 4, pp. 45-49, 97, 135, 174-176. P. Schempp, *Luthers Stellung zur Heiligen Schrift* (Munich, 1929), pp. 70-78.

[13]See *WA, DB* 7, p. 384; *WA* 3, p. 492; *WA* 4, p. 379; *WA* 39 I, p. 47: Theses 41, 49, 51; cf. Ebeling, *Word and Faith*, pp. 82f.

[14]Merk, *Biblische Theologie des NT*, pp. 11f.

[15]See A. Stock, *Einheit des Neuen Testaments* (Zurich/Einsiedeln, Köln, 1969); A. Kümmel, "Mitte des Neuen Testaments," *L'Évangile hier et aujourd'hui. Melanges offerts au F.-J. Leenhardt* (Geneva, 1968), pp. 71-85; F. Courth, "Der historische Jesus als Auslegungsnorm des Glaubens," *Münchener Theologische Zeitschrift* 25 (1974), 301-316; W. Schrage, "Die Frage nach der Mitte und dem Kanon im Kanon des Neuen Testaments in der neueren Diskussion," *Rechtfertigung. Festschrift für E. Käsemann zum 70. Geburtstag*, eds. J. Friedrich, W. Pöhlman, and P. Stuhlmacher (Tübingen, 1976), pp. 415-442.

[16]See E. Käsemann, ed., *Das Neue Testament als Kanon. Dokumentation und kritische Analyse zur Gegenwärtigen Diskussion* (Göttingen, 1970). J. Barr (*The Bible in the Modern World* [New York, 1973], pp. 30-40) claims the Bible is "soteriologically functional." Inge Lönning, *Kanon im Kanon. Zum dogmatischen Grundlagenproblem des neutestamentlichen Kanons* ("Forschungen zur Geschichte und Lehre des Protestantismus" (10/XLIII) (Munich, 1972); F. Mildenberger, "The Unity, Truth, and Validity of the Bible," *Interpretation* 29 (1977), 391-405, esp. 399-404.

Luther and the other Reformers did not apply the hermeneutical consequences of the "sola scriptura" principle to the total realm of theology and thus they did not develop what became known to be the discipline of Biblical theology. The designation "Biblical theology" is in itself ambiguous, because it can be used in a twofold sense: (1) It can designate a theology which has its roots in the teaching of Scripture and bases its foundation on Scripture,[17] or (2) it can designate the theology which the Bible itself contains.[18] In the latter sense it is a specific theological discipline which became bifurcated along the lines of OT theology[19] and NT theology at the turn of the eighteenth to the nineteenth century.[20]

Precursors of those who developed the term "Biblical theology" belonged to the Radical Reformation, i.e., the Anabaptist movement,[21] notably Oswald Glait and Andreas Fischer in the early 1530s.[22] But it was not

[17]In this sense F. C. Baur (*Vorlesungen über neutestamentliche Theologie,* ed. F. F. Baur [Leipzig, 1864], p. 2) and before him D. Schenkel ("Die Aufgabe der Biblischen Theologie in dem gegenwärtigen Entwicklungsstadium der theologischen Wissenschaft," *Theologische Studien und Kritiken* 25 [1852], 40-66, esp. 42-44) suggested that the Reformers engaged in "Biblical theology."

[18]W. Wrede, *Über Aufgabe und Methode der sogenannten Neutestamentlicher Theologie* (Göttingen, 1897), p. 79, reprinted in *Das Problem der Theologie des Neuen Testament,* ed. G. Strecker (Darmstadt, 1975), pp. 81-154, esp. p. 153; Eng. trans. "The Task and Methods of 'New Testament Theology,' " by R. Morgan, *The Nature of New Testament Theology* (SBT 2/25; London, 1973), pp. 68-116, esp. p. 115; Ebeling, *Word and Faith,* pp. 79-81; K. Stendahl, "Method in the Study of Biblical Theology," *The Bible in Modern Scholarship,* ed. J. P. Hyatt (Nashville, 1965), pp. 202-205; Merk, *Biblische Theologie des NT,* pp. 7f.

[19]The development and current issues of OT theology are described in the companion volume of the present book, G. F. Hasel, *Old Testament Theology: Basic Issues in the Current Debate* (2nd ed.; Grand Rapids, Mich., 1975).

[20]G. L. Bauer was the first to treat the theology of the two Testaments separately. See above, n. 2.

[21]See W. Klassen, "Anabaptist Hermeneutics," *Mennonite Quarterly Review* 40 (1966), 83-111; idem, *Covenant and Community* (Grand Rapids, Mich., 1967).

[22]G. F. Hasel, "Capito, Schwenckfeld and Crautwald on Sabbatarian Anabaptist Theology," *Mennonite Quarterly Review* 46 (1972), 41-57.

until one hundred years later that the expression "Biblical theology" actually appears for the first time in Wolfgang Jacob Christmann's *Teutsche Biblische Theologie* (Kempten, 1629). His work is presently not extant.[23] But the work of Henricus A. Diest entitled *Theologia biblica* (Daventri, 1643) is available and permits the earliest insight into the nature of an emerging discipline. "Biblical theology" is understood to consist of "proof-texts" from Scripture, taken indiscriminately from both Testaments in order to support the traditional "systems of doctrine" of early Protestant Orthodoxy. The subsidiary role of "Biblical theology" over against dogmatics was firmly established by Abraham Calovius, one of the most significant representatives of Protestant Orthodoxy, when he applied "Biblical theology" as a designation of what was before called *theologica exegetica*.[24] In his work Biblical "proof-texts," which were called *dicta probantia* and later designated *collegia biblica*, had the role of supporting dogmatics. Calovius' lasting contribution was to assign to Biblical theology the role of a subsidiary discipline that supported Protestant orthodox doctrines. Biblical theology as a subsidiary discipline of orthodox dogmatics is evident in the Biblical theologies of Sebastian Schmidt (1671), Johann Hülsemann (1679), Johann Heinrich Maius (1689), Johann Wilhelm Baier (1716-19), and Christian Eberhard Weismann (1739).[25]

The back-to-the-Bible emphasis of German Pietism brought about a changing direction for Biblical theology.[26] In Pietism Biblical theology became a tool

[23]Quoted in M. Lipenius, *Bibliotheca realis theologica omnium materiarum* (Frankfurt, 1685), tom. I, col. 1709, and first referred to by Ebeling, *Word and Faith*, p. 84 n. 3.

[24]Calovius, *Systema locorum theologicorum I* (Wittenbergae, 1655).

[25]Schmidt, *Collegium Biblicum in quo dicta et Novi Testamenti iuxta seriem locorum comunium theologicorum explinatur* (Strassburg, 1671); Hülsemann, *Vindiciae Sanctae Scripturae per loca classica systematis theologici* (Lipsiae, 1679); Maius, *Synopsis theologiae judicae veteris et nova* (Giessen, 1698); Baier, *Analysis et vindicatio illustrium scripturae* (Altdorf, 1716-19); Weismann, *Institutiones theologiae exegetico-dogmaticae* (Tuebingen, 1739).

[26]O. Betz, "History of Biblical Theology," *IDB*, I, 432.

of the reaction against arid Protestant Orthodoxy.[27] Philipp Jacob Spener (1635-1705), a founding father of Pietism, opposed Protestant scholasticism with "Biblical theology."[28] The influence of Pietism is reflected in the works of Carl Haymann (1708), J. Deutschmann (1710), and J. C. Weidner (1722), which oppose orthodox systems of doctrine with "Biblical theology."[29]

As early as 1745 "Biblical theology" is clearly separated from dogmatic (systematic) theology, and the former is conceived of as being the foundation of the latter.[30] This means that Biblical theology is emancipated from a role merely subsidiary to dogmatics. Inherent in this new development is the possibility that Biblical theology can become the rival of dogmatics and turn into a completely separate and independent discipline. These possibilities were realized under the influence of rationalism in the age of Enlightenment.

B. The Age of Enlightenment

In the age of Enlightenment (*Aufklärung*) a totally new approach for the study of the Bible was developed under several influences. First and foremost was rationalism's reaction against any form of supernaturalism.[31]

[27]R. C. Dentan, *Preface to OT Theology* (2nd ed.; New York, 1963), p. 17; Merk, *Biblische Theologie des NT*, pp. 18-20; Kraus, *Biblische Theologie*, pp. 24-30.

[28]P. J. Spener, *Pia Desideria* (Frankfurt, 1675), trans. and ed. by T. G. Tappert (Philadelphia, 1964), pp. 54f.

[29]Haymann, *Biblische Theologie* (Leipzig, 1708); Deutschmann, *Theologia Biblica* (1710); Weidner, *Deutsche Theologie Biblica* (Leipzig, 1722).

[30]So in an unsigned article published in J. H. Zeller, ed., *Grosses vollständiges Universallexikon* (Leipzig und Halle, 1754; reprinted Graz, 1962), Vol. 43, cols. 849, 866f., 920f. Cf. Merk, *Biblische Theologie des NT*, p. 20.

[31]English deism as represented by John Locke (1632-1704), John Toland (1670-1722), Matthew Tindal (1657-1733), and Thomas Chubb (1679-1747) with its emphasis on reason's supremacy over revelation was paralleled on the Continent with the "rational orthodoxy" of Jean A. Turretini (1671-1737), and such figures as S. J. Baumgarten, J. S. Semler (1725-1791), J. D. Michaelis (1717-1791). See W. G. Kümmel, *The NT: The History of the Investigation of*

Human reason was set up as the final criterion and chief source of knowledge, which meant that the authority of the Bible as the infallible record of divine revelation was rejected. The second major departure of the period of the Enlightenment was the development of a new hermeneutic, the historical-critical method[32] which holds sway to the present day in liberal scholarship and beyond,[33] even though it should not be overlooked that a new stage of criticism is levelled against it[34] and that it is caught up in a methodological crisis.[35]

Its Problem (Nashville, 1972), pp. 51-72; H.-J. Kraus, *Geschichte der historisch-kritischen Erforschung des AT* (2nd ed.; Neukirchen-Vluyn, 1969), pp. 70ff.

[32]G. Ebeling, "The Significance of the Critical Historical Method for Church and Theology in Protestantism," *Word and Faith,* pp. 17-61; U. Wilckens, "Über die Bedeutung historischer Kritik in der Bibelexegese," *Was heisst Auslegung der Heiligen Schrift?,* eds. W. Joest et al. (Regensburg, 1966), pp. 85ff.; J. E. Benson, "The History of the Historical-Critical Method in the Church," *Dialog* 12 (1973), 94-103; K. Scholder, *Ursprünge und Probleme der Bibelkritik in 17. Jahrhundert. Ein Beitrag zur Entstehung des historisch-kritischen Theologie* (Munich, 1966); E. Krentz, *The Historical-Critical Method* (Philadelphia, 1975); G. Maier, *Das Ende der historisch-kritischen Methode* (2nd ed.; Wuppertal, 1975), Eng. trans. *The End of the Historical-Critical Method* (St. Louis, 1977).

[33]Krentz (*The Historical-Critical Method,* p. 76) speaks of "the uneasy truce of conservatism" with the historical-critical method. He refers to G. E. Ladd (*The New Testament and Criticism* [Grand Rapids, Mich., 1967]) who changes certain rationalist presuppositions.

[34]See especially H. Frey, "Um den Ansatz theologischer Arbeit," *Abraham unser Vater. Festschrift für O. Michel* (Stuttgart, 1963), pp. 153-180; A. Nitschke, "Historische Wissenschaft und Bibelkritik," *EvTh* 27 (1967), 225-236; W. Marxsen, *Der Streit um die Bibel* (Gladbeck, 1965); R. M. Frye, "A Literary Perspective for the Criticism of the Gospels," *Jesus and Man's Hope* (Pittsburgh, 1971), II, 193-221; idem, "On the Historical-Critical Method in New Testament Studies: A Reply to Professor Achtemeier," *Perspective* 14 (1973), 28-33; G. Maier, *Das Ende der historisch-kritischen Methode.*

[35]The following provide an introduction to the crisis: W. Pannenberg, *Grundfragen systematischer Theologie* (Göttingen, 1967), pp. 44-78, Eng. trans. *Basic Questions in Theology* (Philadelphia, 1971), pp. 38-80; F. Hahn, "Probleme historischer Kritik," *ZNW* 63 (1972), 1-17; K. Lehmann, "Der hermeneutische Horizont der historisch-kritischen Exegese," *Einführung in die Methoden der biblischen Exegese,* ed. J. Schreiner (Tyrolia, 1971), pp. 40-80; M. Hengel, "Historische Methoden und theologische Auslegung des Neuen Testaments," *Kerygma und Dogma* 19 (1973), 85-90; F. Beisser, "Irrwege

The third is the application of radical literary criticism of the Bible as developed by J. B. Witter (1711) and J. Astruc (1753) for the OT, and J. J. Griesbach (1776), G. E. Lessing (1776), and J. G. Eichhorn (1794) for the NT. Finally, rationalism by its very nature was led to abandon the orthodox view of the inspiration of the Bible so that ultimately the Bible became simply one of the ancient documents, to be studied as any other ancient document.[36]

Under the partial impetus of Pietism and with a strong dose of rationalism Anton Friedrich Büsching's publications (1756-58) reveal for the first time that "Biblical theology" becomes the rival of dogmatics.[37] Protestant dogmatics, also called "scholastic theology," is criticized for its empty speculations and lifeless theories. G. Ebeling has aptly summarized that "from being merely a subsidiary discipline of dogmatics 'biblical theology' now became a rival of the prevailing dogmatics."[38]

A chief catalyst in the "revolution of hermeneutics"[39] was the rationalist Johann Solomo Semler (1725-1791), whose four-volume *Treatise on the Free Investigation of the Canon* (1771-75) claimed that the Word of God

---

und Wege der historisch-kritischen Bibelwissenschaft: Auch ein Vorschlag zur Reform des Theologiestudiums," *Neue Zeitschrift für system. Theologie und Religionsphilosophie* 15 (1973), 192-214; R. Surburg, "Implications of the Historical-Critical Method in Interpreting the OT," *Crisis in Lutheran Theology*, ed. J. W. Montgomery (Minneapolis, Minn., 1973), II, 48-80; Hasel, *OT Theology*, pp. 59-61, 72-75, 132-137; P. Stuhlmacher, *Schriftauslegung auf dem Wege zur biblischen Theologie* (Göttingen, 1975), pp. 59-127.

[36]The key figure is J. S. Semler, whose four-volume *Abhandlung von der freien Untersuchung des Kanons* (1771-75) fought the orthodox doctrine of inspiration. H.-J. Kraus, *Geschichte der historisch-kritischen Erforschung des AT*, pp. 103-113.

[37]A. F. Büsching, *Dissertatio inauguralis exhibens epitomen theologiae e solis literis sacris concinnatae* (Goettingen, 1756); idem, *Epitome Theologiae* (Lemgo, 1757); idem, *Gedanken von der Beschaffenheit und dem Vorzug der biblisch-dogmatischen Theologie vor der scholastischen* (Lemgo, 1758).

[38]Ebeling, *Word and Faith*, p. 87.

[39]Dentan, *Preface*, p. 19.

and Holy Scripture are not at all identical.[40] This implied that not all parts of the Bible were inspired[41] and that the Bible is a purely historical document which, as any other such document, is to be investigated with a purely historical and thus critical methodology.[42] As a result Biblical theology can be nothing else but a historical discipline which stands in antithesis to traditional dogmatics.[43]

A highly significant step toward a separation of Biblical theology from dogmatics came in the four-volume work of Biblical theology (1771-75) by Gotthilf Traugott Zachariä (1729-1777).[44] Under the influence of the new orientation in dogmatics and hermeneutics he attempted to build a system of theological teachings based upon careful exegetical work. Each book of Scripture has its own time, place, and intention. But Zachariä held to the inspiration of the Bible,[45] as did J. A. Ernesti (1707-1781)[46] whose Biblical-exegetical method he followed.[47] Historical exegesis and canonical understanding of Scripture do not collide in Zachariä's thought because "the historical aspect is a matter of secondary importance in theology."[48] On this basis there is no need to distinguish between the Testaments; they stand in reciprocal relationship to each other. Most basically Zachariä's interest was still in the dogmatic system, which he wished to cleanse from impurities.

[40]Kümmel, The NT: The History, p. 63.
[41]G. Hornig, Die Anfänge der historisch-kritischen Theologie (Göttingen, 1961), pp. 56ff.
[42]Merk, Biblische Theologie des NT, p. 22.
[43]Hornig, Die Anfänge, pp. 57f.; Merk, Biblische Theologie des NT, pp. 23f.
[44]G. T. Zachariä, Biblische Theologie oder Untersuchung des biblischen Grundes der vornehmsten theologischen Lehren (Göttingen and Kiel, 1771-75); Dentan, Preface, p. 21; Kraus, Biblische Theologie, pp. 31-39; Merk, Biblische Theologie, pp. 23-26.
[45]Zachariä, Biblische Theologie, I, vi.
[46]J. A. Ernesti, Institutio interpres Novi Testamenti (Leipzig, 1761); Kümmel, The NT: The History, pp. 60f.
[47]Kraus, Biblische Theologie, p. 35.
[48]Zachariä, Biblische Theologie, I, lxvi.

The works of W. F. Hufnagel (1785-89)[49] and the rationalist C. F. von Ammon (1792)[50] hardly distinguish themselves in structure and design from that of Zachariä. Hufnagel's Biblical theology consists of a "historical-critical collection of Biblical proof-texts supporting dogmatics."[51] Von Ammon took up ideas of Semler and the philosophers Lessing and Kant and presented actually more a "philosophical theology." Significant in his treatment is the higher evaluation of the NT than the OT,[52] which is a first step toward an independent treatment of OT theology[53] which was realized four years later by G. L. Bauer.

The late Neologist and rationalist Johann Philipp Gabler (1753-1826), who never wrote or even intended to write a Biblical theology, made a most decisive and far-reaching contribution to the development of the new discipline in his inaugural lecture at the University of Altdorf on March 31, 1787.[54] This year marks the beginning of Biblical theology's role as a purely historical discipline, completely independent from dogmatics. Gabler's famous definition reads: "Biblical theology possesses a historical character, transmitting what the sacred writers thought about divine matters; dogmatic theology, on the contrary, possesses a didactic character, teaching what a particular theologian philosophizes about divine matters in accordance to his ability, time,

[49]W. F. Hufnagel, *Handbuch der biblischen Theologie* (Erlangen, Vol. I, 1785; Vol. II, 1789).

[50]C. F. von Ammon, *Entwurf einer reinen biblischen Theologie,* 3 vols. (Erlangen, 1792). Cf. Kraus, *Biblische Theologie,* pp. 40-51.

[51]D. G. C. von Cölln, *Biblische Theologie* (Leipzig, 1836), I, 22.

[52]Kraus, *Biblische Theologie,* p. 51.

[53]Dentan, *Preface,* p. 26.

[54]J. P. Gabler, "Oratio de iusto discrimine theologicae biblicae et dogmaticae regundisque recte utriusque finibus" ["About the Correct Distinction of Biblical and Dogmatic Theology and the Right Definition of their Goals"] in *Kleine theologische Schriften,* eds. Th. A. Gabler and J. G. Gabler (Ulm, 1831), II, 179-198. A complete German translation is provided by Merk, *Biblische Theologie des NT,* pp. 273-284, and reprinted in *Das Problem der Theologie des NT,* ed. G. Strecker (Darmstadt, 1975), pp. 32-44; a partial English translation is found in Kümmel, *The NT: The History,* pp. 98-100.

age, place, sect or school, and other similar things."[55]
Gabler's inductive, historical, and descriptive approach
to Biblical theology is based on three essential methodological considerations: (1) Inspiration is to be left out
of consideration, because "the Spirit of God most emphatically did not destroy in every holy man his own
ability to understand and the measure of natural insight
into things."[56] What counts is not "divine authority"
but "only what they [Biblical writers] thought."[57]
(2) Biblical theology has the task of gathering carefully
the concepts and ideas of the individual Bible writers,
because the Bible does not contain the ideas of just
a single man. Therefore the opinions of Bible writers
need to be "carefully assembled from Holy Writ, suit-
ably arranged, properly related to general concepts, and
carefully compared with one another. . . ."[58] This task
can be accomplished by means of a consistent application of the historical-critical method with the aid of
literary criticism, historical criticism, and philosophical
criticism.[59] (3) Biblical theology as a historical discipline is by definition obliged to "distinguish between
the several periods of the old and new religion."[60] The
main task is to investigate which ideas are of importance for Christian doctrine, namely which ones "apply
today" and which ones have no "validity for our
time."[61] These programmatic declarations gave direction
to the future of Biblical(OT and NT) theology dispite
the fact that Gabler's program for Biblical theology

[55]"Oratio" in *Kleine theologische Schriften*, II, 183-184. Cf. R.
Smend, "J. P. Gablers Begründung der biblischen Theologie," *EvTh*
22 (1962), 345-367; Kraus, *Biblische Theologie*, pp. 52-59; Merk,
Biblische Theologie des NT, pp. 29-140.
[56]*Kleine theologische Schriften*, II, 186.
[57]P. 186; Kümmel, *History*, p. 99.
[58]P. 187; Kümmel, *History*, p. 100.
[59]Merk, *Biblische Theologie*, pp. 68-81.
[60]Gabler, "Oratio," in *Kleine theologische Schriften*, II, 186; Kümmel, *History*, p. 99.
[61]P. 191; Kümmel, *History*, p. 100.

was conditioned by his time and contains significant limitations.[62]

The goal of a "purely historical" Biblical theology is for the first time realized by Georg Lorenz Bauer (1755-1806),[63] like J. P. Gabler a student of J. G. Eichhorn, and with Gabler a professor at Altdorf. Bauer is to be credited as the first scholar to publish a NT theology.[64] Although he is influenced by Gabler, Bauer's understanding of Biblical theology advances significantly beyond that of the former because he goes beyond the historical-critical interpretation advocated by Gabler to the issues of philosophical questions.[65] For Bauer "Biblical theology is to be a development — pure and purged of all extraneous concepts — of the religious theory of the Jews prior to Christ and of Jesus and his apostles, a development traced from the writings of the sacred authors and presented in terms of the various periods and the various viewpoints and levels of understanding they reflect."[66] Accordingly he treats separately and in sequence (1) the theory of religion of the synoptics, (2) the theory of religion of the gospel of John and the letters of John, (3) the concept of religion of the Apocalypse and (4) of Peter, (5) the epistles of 2 Peter and Jude, and (6) the doctrine of Paul.

As a "historical-critical rationalist"[67] Bauer's determining position in the development of Biblical (OT and NT) theology was his consistent application of the historical-critical method supported with rational-

[62]Merk, *Biblische Theologie,* pp. 87-90, 111-113.

[63]See especially Kraus, *Biblische Theologie,* pp. 87-91, and Merk, *Biblische Theologie,* pp. 141-203.

[64]*Biblische Theologie des Neuen Testaments,* 2 vols. (Leipzig, 1800-1802). Shortly earlier he published a *Biblische Theologie des Alten Testaments* (Leipzig, 1796). Cf. Hasel, *OT Theology,* pp. 22f.; Merk, *Biblische Theologie,* pp. 157-167.

[65]Merk, *Biblische Theologie,* pp. 172f.

[66]Bauer, *Biblische Theologie des NT* (Leipzig, 1800), I, 6. The translation is that in Kümmel, *The NT: The History,* p. 105.

[67]Merk, *Biblische Theologie,* p. 202.

ism's emphasis on historical reason.[68] His historical-critical reconstruction of the manifoldness of the Biblical witnesses raised, among other problems, the matter of the relationship between the Testaments, a problem under vigorous debate today. Furthermore, the whole issue of Biblical theology's nature as a purely historical discipline as vigorously maintained by Gabler and consequently by Bauer and others is again questioned in the recent debate, as is the question of the nature of the descriptive task. Nevertheless, Gabler and Bauer are the founders of the independent discipline of Biblical and NT theology.

It was in the period of the Enlightenment that the historical-critical method was developed and applied to the study of the Bible.[69] The influence of the scientific revolution as pioneered by N. Copernicus (1473-1543) and advanced by J. Kepler (1571-1630)[70] and Galileo Galilei (1564-1642)[71] brought about a new understanding of Scripture.[72] The suggestions of the two latter scholar-scientists related to the independence of the study of nature. Science is no longer informed by Scripture, but Scripture is to be interpreted by means

[68]P. 199.

[69]The history of these developments is described by A. Richardson (*The Bible in the Age of Science* [London, 1961], pp. 9-31), Scholder (*Ursprünge und Probleme der Bibelkritik im 17. Jahrhundert,* pp. 60ff.) who is summarized by Krentz (*The Historical-Critical Method,* pp. 10-22), and Stuhlmacher (*Schriftauslegung,* pp. 75-99).

[70]J. Hübner, *Die Theologie Johannes Keplers zwischen Orthodoxie und Naturwissenschaft* (Tübingen, 1975); A. Deissmann, *Johann Kepler und die Bibel* (Giessen, 1910).

[71]J. J. Langford, *Galileo, Science and the Church* (New York, 1966); O. Loretz, *Galilei und der Irrtum der Inquisition* (Münster, 1966).

[72]See especially C. F. von Weizsäcker, "Kopernikus, Kepler, Galilei," *Einsichten, Gerhard Krüger zum 60. Geburtstag* (Frankfurt, 1962), pp. 376-394; H. Karpp, "Die Beiträge Keplers und Galileis zum neuzeitlichen Schriftverständnis," *ZThK* 67 (1970), 40-55; R. Hooykaas, *Religion and the Rise of Modern Science* (Grand Rapids, Mich., 1972), pp. 35-39; G. F. Hasel, "Founders of the Modern Understanding of the Relation Between Science and Religion" (unpublished paper read at the Michigan Academy of Science, Arts, and Letters, April 6, 1973).

of the conclusions of science.[73] Thus "the Bible's authority was diminished."[74] It pertained to matters of faith and morals[75] but not to matters of science. A similar development with regard to history is seen in the writings of the French political philosopher Jean Bodin (1530-1596) who argued for the use of reason in the writing of history[76] and in Joachim Vadian's insistence on observance in regard to the science of geography.[77] The following Pre-Adamite controversy[78] was triggered by Isaac de la Peyrère in 1655[79] who applied literary criticism to the Pentateuch. These events were joined with developments in the field of philosophy. René Descartes made reason the sole criterion of truth and elevated doubt to range unchecked through the whole fabric of customary convictions.[80] Shortly later Benedict de Spinoza[81] published his famous *Tractatus Theologico-Politicus* (1670) in which he dealt with the question of the relation of theology to philosophy. He argued that both needed to be carefully separated and suggested that reason is men's guide to truth. All of these influences were powerful catalysts toward the formation of the full-fledged historical-critical method.

In 1728 the Geneva theologian of "rational ortho-

---

[73]Galileo writes, "Having arrived at any certainties in physics, we ought to utilize these as the most appropriate aids in the true exposition of the Bible" (*Opere* as translated by S. Drake, ed., *Discoveries and Opinions of Galileo* [Garden City, N.Y., 1957], p. 183). Kepler states that the inspired writers "had nowhere the intention to teach men in the things of nature, except in the first chapter of Genesis where it deals with the supernatural origin of the world" (*Opera omnia*, ed. Chr. Frisch [1858ff.], II, 86).

[74]Krentz, *The Historical-Critical Method*, p. 13.

[75]Hasel, "Founders of the Modern Understanding of the Relation Between Science and Religion," pp. 9f.

[76]Scholder, *Ursprünge und Probleme der Bibelkritik im 17. Jahrhundert*, p. 91.

[77]P. 96.

[78]Pp. 98-104.

[79]Kraus, *Geschichte*, pp. 59-61.

[80]Scholder, *Ursprünge und Probleme der Bibelkritik im 17. Jahrhundert*, pp. 132-158.

[81]R. M. Grant, *A Short History of the Interpretation of Scripture* (2nd ed.; New York, 1966), pp. 146-150.

doxy" Jean A. Turretini is said to have claimed that "the [Holy] Scriptures are to be explained in no other way than other books."[82] He stated:

> Since God, as we have already often noted, is quite certainly the author of both reason and of revelation, it is therefore impossible that these should contradict each other. . . . Consequently, if a meaning seems to be passed on in certain passages [of Scripture], which openly contradicts all conceptions, then everything must be attempted or imputed, rather than that this dogma should be accepted. Therefore those passages are to be explained otherwise, or, if that be impossible, as not genuine, or the book is to be reckoned not to be divine.[83]

The priority of reason over Scriptural revelation is here fully realized at the expense of the authority of the Bible. Of course, Turretini "did not yet know that the general principles of natural reason which he attempted to raise as criteria for interpretation were themselves a completely historically determined 'understanding' that is brought to the text."[84]

The ideas of Turretini were of little influence in his own day. The epoch-making work on the canon and inspiration by J. J. Semler, as briefly referred to above, which appeared about five decades after Turretini's *Bipartite Tractatus Concerning the Method by Which the Sacred Scriptures Are to Be Interpreted,* proved to be of permanent significance for the foundation of the historical-critical method in the study of Scripture. The separation of the Word of God and Scripture[85]

---

[82]Turretini's lectures were published by others under the title *De Sacrae Scripturae interpretandae methodo tractatus bipartitus* (Trajecti Thuviorum, 1728), p. 196.

[83]P. 312. Cf. Kümmel, *History,* pp. 58-61.

[84]U. Wilckens, "Über die Bedeutung der historischen Kritik in der modernen Bibelexegese," *Was heisst Auslegung der Heiligen Schrift?,* p. 94.

[85]Semler declares, "Holy Scripture and Word of God are clearly to be distinguished, for we know the difference. . . . To Holy Scripture belong Ruth, Esther, Song of Songs, etc., but not all these books that are called holy belong to the Word of God. . . ." *D. Joh. Salomo Semlers Abhandlung von freier Untersuchung des Canons,* 4 vols. (Halle, 1771-1775), I, 75.

and the consistent application of the basic rules of the *critica profana* to the Bible[86] together with the sharp distinction between the divine content and human form of Scripture[87] put the Biblical text deliberately into the ancient setting and explain it as a witness to its own time without intending to speak to the modern reader.[88] These conceptions remain fundamental for historical criticism and have earned Semler the designation of father of historical-critical theology.[89] Semler's distinction between theology and religion, a distinction which separated the "locally" and "temporally" determined theologoumena from the lasting religion, was realized by F. C. Baur in the nineteenth century and reached its classic formulation by E. Troeltsch in the beginning of the twentieth century.

C. From the Enlightenment to Dialectical Theology

The age of the Enlightenment brought about changes in theology of lasting influence. Biblical theology freed itself from a subsidiary role to dogmatics to become its rival. Biblical theology turned into a descriptive discipline and became a historical science describing what Biblical writers thought, i.e., "what it meant."[90] The interpretation ("what it means") is by its very nature dependent upon the prevailing philosophy of the time. Aside from the "purely historical" approaches there developed also "positive historical" approaches, the "history-of-religions" approach, and the "history of salvation" approach. The years 1813-1821 witness the appearance of Gottlob Philipp Christian Kaiser's *Die biblische Theologie* in three volumes. He constructs his work with what he calls "the grammatico-historical

[86]Kraus, *Geschichte,* p. 113.

[87]Semler as quoted by Kümmel, *History,* p. 64.

[88]J. S. Semler, *Vorbereitung zur theologischen Hermeneutik* (Halle, 1760), pp. 6-8, 149f., 160-162.

[89]Krentz, *The Historical-Critical Method,* p. 19.

[90]The terminology of K. Stendahl, "Biblical Theology, Contemporary," *IDB,* I, 418-432.

method of interpretation" combined with "the point of view of a philosophical universal history of religion."[91] This means a total rejection of any kind of supernaturalism. He is the first to apply a "history-of-religions" approach and to subordinate all Biblical and nonbiblical aspects under the principle of universal religion.[92]

Wilhelm Martin Leberechte de Wette published his *Biblische Dogmatik des Alten und Neuen Testaments* in 1813.[93] He was a student of Gabler. His work marks a move away from rationalism by adopting Kantian philosophy as mediated by J. F. Fries,[94] combining Biblical theology with a system of philosophy. His higher synthesis of faith and feeling moved in a "genetic development" of religion from Hebraism via Judaism to Christianity.[95] This means a shattering of the material unity of OT and NT,[96] and NT theology comes to be understood as a phenomenon of the history-of-religions. Everything local and temporal, everything individual and particular, must be peeled off in order to arrive at that which is timeless, general, and lasting. Nevertheless, de Wette's attempt indicates that there is an unresolved methodological problem, because he attempted to combine Biblical theology with dogmatic interests.

The approach of de Wette received a radical rebuttal from K. W. Stein, who argued that it is a departure from Gabler's program and Bauer's NT theology. The insistence that "only a historical-critical approach can lead to a pure and complete Biblical theology"[97] and

[91]Kaiser, *Die biblische Theologie* (Erlangen, 1813), I, iii.

[92]See Dentan, *Preface*, pp. 28f.; Kraus, *Biblische Theologie*, pp. 57f.; Merk, *Biblische Theologie*, pp. 214f.

[93]R. Smend, *W. M. L. de Wettes Arbeit am Alten und am Neuen Testament* (Basel, 1958).

[94]Kraus, *Biblische Theologie*, p. 72.

[95]Merk, *Biblische Theologie*, pp. 210-214.

[96]Strecker, *Das Problem der Theologie des NT*, p. 5.

[97]K. W. Stein, "Über den Begriff und die Behandlungsart der Biblischen Theologie des NT," *Analecten für das Studium der exegetischen und systematischen Theologie*, eds. C. A. G. Keil and H. G. Tzschirner (1816), III, 151-204, esp. p. 180.

that the thoughts of the different NT writers cannot
be brought together in a system points to the problem
that the NT is made up of various theologies but that
there is no NT theology.[98] He seeks to make the
teaching of Jesus, namely that on which the NT writers
agree, the center of the NT.[99] Here the whole issue
of the center and unity of the NT comes to the fore;
this remains a key issue to the present day.

To the tradition of Gabler and Bauer as regards the
"purely historical"[100] nature of Biblical (NT) theology
belongs *Die biblische Theologie des Neuen Testaments*
(Leipzig, 1836) by Daniel G. C. von Cölln.[101] He is
said to be the last one to present a Biblical theology
built upon rationalism.[102] Von Cölln delineated a de-
velopmentalism of Hebraism-Judaism-Christianity and
presented a history of spiritualization, ethical cleansing,
and universal enlargement of the idea of theocracy.[103]
O. Merk points out that von Cölln's end result was a
modified dogmatic theology because he did not sharply
separate the task of a historical-critical (purely historical descriptive) Biblical theology from the task of
interpretation (dogmatics).[104]

The apex of the Gabler and Bauer approach of a
"purely historical" NT theology is reached by Ferdinand Christian Baur's (1792-1860) work.[105] Baur is

[98]Merk, *Biblische Theologie,* p. 214.

[99]Stein, "Über den Begriffe," pp. 189-204.

[100]The distinction of the development of a "purely historical"
method is justified on the basis of the designation as employed by E.
Troeltsch, "Über historische und dogmatische Methode," *Gesammelte
Studien II* (Tübingen, 1913), pp. 729-753, reprinted in *Theologie
als Wissenschaft,* ed. G. Sauter (Munich, 1971), pp. 105-127.

[101]His OT theology appeared as vol. I of which his NT theology
is vol. II under the general title *Biblische Theologie* (Leipzig, 1836).
Cf. Kraus, *Biblische Theologie,* pp. 60-69.

[102]Merk, *Biblische Theologie,* p. 222.

[103]Kraus, *Biblische Theologie,* p. 67.

[104]Merk, *Biblische Theologie,* pp. 225f.

[105]P. C. Hodgson, *The Formation of Historical Theology. A Study
of Ferdinand Christian Baur* (New York, 1966); W. Geiger, *Spekulation und Kritik. Die Geschichtstheologie F. C. Baurs* (Munich,
1964); E. Barnikol, *F. C. Baur als rationalistisch-kirchlicher Theologe*
(Berlin, 1970).

the founder and uncontested head of the Tübingen School. In the year 1835 his student David Friedrich Strauss (1808-1874) published his *Life of Jesus*,[106] a radical reinterpretation of the NT accounts of Jesus. Strauss provided neither a supernatural nor a rationalistic but a mythical interpretation of the Gospel records which give a basis of historical fact transformed and enlarged by the faith of the early Christian community. The Hegelian philosophical method of the thesis of a supernaturalistic interpretation which was countered by the antithesis of the rationalistic interpretation brings Strauss to the synthesis of mythological interpretation. "This Hegelian dialectic determines the method of the work"[107] of Strauss.

F. C. Baur's *Lectures on New Testament Theology* were posthumously published in the year 1864[108] and represent the conclusion of his scholarly efforts.[109] Baur's Hegelian dialectic led him to view the history of Christianity as a struggle between the thesis of Jewish Christianity (Petrine materials, Matt., Rev.) and the antithesis of Gentile Christianity (Gal., 1-2 Cor., Rom., Luke) which resulted in the synthesis of early catholicism (Mark, John, Acts) of the second century.[110] This has a bearing on NT theology, which is "a purely historical science"[111] but is restricted to the writings of the NT.[112] In harmony with his earlier studies he distinguishes three periods: The first is characterized through the "concepts-of-doctrine" (*Lehr-*

[106]*Das Leben Jesu*, 2 vols. (Tübingen, 1835-36), Eng. trans. by G. Eliot, *The Life of Jesus Critically Examined* (from 4th German ed.; London, 1846). Cf. A. Schweitzer, *The Quest of the Historical Jesus* (New York, 1964), pp. 78-120.

[107]Schweitzer, *The Quest of the Historical Jesus*, p. 80.

[108]F. C. Baur, *Vorlesungen über Neutestamentliche Theologie*, ed. F. F. Baur (Leipzig, 1864).

[109]Merk, *Biblische Theologie*, p. 227.

[110]B. Rigaux, *Paulus und seine Briefe* (Munich, 1964), pp. 14f.; R. C. Briggs, *Interpreting the New Testament Today* (Nashville, 1973), pp. 145-148.

[111]Baur, *Vorlesungen*, p. 1.

[112]P. 38.

begriffe) of the four genuine Pauline letters (Gal.,
1-2 Cor., Rom.); the second period includes Hebrews,
the lesser Pauline letters, 1-2 Peter, James, the Synoptics,
and Acts; and the third period encompasses the
Pastoral epistles and the Johannine letters. The "teaching of Jesus" has no room in this strictly historical
sequence, but Baur puts it before the three periods and
reduces it to a "purely moral element."[113] Thus Baur's
emphasis is on reconstruction of the historical concepts
and the progress of development of the several doctrines. In contrast to G. L. Bauer's NT theology, to
which Baur is more indebted than to J. P. Gabler,
Baur considers the "teachings of Jesus" as a prehistory
of NT theology and not a basic part of a theology of
the NT itself. R. Bultmann appears to stand in the
tradition of Baur when he declares, "The message of
Jesus is a presupposition for the theology of the New
Testament rather than a part of that theology itself."[114]
This question remains a pressing issue today. The well-
known major defects of Bauer's approach are the application of the Hegelian dialectic and an overemphasis
on the influence of Judaism in early Christianity.

In contrast to the "purely historical" approaches to
NT theology, there were scholars in the early decades
of the nineteenth century who may be classified as
belonging to the "positive historical"[115] direction of
NT scholarship. Among the initiators of this direction
are M. F. A. Lossius[116] and D. L. Cramer,[117] both of
whom have essentially the same conception. Their
works have had an important influence in the last
century. Lassius combines the dogmatic approach of

---

[113]Kümmel, *History,* p. 142.

[114]R. Bultmann, *Theology of the New Testament* (London, 1965),
I, 3.

[115]See particularly Goppelt, *Theologie des NT,* I, 41-45.

[116]*Biblische Theologie des Neuen Testaments oder die Lehren des
Christenthums aus den einzelnen Schriften des N.T. entwickelt* (Leipzig, 1825).

[117]*Vorlesungen über die biblische Theologie des Neuen Testaments,*
ed. F. A. A. Näbe (Leipzig, 1830).

the "concept-of-doctrines" with the historical one. He suggests that there are but three possibilities of writing a NT theology. Either one treats each NT writer separately or one uses a systematic approach of "concepts-of-doctrine" or one combines both methods.[118] From the perspective of the Gabler-Bauer-Baur approach of a "purely historical" NT theology, the Lossius-Cramer approach of a "positive historical" NT theology may be considered a methodological reversal,[119] but from another perspective this may be viewed as a necessary antithesis to the radical criticism of the NT traditions.[120]

A unique place is to be accorded to the outrightly conservative *Outline of Biblical Theology* (1828) of Ludwig F. O. Baumgarten-Crusius.[121] His highly valued work reflects only to a limited degree Gabler's influence. The two Testaments are considered to belong together. Baumgarten-Crusius seeks "to present a system of purely biblical concepts which is to serve as the foundation and norm for doctrine and as the starting-point for the history of dogma."[122] He recognizes the validity of grammatical-historical interpretation,[123] feels indebted to Kaiser, de Wette, and Lossius,[124] but argues soberly against the excesses of deism's critique of religion with a view to ward off foreign influences on Biblical theology. He suggests that the unity of the Bible is recognized on the basis of the common theme of the kingdom of God which unites both Testaments. This center of the Bible has supporters today that belong to a non-conservative line of scholarship.

[118]Lossius, *Biblische Theologie des NT*, pp. 11f. Cf. Merk, *Biblische Theologie*, p. 217.

[119]So Merk, *Biblische Theologie*, p. 218.

[120]So Goppelt, *Theologie des NT*, I, 41.

[121]*Grundzüge der Biblischen Theologie* (Jena, 1828). Cf. Kraus, *Biblische Theologie*, p. 218.

[122]Baumgarten-Crusius, *Grundzüge der Biblischen Theologie*, p. 3.

[123]P. 6.

[124]P. 10.

The problem of unity and diversity within the NT becomes an important issue in the approach of August Neander whose two tomes were published in 1832-33.[125] After tracing the history of the apostolic period (Vol. I) he distinguishes between the different apostles, namely the strands of Paul, James, Peter, and John (Vol. II). The diversity of presentation of the message of these apostles serves to emphasize "the living unity"[126] of the teaching of Christ within its manifold-ness. This understanding made it possible for him to develop in his last section the themes of the NT.[127]

The influence of Neander upon Christian Friedrich Schmid is freely acknowledged by the latter,[128] who considers the method of his Biblical Theology of the NT, 2 vols. (1853)[129] to consist of a "historical-genetic" presentation of the canonical writings of the NT. Schmid believes that there is an essential unity under-lying the NT which is reflected in the different doc-trines of the NT writers.[130] A similar view is maintained in 1854 by George Ludwig Hahn[131] and in 1856 by Hermann Messner.[132] These scholars agree that there is unity in diversity, that NT theology is concerned only with the canonical writings, that the proper method is the "historical-critical" one, and that it is proper to present the teaching of the NT under more or less traditional headings from dogmatics.

The so-called "modern positive" direction of NT theology has been pioneered by an opponent of the

[125]Geschichte der Pflanzung und Leitung der christlichen Kirche durch die Apostel, als selbständiger Nachtrag zu der allgemeinen Geschichte der christlichen Religion und Kirche, 2 vols. (Hamburg, 1832-1833).

[126]II, 501.

[127]II, 501-711.

[128]C. F. Schmid, "Über das Interesse und den Stand der biblischen Theologie des Neuen Testaments in unserer Zeit," Tübinger Zeit-schrift für Theologie 4 (1838), 125-160, esp. 159.

[129]Biblische Theologie des Neuen Testaments, ed. C. von Weiz-säcker, 2 vols. (Stuttgart, 1853).

[130]Merk, Biblische Theologie, pp. 219f.

[131]Die Theologie des Neuen Testaments (Leipzig, 1854).

[132]Die Lehre der Apostel (Leipzig, 1856).

Tübingen School. Bernhard Weiss's *Textbook of the Biblical Theology of the New Testament* (1868)[133] enjoyed a great popularity with seven editions over a period of almost four decades.[134] In contrast to the radical views of F. C. Baur, the approach of Weiss was conservative,[135] because he considered most NT writings as genuine; in contrast to A. Neander, C. F. Schmid, G. L. Hahn, and F. Messner, the approach of Weiss is less conservative, though still positive, because he does not address himself fully to the relationship of the OT to the NT and the Gospel of John is totally excluded from serving as a source for the teachings of Jesus.[136]

Weiss suggests that "the Biblical theology of the NT has to describe the manifoldness of the forms of teaching of the different NT writings."[137] Extra-canonical documents have no place in a Biblical theology of the NT.[138] "The most important aid for Biblical theology is one of method, i.e., an exegesis that follows the rules of grammatical-historical interpretation."[139] This means for Weiss that the hermeneutical foundation is rooted in the position which "interprets each writer from within himself"[140] and neither from dogmatic nor philosophical systems nor from so-called parallel texts from Scripture. On the other hand, the particular words of the individual authors have to be provided by Biblical theology.

On the whole the method of Weiss is characterized through a theological "concept-of-doctrine" (*Lehrbe-*

---

[133]*Lehrbuch der Biblischen Theologie des Neuen Testaments* (Berlin, 1868). Eng. trans. from 3rd ed. *The Theology of the New Testament* (London, 1892).

[134]7th ed.; Stuttgart/Berlin, 1903. The first sixteen pages of the first edition of 1868 are republished in *Das Problem der Theologie des NT*, pp. 45-66.

[135]Kraus, *Biblische Theologie*, p. 151.

[136]Kümmel, *History*, p. 173.

[137]*Das Problem der Theologie des NT*, p. 52.

[138]P. 60.

[139]P. 61.

[140]P. 62.

griff) approach, even though he recognizes an "inner development" of "the two main strands," namely "the primitive apostolic one" and "the Pauline one."[141] The "concept-of-doctrine" approach in NT theology has been passed on to all scholars who may be considered to be representatives of the "modern positive" direction of NT theology. A programmatic sentence of Weiss is typical of the "modern positive" direction: "Biblical theology cannot concern itself with the critical and specialized investigations regarding the origin of NT writings, because it is only a historical-descriptive science and not a historical-critical one."[142] This definition is more or less in the background of the NT theologies of W. Beyschlag,[143] P. Feine,[144] F. Büchsel,[145] and in the English language in the works of F. Weidner,[146] E. P. Gould,[147] G. B. Stevens,[148] and others.

Another "conservative" reaction to the "purely historical" approach to NT theology came to expression in the "salvation-history school" which was connected with Gottfried Menken (1768-1831),[149] Johann T. Beck (1804-1878),[150] and its dominating figure J. Ch. Konrad von Hofmann (1810-1877).[151] The "salvation-

---

[141]P. 56.

[142]Weiss, *Lehrbuch,* p. 8. Cf. *Das Problem der Theologie des NT,* p. 53.

[143]Willibald Beyschlag, *Neutestamentliche Theologie oder geschichtliche Darstellung der Lehren Jesu und des Urchristenthums nach den neutestamentliche Quellen,* 2 vols. (Halle, 1891-1892). Cf. Merk, *Biblische Theologie,* pp. 240f.

[144]Paul Feine, *Theologie des Neuen Testaments* (Leipzig, 1910). The 8th ed. was published in 1951.

[145]F. Büchsel, *Theologies des Neuen Testaments. Geschichte des Wortes Gottes im Neuen Testament* (Gütersloh, 1935).

[146]F. Weidner, *Biblical Theology of the New Testament,* 2 vols. (Chicago/London, 1891).

[147]E. P. Gould, *The Biblical Theology of the New Testament* (New York, 1900).

[148]G. B. Stevens, *The Theology of the New Testament* (Edinburgh, 1901; 2nd. ed., 1906).

[149]Kraus, *Biblische Theologie,* pp. 240-244.

[150]Pp. 244-247.

[151]J. Ch. K. von Hofmann, *Weissagung und Erfüllung im Alten*

history school" of the nineteenth century is based upon
(1) the history of the people of God as "expressed in
the Word"; (2) the idea of the inspiration of the Bible;
and (3) the (preliminary) result of the history between
God and man in Jesus Christ. Von Hofmann found in
the Bible a record of linear saving history in which the
active Lord of history is the triune God whose purpose
and goal it is to redeem mankind. Since Jesus Christ
is the primordial goal of the world to which salvation
history aims and from which it receives its meaning,[152]
the OT and NT contain salvation-historical proclamation. This a Biblical theology has to expound. Each
book of the Bible is assigned its logical place in the
scheme of salvation history. The Bible is not to be
regarded primarily as a collection of proof-texts or a
repository of doctrine, but a witness to God's activity
in history which will not be fully completed until the
eschatological consummation.[153]

The "salvation-historical" approach of von Hofmann
has been hailed by P. Feine as "the most fruitful theological development of the 19th century."[154] L. Goppelt
also accords him a significant place,[155] whereas others
seem to underestimate his real importance by treating
him as a part of "the religion of biblicism"[156] or not
mentioning him at all.[157] Von Hofmann's influence has
been significant in many ways. The reasons for this
are several. In contrast to his contemporary F. C. Baur,
von Hofmann did not integrate the NT in the general

und Neuen Testamente (Nördlingen, 1841-44); idem, Der Schriftbeweis (Nördlingen, 1852-56); idem, Biblische Hermeneutik, eds. J.
Hofmeister and Volck (Nördlingen, 1880), Eng. trans. Interpreting
the Bible (Minneapolis, 1959).

[152]Weissagung und Erfüllung, I, 40.

[153]K. G. Steck, Die Idee der Heilsgeschichte. Hofmann-Schlatter-
Cullmann (Zollikon, 1959).

[154]Feine, Theologie des NT, p. 4.

[155]Goppelt, Theologie des NT, I, 45f. So also G. E. Ladd, A Theology of the New Testament (Grand Rapids, Mich., 1974), p. 16.

[156]Betz, IDB, I, 434.

[157]Bultmann, "The History of NT Theology as a Science," Theology
of the NT (London, 1955), II, 241-251.

history of thought but brought it into a historical relation with the OT, i.e., into salvation history. It is pointed out that in doing this he combines the Reformation principle to let Scripture interpret Scripture with a modern understanding of history.[158] On the other hand, it is to be recognized that von Hofmann holds that the history of God's people is one that is "presented in the Word."[159] Thus it cannot be rejected out of hand as a philosophy of history of human origin.[160] It must be emphasized once again that for von Hofmann "the activity of the Holy Spirit has produced the Biblical books, the activity of the Holy Spirit has also brought them together."[161] Since the Holy Spirit is responsible for the origin of the Biblical writings and the formation of the canon, a salvation-history theology has the task to investigate the historical place of the products of the Holy Spirit. This is best achieved through an organic cross-section of the whole Bible along salvation-history lines and not through a proof-text method that is irresponsible to the context.[162]

The influence of von Hofmann is evident in the learned Theodor Zahn,[163] the man whose criticism Adolf von Harnack feared.[164] Zahn does not conceive of NT theology as a scientific system of religion but as a presentation of the theology contained in the Bible,[165] which must be presented in its "historical development" and "ordered according to the steps of salvation history."[166] His NT theology starts with John

[158]Goppelt, *Theologie des NT,* I, 46.
[159]Von Hofmann, *Weissagung und Erfüllung,* I, 49.
[160]Kraus, *Biblische Theologie,* p. 250.
[161]Von Hofmann, *Weissagung und Erfüllung,* I, 49.
[162]Von Hofmann, *Der Schriftbeweis* (Nördlingen, 1852-56); cf. Goppelt, *Theologie des NT,* I, 46.
[163]T. Zahn, *Geschichte des neutestamentlichen Kanons,* 2 vols. (Erlangen/Leipzig, 1888-92); idem, *Einleitung in das Neue Testament,* 2 vols. (Leipzig, 1906-07); idem, *Grundriss der neutestamentlichen Theologie* (Leipzig, 1928). Cf. Kraus, *Biblische Theologie,* pp. 181f.
[164]Kümmel, *History,* p. 197.
[165]Zahn, *Grundriss der ntl. Theologie,* p. 1.
[166]Ibid.

the Baptist, who is the embodiment of prophetic prediction and at the same time the "fulfillment of the promise that points to the final divine revelation and the opener of the final epoch of salvation history."[167] Zahn followed in his presentation the "concept-of-doctrine" (*Lehrbegriff*) approach,[168] but only rarely goes back to the OT.

The place of Adolf Schlatter[169] in the spectrum of the development of NT theology is debated by some.[170] Schlatter "is perhaps the only 'conservative' New Testament scholar since Bengel who can be rated in the same class but not school as Baur, Wrede, Bousset and Bultmann."[171] We include Schlatter in the group of scholars associated with the general rubric of salvation history (*Heilsgeschichte*) because he is to be associated with that movement. In his provocative essay "Atheistic Methods in Theology" (1905)[172] Schlatter rejects the atheism inherent in the modern his-

[167]P. 5.

[168]Merk (*Biblische Theologie*, p. 251 n. 137) claims that Zahn is the last one to use this approach.

[169]A. Schlatter, *Der Glaube im Neuen Testament* (Darmstadt, 1885; 5th ed., 1963), which is called a "NT theology *in nuce*" (Bultmann, *Theology of the NT*, II, 248); idem, *Die Theologie des Neuen Testaments*, 2 vols. (Stuttgart, 1909-10), which appeared under the titles *Geschichte des Christus* (Stuttgart, 1923) and *Die Theologie der Apostel* (Stuttgart, 1922) respectively. Schlatter's important programmatic essay "Die Theologie des Neuen Testaments und die Dogmatik," *Beiträge zur Förderung christlicher Theologie* 13 (1909), 7-82, is reprinted in A. Schlatter, *Kleine Schriften*, ed. U. Luck (Munich, 1969), pp. 203-255, and in *Das Problem der Theologie des NT* (hereafter cited as *PTNT*), pp. 155-214, Eng. trans. "The Theology of the New Testament and Dogmatics," by R. Morgan, *The Nature of New Testament Theology*, pp. 117-166 (hereafter cited as *NNTT*).

[170]Bultmann (*Theology of the NT*, II, 248) states that Schlatter takes "a place by itself in the whole development" of NT theology. O. Betz claims that "Schlatter struck out on a line by himself" (*IDB* I, 436), but Goppelt puts him squarely within the line of the "salvation-history" emphasis of NT scholarship (*Theologie des NT*, I, 47) whereas Harrington (*Path of Biblical Theology*, p. 116) says surprisingly that Schlatter produced "a less satisfactory alternative to the *heilsgeschichtliche* position."

[171]*NNTT*, p. 27.

[172]A. Schlatter, "Atheistische Methoden in der Theologie" (1905), reprinted in *Kleine Schriften*, pp. 134-150.

torical-critical method and maintains that neither culture with its world-view (*Weltanschauung*) nor modern historical method is adequate for NT theology. The methods which attempt to study the development of Christianity on a purely historical basis without the employment of the activity of God are "atheistic."[173] Thus Schlatter's understanding of total reality, including the divine, makes his "solution to the problem of a New Testament theology unacceptable to anyone who wishes to see it as a purely historical discipline to be undertaken by the methods shared by all historians."[174] This raises the fundamental question of the goal of historical research.

First of all, Schlatter conceives of "the object of New Testament theology which wants to remain a science to be the New Testament word."[175] NT theology as such is restricted to the canonical writings of the NT and does not include the entire literature of early Christianity (*contra* Wrede and followers). The Church was the result of NT proclamation and not vice versa.[176] "The fact that New Testament history and the word which witnesses to it is the ground of Christianity's existence is expressed by the fact that the New Testament is its canon."[177] Schlatter supports a canonical NT theology because he considers all NT documents as authentic (except 2 Peter).[178]

Schlatter is highly sensitive to the matter of historical objectivity. He strikes sensitive nerves in claiming that "historical objectivity is illusory,"[179] if NT theology joins in all the debates evoked by philosophical (rationalist, Hegelian, Kantian) questions as had been

[173]P. 139.
[174]Morgan, *NNTT*, p. 33.
[175]*NNTT*, p. 164.
[176]*NNTT*, p. 120: "Since Christianity is based upon the New Testament, the interpretation of the New Testament is an act which touches its foundation."
[177]*NNTT*, p. 120.
[178]Pp. 146-148.
[179]P. 123.

the case. The position that the NT theologian works as a historian who "explains" and "observes the New Testament neutrally" means "to begin at once with a determined struggle against it."[180] Why is this so? Schlatter answers, "The word with which the New Testament confronts us intends to be believed, and so rules out once and for all any sort of neutral treatment. As soon as the historian sets aside or brackets the question of faith, he is making his concern with the New Testament and his presentation of it into a radical and total polemic against it."[181] In rejecting the claim of objectivity on the part of those using a "purely historical" approach, Schlatter anticipated the debate between the OT scholars O. Eissfeldt and W. Eichrodt in the 1920s.[182]

The strictures advanced by Schlatter against a "purely historical" approach to NT theology do not in the least imply that he is insensitive to historical investigation. He defended NT theology as a historical discipline against those who claim that an undertaking that explains the NT historically "is fundamentally irreligious."[183] "If history is excluded from God's influence on the grounds that it is merely transitory and human, there exists no conscious relationship to God granted us in our personal life."[184] Schlatter criticizes on the one front liberalism's understanding of history as a closed continuum of causes and effects which leaves no room for transcendence,[185] and on the other

[180]P. 122.

[181]Ibid.

[182]O. Eissfeldt, "Israelitisch-jüdische Religionsgeschichte und alttestamentliche Theologie," *ZAW* 44 (1926), 1-12; W. Eichrodt, "Hat die alttestamentliche Theologie noch selbständige Bedeutung innerhalb der alttestamentlichen Wissenschaft?" *ZAW* 47 (1929), 83-91; cf. Hasel, *OT Theology*, p. 32.

[183]*NNTT*, p. 151.

[184]P. 152.

[185]See the recent statement relating to the historian by R. W. Funk, "The Hermeneutical Problem and Historical Criticism," *The New Hermeneutic*, eds. J. M. Robinson and J. B. Cobb, Jr. (New York, 1964), p. 185: "The historian cannot presuppose supernatural intervention in the causal nexus as the basis for his work."

front a narrow orthodoxy that claims that God acts beyond history and not in and through it. "So the New Testament utterly repudiates the thesis that revelation and history cannot be united, and this at the same time destroys the view that historical research is a denial of revelation."[186] This statement can be read aright only if one keeps in mind that his understanding of reality has God acting in history. It is quite to the point when R. Morgan[187] observes that Schlatter's position has much in common with some aspects of W. Pannenberg's theological position[188] and the latter's critique of the subsequent "theology of the Word."

Schlatter maintains that one must not go behind the sources of the NT. "Historical thinking is not to encompass beyond that which the sources reveal; otherwise historical research turns into a novel."[189] He takes his departure from the conviction that the NT testimony is unified, in spite of all diversity, and that faith is a presupposition for proper understanding of the NT writings.[190] The unity of the NT testimony has a historical foundation in "the environment of Jesus and his followers [which] was Palestinian Judaism."[191] With regard to the whole Bible Schlatter declares the following:

> The unity, which Scripture needs and has, consists in that all her instructions join themselves to a united whole. I cannot push aside one point without moving the whole; I cannot cast way one point without losing the whole; I cannot unite myself with one point without taking the whole and being guided by the whole. . . .

[186]*NNTT,* p. 152.

[187]*NNTT,* p. 32.

[188]W. Pannenberg, *Basic Questions in Theology,* 2 vols. (Philadelphia, 1970-71). Cf. Hasel, *OT Theology,* pp. 68-75.

[189]Schlatter, *Theologie des NT,* I, 11.

[190]See especially G. Egg, *Adolf Schlatters kritische Position, gezeigt an seiner Matthäusinterpretation* (Stuttgart, 1968), pp. 55, 64-66, 107f.

[191]Pp. 55f., 123-125.

> And Paul who emphasizes the uniqueness of the NT
> word in a most pronounced way takes up with utmost
> vigor the apparently most distant member of the OT,
> the law. In that he experiences with new power what
> the law wants and brings about he arises in the full-
> ness and freedom of faith.[192]

L. Goppelt and H. J. Kraus are quite correct in seeing
in Schlatter's approach a salvation-history conception.[193] Schlatter stands before us as a giant who has
carefully considered the nature of the whole enterprise
of NT theology but whose views have not received the
attention they deserve. He is no narrow Biblicist.[194]
He believes that apostolic authorship does not militate
against the possibility of a development of thought in
the NT. R. Morgan observes correctly, "Since Christian theology, as contemporary interpretation of the
Christian tradition, consists always in this ongoing
argument between conservatives and liberals or modern-
ists, the study of liberal Protestantism can usefully be
balanced by some consideration of Schlatter."[195] Schlatter is a precursor of those for whom the "theological"
concern dominates.

An approach to NT theology which could hardly be
more different than that of Schlatter is the one outlined by William Wrede (1859-1906) in his programmatic essay *Concerning the Task and Method of So-
Called New Testament Theology* first published in
1897.[196] This essay makes Wrede the pioneer of the

[192]A. Schlatter, *Einleitung in die Bibel* (4th ed., 1923), pp. 481f.
as cited by Kraus, *Biblische Theologie*, pp. 177f.
[193]Goppelt, *Theologie des NT*, I, 47f.; Kraus, *Biblische Theologie*,
p. 178.
[194]Kraus (*Biblische Theologie*, p. 177) states that the kind of theology of Schlatter is no "Biblicism" because he does not separate the
act of thought from the act of life and is concerned constantly with
a present reception of what is historical.
[195]*NNTT*, p. 32.
[196]W. Wrede, *Über Aufgabe und Methode der sogenannten Neutestamentlichen Theologie* (Göttingen, 1897), reprinted in *PTNT*,
pp. 81-154, Eng. trans. by R. Morgan in *NNTT*, pp. 68-116, under
the title "The Task and Methods of 'New Testament Theology'."

"religio-historical" phase[197] of NT theology which came
eleven years after the first OT theologies containing
the "history-of-religion" approach were published by
August Kayser (1886) and C. Piepenbring (1886).[198]
Before we consider the major points of Wrede's
arguments, we should briefly consider the work of
H. J. Holtzmann which had just appeared and was the
main object of Wrede's attack.

The monumental two-volume *Textbook of New
Testament Theology* by Heinrich Julius Holtzmann
(1832-1910) appeared in 1897.[199] R. Bultmann calls it
"a model of critical conscientiousness"[200] and R. Morgan "a classic of historical-critical scholarship [which]
rejected Weiss's conservative views about authorship,
his isolation of the New Testament from the surrounding world of thought, and especially his view that
revelation could be presupposed by the discipline."[201]
Holtzmann follows the methodology of F. C. Baur but
leaves out the roughest of Hegelianism. He does not
wish to isolate the NT from its cultural environment,
but falls back to the "concept-of-doctrine" (*Lehrbegriff*) method and places the NT writers side by
side, more or less disconnectedly.[202] Holtzmann retained the traditional name of NT theology and
restricted himself for pragmatic and not for methodological reasons to the canonical writings of the NT,
but claimed that the "separation of the central and the
peripheral will be the unavoidable consequence of
every treatment of the biblical-theological problems
from the historical point of view."[203] This procedure
leads to an atomistic method which is partially tradi-

[197]Harrington, *The Path of Biblical Theology,* p. 115, is totally
off the mark in his statement that "Wrede's essay is the programme
of the *heilsgeschichtlich* school."
[198]Hasel, *OT Theology,* pp. 29-31.
[199]H. J. Holtzmann, *Lehrbuch der Neutestamentlichen Theologie,*
2 vols. (Freiburg/Leipzig, 1897).
[200]Bultmann, *Theology of the NT,* II, 245.
[201]*NNTT,* p. 7.
[202]Merk, *Biblische Theologie,* p. 242; Kümmel, *History,* p. 191.
[203]Holtzmann, *Lehrbuch der Neutestamentlichen Theologie,* I, 25.

tional and partially critical. The doctrines of man, law, sin, corruption, and revolution (conversion) are followed by christology, redemption, and divine righteousness. The concluding chapters discuss ethics, mysticism, and finally eschatology. "At every step it is evident how unnatural is an arrangement of the material which leaves out of account the connexions inherent in the system."[204] In general Holtzmann holds on to the notion that historical research in the field of Biblical theology is a theological undertaking.

Holtzmann's NT theology and his method of justifying the theological task in the laying bare of that which has lasting value make it evident that by the end of the nineteenth century NT theology had departed from the foundation of J. P. Gabler and G. L. Bauer. Surprisingly Adolf Deissmann concludes in his essay "Concerning the Method of the Biblical Theology of the New Testament" (1893)[205] that 100 years after Gabler "there is no longer any doubt about the purely *historical character* of NT theology."[206] Deissmann, however, maintains that one must not superimpose "concepts-of-doctrine" (*Lehrbegriffe*) on the NT.[207] The historical nature of NT theology demands "in principle" that it go beyond the canonical writings so that "the appearance of a predetermined route is removed."[208] The goal of NT theology is "to reproduce the religio-ethical thoughts of early Christianity" which include the following three major tasks: "First, to determine the religio-ethical thought content of the age in which Christendom arose and to which its Gospel is directed";[209] second, to determine "the unique single formations of early Christian consciousness";[210] and

[204]A. Schweitzer, *Paul and His Interpreters. A Critical History* (Schocken ed.; New York, 1964), p. 102.

[205]A. Deissmann, "Zur Methode der biblischen Theologie des Neuen Testaments," *ZThK* 3 (1893), 126-139, reprinted in *PTNT*, pp. 67-80.

[206]Deissmann, *PTNT*, p. 67 (italics his).

[207]Pp. 74-76.

[208]P. 67.

[209]P. 68.

[210]P. 73.

third, to provide "the presentation of the total consciousness of early Christianity."[211] The emphasis lies on the latter, which means on the one hand that it is unavoidable for the historian to strive for a systematic presentation and on the other that there is "historical justification for the attempt to demonstrate unity in the diversity of the classical witness of early Christianity. Certainly there is no uniformity!"[212] The systematization of NT thought is the crown of the enterprise as such. It is a "cross-section" under the headings of "God, man, sin, Christ, salvation."[213]

William Wrede also combatted the "concept-of-doctrine" (*Lehrbegriff*) approach in his epoch-making essay written in 1897.[214] He is much less confident than Deissmann that Gabler's program of Biblical theology as a "purely historical" discipline has come about. Wrede states emphatically, "Biblical theology today . . . is not yet in the true and strict sense a historical discipline at all."[215] Wrede "proclaims clearly and consistently the autonomy of the historical"[216] approach. He rejects Deissmann's third task of a "cross-section" because it "would only be an abstraction of real history" and "we are not accustomed to making similar demands for other areas in the history of religion."[217] He attacks historical NT research of the nineteenth century, particularly the Tübingen School of F. C. Baur but also the theology of A. Ritschl (1822-1889). The latter is said to build upon

[211]P. 78.

[212]P. 79.

[213]Ibid.

[214]See above, n. 196. For assessments of Wrede's essay, see M. Dibelius, "Biblische Theologie und biblische Religionsgeschichte II. des NT," *Religion in Geschichte und Gegenwart* (2nd ed.; Tübingen, 1927), I, 1191-1194, esp. 1192f.; G. Strecker. "William Wrede. Zur hundertsten Wiederkehr seines Geburtstages," *ZThK* 57 (1960), 67-91; Kümmel, *History*, pp. 304f.; Kraus, *Biblische Theologie,* pp. 163-166; R. Morgan, *NNTT*, pp. 8-26.

[215]*PTNT*, p. 154; *NNTT*, p. 116.

[216]Kraus, *Biblische Theologie*, p. 164.

[217]*PTNT*, p. 152 n. 96; *NNTT*, p. 193 n. 96.

historical foundations but abandoned these arbitrarily when they conflicted with doctrine or the canon. Wrede argued for a consistent application of the historical-critical method, i.e., the NT writings must be understood and interpreted solely on the basis of the culture of their own times.[218] This means both that the Reformation principle of the self-interpretation of Scripture is completely rejected and that there is no such thing as inspiration,[219] but that the historical picture of early Christianity can be derived from the three principles enumerated by "the dogmatician of the history-of-religions school"[220] Ernst Troeltsch (1865-1923), namely, historical criticism, analogy, and the correlation between historical processes.[221] This affirmation leads Wrede to the declaration that the dominating method of NT theology as manifested in the works of F. C. Baur, B. Weiss, and H. J. Holtzmann, i.e., the method of "concepts-of-doctrine" (*Lehrbegriffe*), is to be rejected.[222] "So long as New Testament theology retains a direct link with dogmatics as its goal, and expects from it material for dogmatics to work on—and that is a common view—it will be natural for biblical theological work to have an eye on (*hinschielen*) dogmatics. Biblical theology will be pressed for an answer to questions from dogmatics which the Biblical documents do not really give and will be tempted to eliminate results which are troublesome for dogmatics."[223] Wrede gives the impression

[218]*PTNT*, pp. 108-123; *NNTT*, pp. 84-95.

[219]*PTNT*, p. 83: "The old doctrine of inspiration is recognized by academic theology, including very largely also those standing at the 'right,' to be untenable. For logical thinking there can be no middle position between inspired writings and historical documents, although there is in fact no lack of one quarter and three quarter doctrines of inspiration." The resultant corollary is the following: "Where the doctrine of inspiration has been discarded, one can no longer maintain the dogmatic conception of the canon" (*PTNT*, p. 85). Cf. *NNTT*, pp. 69f., with an inexact translation.

[220]Morgan, *NNTT*, p. 10.

[221]Troeltsch in *Theologie als Wissenschaft*, ed. G. Sauter, p. 107.

[222]*PTNT*, pp. 91-108; *NNTT*, pp. 73-84.

[223]*PTNT*, p. 82 (my trans.); *NNTT*, p. 69.

that NT theology is an enterprise that has "an eye on" dogmatics and receives its questions from it. Whether or not this is so is quite debatable. In any case, Wrede maintains that the scholar who works consistently with the historical-critical method does not study the theology or doctrine of a movement (early Christianity) but investigates and presents its "religion."

Wrede's "history-of-religions" method[224] brought about also a new assessment of the title of the discipline of NT theology. Wrede points out as others had before him that "the name 'Biblical theology' originally meant not a theology which the Bible contained, but a theology which has Biblical character, and got it from the Bible. That can be set aside as irrelevant to us."[225] Kraus finds this irrelevance surprising, "for Wrede projects nevertheless his own conceptions without further reflection—as he thinks—into the 'original meaning' of 'Biblical theology'."[226] Indeed the matter is not quite as irrelevant as it is claimed. Wrede proposes a new title for the discipline under the influence of G. Krüger,[227] because the name is controlled by the subject matter. "The name New Testament theology is wrong in both its terms. The New Testament is not concerned merely with theology, but is in truth far more concerned with religion. . . . The appropriate name for the subject matter is: early Christian history of religion, or the history of early Christian religion and theology."[228] This means that NT theology in the widely practiced sense is dead.

In harmony with the renaming and transformation of the discipline, the incisive task is defined by Wrede

---

[224]Good discussions of the "history-of-religion" method and school are found in S. Neill, *The Interpretation of the New Testament 1861-1961* (London, 1964), pp. 157-190; Kümmel, *History,* pp. 206-324; Kraus, *Biblische Theologie,* pp. 160-169.

[225]*PTNT,* p. 153; *NNTT,* p. 115.

[226]Kraus, *Biblische Theologie,* p. 165.

[227]Gustav Krüger, *Das Dogma vom Neuen Testament, Programm der Universität Giessen* (Giessen, 1896), p. 34. Cf. Merk, *Biblische Theologie,* p. 245.

[228]*PTNT,* pp. 153f. (my trans.); *NNTT,* p. 116.

in answer to his own question: "What are we really looking for? In the last resort, we at least want to know *what was believed, thought, taught, hoped, required, and striven for* in the earliest period of Christianity; not what certain writings say about faith, doctrine, hope, etc."[229] The subject matter determines the task.

> On the whole it is not within the historical researcher's power to serve the church through his work. The theologian who obeys the historical object as his master is not in a position to serve the church through his properly scientific-historical work even if he were personally interested in doing so. One would then have to consider the investigation of historical truth as such as serving the church. That is where the chief difficulty of our whole theological situation lies, and it is not created by individual wills: the church rests on history, but history cannot escape investigation, and the investigation of history possesses its own laws within itself.[230]

History is thus autonomous. The theologian has as "his master" none but "the historical object." Kraus emphasizes rightly, "Wrede announces an exchange of masters. Until now the 'concepts-of-doctrine' were masters; from now on history is the master."[231] But Wrede himself admits that "concepts must no doubt play a leading role in NT theology. They are the easiest part of early Christian religion for us to grasp, and most of the results of the religious development are summed up in them. Our discipline, however, is not concerned with every single concept, but only with the normative and dominant, and hence the characteristic and indicative ones."[232] Wrede expects from a NT theology that it "must show us the special character of early Christian ideas and perceptions, sharply profiled, and help us to understand them his-

---

[229]*PTNT*, p. 109; *NNTT*, pp. 84f. (italics his).
[230]*PTNT*, p. 90 (my trans.); *NNTT*, p. 73.
[231]Kraus, *Biblische Theologie*, p. 164.
[232]*PTNT*, pp. 95f.; *NNTT*, pp. 76f.

torically."[233] The new program of Wrede is thus (1) totally freed from church interests and from questions raised by dogmatics, (2) supposedly disinterested in theology as such, (3) fully committed to a consistent historical methodology, (4) seeking to present the religion of earliest Christianity, (5) bound to study the sources without regard to the canon, (6) attempting to show the special character of early Christian ideas and perceptions, (7) describing "concepts" of early Christian religion with a view to indicate development, and (8) built upon the history-of-religions approach.

How would Wrede structure his proposed "early Christian history of religion"? "The first main theme of NT theology is *Jesus' preaching*,"[234] even though "we do not possess the *ipsissima verba* [very words] of Jesus."[235] This is to be followed by a description of the faith and doctrine of the Jewish and Gentile Christian communities. "Next comes a special chapter on Paul."[236] A section on "Johannine theology" will form the concluding chapter.[237]

Wrede's religio-historical program did not find its realization in a publication of his own. He died in 1906. But his influence was permanent. Heinrich Weinel was the first to take up the new program in a work which he surprisingly entitled *Biblical Theology of the New Testament* (1911).[238] The subtitle, "The Religion of Jesus and Early Christianity," reveals clearly its religio-historical intention. He announces that "in place of a Biblical theology of the NT there must be put a history of the religion of earliest Christianity."[239] Weinel puts greatest emphasis on the "religion of

[233]*PTNT*, p. 104; *NNTT*, p. 83.
[234]*PTNT*, p. 135; *NNTT*, p. 103.
[235]*PTNT*, p. 136; *NNTT*, p. 104.
[236]*PTNT*, p. 139; *NNTT*, p. 106.
[237]*PTNT*, pp. 147-150; *NNTT*, pp. 112-114.
[238]H. Weinel, *Biblische Theologie des Neuen Testaments* (Tübingen, 1911; 4th ed., 1928).
[239]P. 3.

Jesus" as an "ethical religion of redemption" in contrast to the "mythical religion of redemption,"[240] both of which united in the "religion" of earliest Christianity. The influence of Hegelian dialectics is apparent. Weinel has also emphasized again the "special theological character" which was denied by Wrede.[241] The reason for this movement from description (reconstruction) to interpretation (theology) was ultimately caused by the "fact that a clear concept of faith and religion was missing"[242] in the history-of-religions school.[243]

Two years after the publication of Weinel's tome, Wilhelm Bousset's (1865-1920) significant *Kyrios Christos* (1913)[244] appeared. Bousset overcomes the clearly delineated epoch of F. C. Baur through a subtle history of the origin and development of the religion of Christianity. The application of radical tradition criticism reduces to a bare minimum the picture of Jesus. Bousset claims that in many cases Christians were mystery-worshippers before they were converted. All that happened was the transference of the concepts of the mystery-gods to Jesus of Nazareth. The *Kyrios* of the early Hellenistic chuches is a power which is present in cult and worship where the believers have sacramental communion with him. Thus Paul or his successors transformed earliest Christianity into a mystery cult. "Such processes take place in unconsciousness, in the uncontrollable depth of the total psyche of the community."[245]

Karl Holl and L. Goppelt raise the question whether

[240]Pp. 130ff.

[241]Merk, *Biblische Theologie*, p. 247.

[242]Bultmann, *Theology of the NT*, II, 246.

[243]J. Kaftan (*Neutestamentliche Theologie im Abriss dargestellt* [Berlin, 1927]) also belongs to the history-of-religions school. He conceives the religion of the NT as an "ethical religion of redemption."

[244]W. Bousset, *Kyrios Christos. Geschichte des Christusglaubens von den Anfängen des Christentums bis Irenaeus* (Göttingen, 1913; 6th ed.; Darmstadt, 1967), Eng. trans. *Kyrios Christos* (Nashville, 1970).

[245]Bousset, *Kyrios Christos*, p. 99.

the origin of the early catholic church has been really explained by Bousset and the history-of-religion approach.[246] "Why were Judaism and Hellenism rejected as foreign elements, if, as has been declared here, the early church has grown from them in historical continuity? The purely historical presentation is unable to explain this hiatus and thus the total picture, because it makes historical continuity the presupposition. Likewise the picture of early Christology is presupposed in the historical principle of correlation: The redeemer myths of the surroundings are 'transferred' to Jesus!"[247] It is evident that a "purely historical" approach is not exactly identical with "pure objectivity" or objective science. E. Troeltsch had indeed declared that the historical-critical method itself has as its mental presupposition "a whole world view."[248] This implies that historical research is always conditioned by the current philosophy of the time.

Let us summarize. At the turn of the twentieth century Protestant theology is represented in a rich panorama. First, there is Franz Overbeck who leaves voluntarily his professional chair for NT exegesis and ancient church history at the University of Basel in 1897 because of the pure historical methodology which led to his "basic unbelief."[249] His radical unbelief denies the theological task in a purely historical study of the NT. Second, there is the history-of-religions school with its program of a religio-historical theology based upon a consistent historical-critical method (Wrede, Troeltsch, Weinel, Bousset, etc.). And finally, there is the incisive theological critique of the "purely historical" method by Schlatter, an extremely erudite scholar with a solid interest in the approach of salva-

---

[246]K. Holl, "Urchristentum und Religionsgeschichte," *Gesammelte Aufsätze zur Kirchengeschichte* (Tübingen, 1928), II, 1-32; Goppelt, *Theologie des NT*, I, 31.

[247]Goppelt, *Theologie des NT*, I, 31.

[248]As cited by Goppelt, ibid.

[249]Kümmel, *History*, p. 203.

tion history (*Heilsgeschichte*). Thus is reached the time of the rise of dialectical theology.

D. From Dialectical Theology to the Present

In the period following World War I several factors, including a changing *Zeitgeist*, brought about a new situation in the theological world. R. C. Dentan points to the following factors: (1) A general loss of faith in evolutionary naturalism; (2) a reaction against the conviction that historical truth can be attained by pure scientific "objectivity" or that such objectivity is indeed attainable; (3) the trend of a return to the idea of revelation in dialectical (neo-orthodox) theology;[250] and to this may be added (4) the renewed interest in theology as such. The historicism of liberalism[251] was found to be inadequate and new developments were at the horizon.

The famous Karl Barth signaled a radical change in both hermeneutics[252] and theology. World War I taught him the inadequacy of liberal theology. His disenchantment was expressed in provocative words in the Preface of his powerful commentary on Romans published in German in 1918:

> The historical-critical method of Biblical investigation has its validity. It points to the preparation for understanding that is never superfluous. But if I had to choose between it and the old doctrine of inspiration, I would decidedly lay hold of the latter. It has the greater, deeper, *more important* validity, because it points to

[250]Dentan, *Preface,* p. 61.

[251]See especially C. T. Craig, "Biblical Theology and the Rise of Historicism," *JBL* 62 (1943), 281-294; M. Kähler, "Biblical Theology," *The New Schaff-Herzog Encyclopedia of Religious Knowledge* (reprint, Grand Rapids, Mich., 1952), II, 183ff.; C. R. North, "OT Theology and the History of Hebrew Religion," *Scottish Journal of Theology* 2 (1949), 113-126.

[252]H.-G. Gadamer, "Hermeneutik und Historismus," *Philosophischer Revue* 9 (1962), 246ff.; J. M. Robinson, "Hermeneutic Since Barth," *The New Hermeneutic. New Frontiers in Theology,* eds. J. M. Robinson and J. B. Cobb, Jr. (New York, 1964), pp. 1-77, esp. 22-29.

the work of understanding, without which all preparation is worthless. I am happy not to choose between the two. But my whole attention was directed to looking *through* the historical into the Spirit of the Bible, which is the Eternal Spirit.[253]

These bold strokes of Barth's pen were part of what gave birth to dialectical (neo-orthodox) theology which raised the question of interpretation and theology in a new way. Barth emphasized the divine side of the God-man relationship, i.e., God as the source of revelation, and demands and practices a "postcritical interpretation of Scripture."[254] This means an interpretation of the Bible which is not stuck with historical-critical problems but penetrates to the witness of revelation contained in the Bible.

A most dominating figure of NT studies in the twentieth century emerges with and departs from dialectical theology. Rudolf Bultmann's scholarly career lasted over six decades. He pioneered in both form criticism[255] and the program of demythologization,[256]

[253]K. Barth, *Der Römerbrief* (Bern, 1918), p. v. (italics his). There is an Eng. trans. by E. C. Hoskyns, *The Epistle to Romans* (London, 1933).

[254]R. Smend, "Nachkritische Schriftauslegung," *PARRHESIA. Festschrift für K. Barth zum 80. Geburtstag* (Zurich, 1966), pp. 215-237.

[255]R. Bultmann, *Die Geschichte der synoptischen Tradition* (Göttingen, 1921; 2nd ed., 1931), Eng. trans. *The History of the Synoptic Tradition* (New York, 1963); R. Bultmann and K. Kundsin, *Form Criticism. Two Essays on NT Research* (New York, 1962). Bultmann was preceded in the form-critical method by M. Dibelius, *Die Formgeschichte des Evangeliums* (Tübingen, 1919; 3rd ed., 1959), Eng. trans. *From Tradition to Gospel* (New York, 1934) and by K. L. Schmidt, *Der Rahmen der Geschichte Jesu* (Berlin, 1919). Important assessments of this method of research are provided by G. Iber, "Zur Formgeschichte der Evangelien," *Theologische Rundschau* 24 (1957/58), 282-338; W. E. Barnes, *Gospel Criticism and Form Criticism* (Edinburgh, 1936); E. B. Redlich, *Form Criticism, Its Value and Limitation* (2nd ed., Edinburgh, 1948); E. Güttgemanns, *Offene Fragen zur Formgeschichte des Evangeliums* (Munich, 1970); H. Koester, "One Jesus and Four Primitive Gospels," *Trajectories through Early Christianity*, eds. J. M. Robinson and H. Koester (New York, 1970), pp. 158-204; D. Lührmann, *Die Redaktion der Logienquelle* (Neukirchen-Vluyn, 1969); C. E. Carlston, *The Parables of the Triple Tradition* (Philadelphia, 1975).

and contributed to the debate about the new quest of the historical Jesus,[257] among many other things. His work has brought about a flood of literature both for and against his views.

Bultmann appears to have absorbed and combined several major influences. First, he comes from the "purely historical" direction of research, i.e., from the history-of-religions school.[258] He remains within the strand of "consistent eschatology."[259] He stands with both feet planted in the historical-critical tradition.[260] Second, Bultmann adopts as his mental presupposition the prevailing philosophy of his time in the form of

---

[256]R. Bultmann's talk "Neues Testament und Mythologie" was originally presented in 1941 and is published in Eng. trans. "New Testament and Mythology," in *Kerygma and Myth*, ed. H.-W. Bartsch (London, 1954), I, 1-44. The early debate roused by this issue is collected in the volumes *Kerygma und Mythos*, ed. H.-W. Bartsch of which an Eng. trans. appeared in the two volumes of *Kerygma and Myth* (London, 1954, 1962). See also the essays by E. Kinder, W. Künneth, R. Prenter, G. Bornkamm in *Kerygma and Myth*, eds. C. E. Braaten and R. A. Harrisville (Nashville, 1962), pp. 55-85, 86-119, 120-137, 172-196. See also R. H. Fuller, *The New Testament in Current Study* (New York, 1962), pp. 1-24.

[257]R. Bultmann opposed it in *Das Verhältnis der urchristlichen Christusbotschaft zum historischen Jesus* (Heidelberg, 1960; 4th ed., 1965), trans. in *The Historical Jesus and the Kerygmatic Christ*, eds. C. E. Braaten and R. A. Harrisville (Nashville, 1964), pp. 15-42. The latter volume also contains essays on the subject by E. Stauffer, H. Conzelmann, H. Braun, C. E. Braaten, H.-W. Bartsch, H. Ott, R. A. Harrisville, Van A. Harvey, and S. M. Ogden. See also J. M. Robinson, *A New Quest of the Historical Jesus* (SBT, 25; London, 1959); K. Schubert, ed., *Der historische Jesus und der Christus unseres Glaubens* (Vienna, 1962); E. Fuchs, *Studies on the Historical Jesus* (SBT, 42; London, 1964); Fuller, *NT in Current Study*, pp. 25-53; L. E. Keck, *A Future for the Historical Jesus: The Place of Jesus in Preaching and Theology* (Nashville, 1971); G. Aulén, *Jesus in Contemporary Historical Research* (Nashville, 1976).

[258]Bultmann, *Theology of the NT*, II, 250.

[259]See Johannes Weiss, *Die Predigt Jesu vom Reich Gottes* (Göttingen, 1892; 2nd ed., 1900) and especially Bousset's views which Bultmann states were essentially correct (*Glauben und Verstehen*, I [Göttingen, 1933], pp. 256f.). Cf. Kümmel, *History*, pp. 226-244; G. E. Ladd, *Jesus and the Kingdom. The Eschatology of Biblical Realism* (2nd ed.; Waco, Texas, 1970), pp. 3-38.

[260]Bultmann, *Theology of the NT*, II, 250.

the existentialism of M. Heidegger,[261] his colleague at the University of Marburg from 1923 to 1928. His attempt is to reinterpret the NT message (kerygma) into the thought world of modern man. He seeks to prevent modern man from making an existential decision on the basis of the mythological language of the NT. This means for Bultmann "to interpret the theological thoughts of the New Testament in their connection with the 'act of living'—i.e. as explication of believing self-understanding."[262] Bultmann, for example, believes it possible to detect with historical research that Jesus proclaimed "the eschatological message of the irruption of God's Reign" with the certainty of the imminent end. This apocalyptic myth must be demythologized, i.e., decoded and reinterpreted. It means in existentialist terms "to direct him [man] into his NOW as the hour of decision for God."[263] Third, Bultmann seeks to combine the historical question with the theological one. He does not wish to separate "reconstruction" from "interpretation" as O. Merk puts it,[264] or to keep apart the "what it meant" from the "what it means" in the terms of K. Stendahl.[265] Bultmann seeks to avoid the mistake "of the tearing apart of the act of thinking from the act of living and hence of a failure to recognize the intent of theological utterance."[266] This is where Bultmann departs from Wrede and the aims of a "purely historical" direction of research. The goal of the latter

[261]Particularly as expressed in Heidegger's *Being and Time* (New York, 1962). First German edition 1927. An incisive discussion of the influence of Heideggerian existentialism on Bultmann is by J. Macquarrie, *An Existentialist Theology: Comparison of Heidegger and Bultmann* (New York, 1955). See also J. M. Robinson and J. B. Cobb, Jr., eds., *The Later Heidegger and Theology,* "New Frontiers in Theology I" (New York, 1963).

[262]Bultmann, *Theology of the NT,* II, 251.

[263]Vol. I, 21; cf. *Kerygma and Myth,* I, pp. 42f.: "Through the word of Preaching the cross and resurrection are made present: the eschatological 'now' is here. . . ."

[264]Merk, *Biblische Theologie,* pp. 257f.

[265]K. Stendahl, "Biblical Theology, Contemporary," *IDB,* I, 419.

[266]Bultmann, *Theology of the NT,* II, 250f.

direction of research is enlarged so that it may encompass the theological question. This is analyzed at greater depth in the following chapter.

The so-called Bultmann School is presented with variations and changes in some basic questions particularly by Hans Conzelmann, who is the only one of the so-called Bultmannians to have written *An Outline of the Theology of the New Testament* (1967),[267] P. Vielhauer and his students Günther Klein,[268] Georg Strecker,[269] and Walter Schmithals.[270]

The most significant reaction against Bultmann came in the 1950s from his own disciples who are customarily called the post-Bultmannians.[271] The most important of them are Ernst Käsemann, who formally launched the new quest of the historical Jesus in 1953,[272] Ernst Fuchs, J. M. Robinson,[273] and Günther Bornkamm.[274] It is well to keep in mind that Martin Kähler (1835-1912) was a forerunner of the new questers.[275] The post-Bultmannians objected to Bultmann's claim that the Jesus of history was irrelevant for faith. For some of the post-Bultmannians the historical Jesus is the ground of the kerygma (Käsemann, Bornkamm, etc.), while for others he is the ground of faith (Fuchs,

[267]H. Conzelmann, *Grundriss der Theologie des Neuen Testaments* (Munich, 1967), Eng. trans. (New York, 1969).

[268]G. Klein, "Das Ärgernis des Kreuzes," *Streit um Jesus,* ed. F. Lorenz (Munich, 1969), pp. 61-71.

[269]G. Strecker, "Die historische und theologische Problematik der Jesus-frage," *EvTh* 29 (1969), 453-476; idem, "Das Problem der Theologie des Neuen Testaments," *PTNT,* pp. 1-31.

[270]W. Schmithals, "Kein Streit um Kaisers Bart," *Evangelische Kommentare* 3 (1970), 76-85.

[271]W. G. Doty, *Contemporary New Testament Interpretation* (Englewood Cliffs, N.J., 1972), pp. 28-51.

[272]Published under the title "Das Problem des historischen Jesus," *ZThK* 51 (1954), 125-153; Eng. trans. E. Käsemann, *Essays on New Testament Themes* (SBT, 41; London, 1964), pp. 15-47.

[273]See above, n. 257, for literature.

[274]See his *Jesus of Nazareth* (New York, 1960).

[275]In 1896 he published his book *Der sogenannte historische Jesus und der geschichtliche, biblische Christus* (Leipzig, 1896); Eng. trans. *The So-Called Historical Jesus and the Historic Biblical Christ* (Philadelphia, 1964).

Ebeling,[276] etc.). It has recently been stated that "the failure to achieve clear results in the so-called new quest of the historical Jesus has resulted in a scaling down of critical expectations."[277]

In the early 1960s several post-Bultmannians, notably E. Fuchs, G. Ebeling, J. M. Robinson, and also R. W. Funk,[278] went beyond Bultmann's hermeneutic,[279] particularly his adoption of the existentialism of the earlier Heidegger,[280] criticizing Bultmann's understanding of the way language functions. In traditional hermeneutics the text is to be interpreted. The new hermeneutic reverses this process. Man is to be interpreted or addressed through the medium of the text. An adequate discussion of the complexity of the new hermeneutic would lead us too far afield. Enough has been said to indicate that critical scholarship has moved far beyond Bultmann and has seen decisive weaknesses in his approach.[281]

The essay published in English in 1976 by a post-Bultmannian who is a known member of both the movement of the new quest and the movement of the new hermeneutic is symptomatic of NT theology among one of them. J. M. Robinson has given it the provocative title "The Future of New Testament Theology."[282] He states that with Wrede "New Testament Theology

[276]Gerhard Ebeling, *Word and Faith* (London, 1963); idem, *The Nature of Faith* (London, 1961); idem, *Theology and Proclamation: Dialogue with Bultmann* (Philadelphia, 1966).

[277]H. C. Kee, "Biblical Criticism, NT," *IDB Suppl.* (1976), pp. 103f.

[278]R. W. Funk, *Language, Hermeneutic, and Word of God* (New York, 1966). See above, nn. 261-276.

[279]A concise summary is provided by Doty, *Contemporary NT Interpretation*, pp. 28-51; P. J. Achtemeier, *An Introduction to the New Hermeneutic* (Philadelphia, 1969); G. Stachel, *Die neue Hermeneutik. Ein Überblick* (Munich, 1968).

[280]Robinson and Cobb, eds., *The Later Heidegger and Theology*.

[281]See the summary by N. Perrin, "The Challenge of New Testament Theology Today," *New Testament Issues,* ed. R. Batey (New York, 1970), pp. 15-34, and the points of criticism mentioned by Doty, *Contemporary NT Interpretation,* pp. 43f.

[282]See above, n. 5.

was brought to its end. . . ."[283] "After many detours and evasions we should simply concede Wrede to have been right and hence deny any future to New Testament theology; we should . . . channel New Testament Theology into the less problematical discipline of the history-of-religions. . . . Yet an exclusive concentration on the historical task, as the form of New Testament theology suited to the twentieth century, should admittedly be named 'History of Primitive Christian Religion,' not 'New Testament Theology'."[284] But Robinson feels that Bultmann opened up another possible expanding front toward a future of NT theology. "This procedure, which actually points to the new hermeneutic and its presuppositions in the philosophy of language, . . . achieve [sic] important results for New Testament theology."[285] On the basis of a "cosmological" path, not an "anthropological" one as in the case of Bultmann, NT theology can be carried through "in terms of the otherworldly fanaticism of the primitive congregation moving toward the Pauline and Johannine unworldliness, but also to the Lucan and Constantinian worldliness, a trend that was constantly accompanied by a left wing of increasingly gnostic flight from the world."[286] Thus Robinson calls for a "move beyond New Testament doctrinal constructs . . . into the movements of language that can be interpreted in terms of alternatives in the modern world, by extending them 'theologically,' 'ontologically,' 'cosmologically,' 'politically,' etc."[287] Does this intended renewal of the old program with an understanding of history which is oriented on the totality of society and the current philosophy of language not integrate the NT into history in such a way that its significance is removed through an a priori world view?[288]

[283]"The Future of NT Theology," p. 17.
[284]P. 20.
[285]Ibid.
[286]P. 21.
[287]P. 22.
[288]See Goppelt, *Theologie des NT,* I, 40f.

The opposite direction from the one just summarized is followed by Peter Stuhlmacher of the University of Tübingen, one of whose teachers was the post-Bultmannian E. Käsemann. Stuhlmacher's book *Interpretation of Scripture on the Way to Biblical Theology* (1975)[289] contains his basic reflections and suggestions. He deals extensively with the Bultmannian heritage but concludes that "the integrating power of Bultmann's hermeneutical scheme is largely exhausted,"[290] and points out in addition that "we do not yet have the new hermeneutic which we are in need of."[291] This implies a No to the Bultmannians and post-Bultmannians. In contrast to them Stuhlmacher speaks of a "hermeneutic of approval" (*Hermeneutik des Einverständnisses*)[292] which is to contain ample room for (1) the "inherent power of the word of Scripture"; (2) the "horizon of faith and experience of the church"; (3) an "openness for a meeting with the truth of God which comes to us from transcendence"; and (4) an "openness for the possibility of faith."[293] He sees himself as holding a middle position as "one on the borderline between kerygmatic theology, Pietism, and a biblically oriented Lutheranism."[294]

It may be startling for some to note that Stuhlmacher puts forth proposals toward a "Biblical theology of the New Testament."[295] He follows the lead of OT scholars (G. von Rad, W. Zimmerli, and esp. H. Gese) and raises the question whether a NT theology "should not again be projected as a Biblical theology, i.e. as a New Testament theology which is open towards the Old Testament and which seeks to rework the connection of tradition and interpretation of the OT

[289]P. Stuhlmacher, *Schriftauslegung auf dem Wege zur biblischen Theologie* (Göttingen, 1975).

[290]P. 99.

[291]P. 48.

[292]Pp. 120-125.

[293]Pp. 125f.

[294]P. 61.

[295]Pp. 127, 138, 163.

and NT traditions."[296] The center of such a Biblical theology of the NT is the proclamation of reconciliation rooted in the message of Jesus Christ,[297] because "the message of reconciliation (*Versöhnungsbotschaft*) [is] the determining center of Holy Scripture as a whole. . . ."[298]

The positions of J. M. Robinson and P. Stuhlmacher reflect in their conceptions of NT theology the radical divergence of those coming out of the Bultmann School. The program of the former seems to lead back to the "purely historical" direction, whereas the program of the latter leads closer to the so-called "salvation-history" movement of scholarship. Before we return to the *heilsgeschichtliche* (salvation-historical) approaches to NT theology, we must note also developments in Roman Catholic scholarship and those approaches that are classified as representing the "modern positive" tendency of NT scholarship.

Roman Catholic scholarship produced its first NT theology in 1928. The French scholar A. Lemonnyer presented in his *The Theology of the New Testament*[299] a thematic approach. This is also the method of the popularly written *The Theology of the New Testament* (1936) by O. Kuss.[300] Much more significant works appeared in the early 1950s. M. Meinertz published in 1950 a two-volume NT theology[301] which he had finished already eight years earlier. Although he discusses the relationship of NT theology to dogmatics,

[296]P. 138.

[297]Pp. 127, 175.

[298]P. 178.

[299]A. Lemonnyer, O. P., *La Théologie du Nouveau Testament* (Paris, 1928), Eng. trans. *The Theology of the New Testament* (London, 1930). A revised edition and enlarged by L. Cerfaux was published in Paris, 1963. Cf. Harrington, *Path*, pp. 117f.

[300]O. Kuss, *Die Theologie des Neuen Testaments. Eine Einführung* (Regensburg, 1936).

[301]M. Meinertz, *Theologie des Neuen Testaments*, 2 vols. (Bonn, 1950); idem, "Randglossen zu meiner Theologie des NT," *ThQ* 132 (1952), 411-432; idem, "Sinn und Bedeutung der neutestamentlichen Theologie," *Münchener theologische Zeitschrift* 5 (1954), 159-170.

he does not discuss the origin and development of the discipline of NT theology. Jesus Christ has a unifying role in the variegated theologies of the individual NT writers. The record of divine revelation exhibits in the different books of the NT a richness which finds different forms of expression, but which is united in the person Jesus Christ.[302]

Meinertz has divided his volumes into four parts. The first deals with "Jesus" in which John the Baptist also figures as Jesus' precursor.[303] The second part discusses the early Christian community (with Acts, James, Jude).[304] The third part with the teaching of Paul is the longest,[305] and it is followed by the last part on Johannine thought.[306] His concluding sentence sums up the emphasis of his two tomes: "The living Christ unites ultimately all the rays of the New Testament."[307]

J. Bonsirven presented his *Theology of the New Testament* in 1951[308] and is also interested in a unified presentation of NT theology. The task of NT theology "is to bring together the revealed truths contained in the New Testament, to define their meaning as the authors understood it, and to attempt to classify these truths in order of importance, so as to provide a basis for Christian dogma."[309] This reveals an essentially historical-descriptive approach which "follows the chronology of history, not of the documents we are drawing on."[310]

Bonsirven also divides his NT theology into four

[302]Meinertz, *Theologie des NT*, I, 3f.
[303]I, 8-211.
[304]Pp. 212-247.
[305]II, 1-254.
[306]Pp. 267-338.
[307]P. 346.
[308]J. Bonsirven, S. J. *Théologie du Nouveau Testament* (Paris, 1951), Eng. trans. *Theology of the New Testament* (Westminister, Md., 1963).
[309]*Theology of the NT*, p. xiii.
[310]P. xvi.

parts. The first treats Jesus Christ.[311] The short second one is on "primitive Christianity."[312] The third discusses the teachings of Paul,[313] and finally comes a section on the other apostolic witnesses under the headings of theology, Christian life, and eschatology.[314]

The modern Catholic Biblical movement was inaugurated by the encyclical *Divino Afflante Spiritu* (1943) of Pius XII which instructed Roman Catholic scholars to use modern methods in the study of Scripture. In the mid-1950s faculty trained in the methods of Biblical criticism moved in large numbers into college, seminary, and university teaching positions. The Pontifical Biblical Commission's secretary stated in 1955 that now Roman Catholic scholars had "complete freedom" (*plena libertate*) concerning the decrees of 1905-1915, except where they touched on faith and morals.[315] In the mid-1970s one can hardly speak of any differences in the application of the methods of Biblical criticism between non-Roman Catholic scholars and Roman Catholic scholars. Two of the Roman Catholic NT theologies written since the reorientation of Roman Catholic scholarship use the thematic approach. There is the four-volume work of the German Karl H. Schelkle (1968-1974) and the two-volume work of the Spaniard M. García Cordero (1972).[316] Aside from these there have been studies on the nature and method of NT theology by Rudolf Schnackenburg (1961),[317] and Biblical (OT and NT) theology by

[311]Pp. 3-152.
[312]Pp. 153-189.
[313]Pp. 191-368.
[314]Pp. 369-405.
[315]R. E. Brown, *Biblical Reflections on Crises Facing the Church* (New York, 1975), p. 111.
[316]K. H. Schelkle, *Theologie des Neuen Testaments,* 4 vols. (Düsseldorf, 1968-74), Eng. trans. *Theology of the New Testament* (Collegeville, Minn., 1971ff.); M. G. Cordero, *Teología de la Biblia II et III: Nuevo Testamento,* 2 vols. (Madrid, 1972).
[317]R. Schnackenburg, *La Théologie du Nouveau Testament* (Bruges, 1961), Germ. trans. *Neutestamentliche Theologie. Der Stand der Forschung* (Munich, 1963; 2nd ed., 1965), Eng. trans. *New Testament Theology Today* (London, 1963).

Wilfrid Harrington (1973).[318] There are many highly
significant essays touching on all the major issues of
NT theology,[319] but there is still no NT theology
written by a Roman Catholic which builds on modern
methods of Biblical criticism.[320]

There are several NT theologies which may be
loosely classified as belonging to the "modern positive" direction of NT theology. In its earlier stages
this direction was represented by B. Weiss, W. Beyschlag, P. Feine, F. Büchsel, F. Weidner, E. P. Gould,
and G. B. Stevens. E. Stauffer published his *New
Testament Theology* in 1941[321] and explicitly points
to B. Weiss as the point of departure for his work.[322]

[318]See above, n. 1.

[319]The essays by the following seem to be among the most important: W. Hillman, "Wege zur neutestamentlichen Theologie," *Wissenschaft und Weisheit* 14 (1951), 56-67, 200-211; 15 (1952), 15-32,
122-136; C. Spicq, "L'avenement de la théologie biblique," *RSPT*
35 (1951), 561-574; idem, "Nouvelles réflexions sur la théologie biblique," *RSPT* 42 (1958), 209-219; F.-M. Braun, "La théologie biblique," *Revue Thomiste* 61 (1953), 221-253; H. Schlier, "Über Sinn
und Aufgabe einer Theologie des Neuen Testaments," *Biblische Zeitschrift* 1 (1957), 5-23, Eng. trans. "The Meaning and Function of a
Theology of the New Testament," *Dogmatic vs. Biblical Theology,* ed.
H. Vorgrimler (Baltimore/Dublin, 1964), pp. 87-113; A. Descamps,
"Réflexions sur la méthode en théologie biblique," *Sacra Pagina* I
(Gembloux, 1959), pp. 132-157; A. Vögtle, "Progress and Problems in
NT Exegesis," *Dogmatic vs. Biblical Theology,* pp. 31-65; D. M. Stan-
ley, "Towards a Biblical Theology of the New Testament. Modern
Trends in Catholic Biblical Scholarship," *Contemporary Developments
in Theology* (West Hartford, 1959), pp. 267-281; A. Vögtle, "New
Testament Theology," *Sacramentum Mundi* (London, 1969), IV, 216-
220; K. H. Schelkle, "Was bedeutet 'Theologie des Neuen Testaments'?" *Evangelienforschung,* ed. J. Bauer (Würzburg, 1968), pp.
299-312; P. Grech, "Contemporary Methodological Problems in New
Testament Theology," *BTB* 2 (1972), 262-280.

[320] There are three short but significant essays on aspects of NT
theology in *The Jerome Biblical Commentary,* eds. R. E. Brown,
J. A. Fitzmyer, and R. E. Murphy (Englewood Cliffs, N.J., 1968):
D. M. Stanley, S. J., and R. E. Brown, S. S., "Aspects of New Testament Thought" (II, 768-799); J. A. Fitzmyer, S. J., "Pauline Theology" (II, 800-827); and B. Vawter, C.M., "Johannine Theology"
(II, 828-839).

[321]E. Stauffer, *Die Theologie des Neuen Testaments* (Gütersloh,
1941; 5th ed., 1948), Eng. trans. from 5th ed. *New Testament Theology* (London, 1955). .

[322]Stauffer, *NT Theology,* p. 49.

Stauffer does not organize his work along the lines of the chronological order of the NT writings or blocks of writings, but chooses a systematic approach organized along theological themes. His material order follows the line of "the Christocentric theology of history in the New Testament." This approach has a basic "salvation-historical" outlook[323] and the method is "strictly descriptive."[324] Stauffer's "theology of history" leaves no room for the theology of the Synoptics,[325] or of Jesus, Paul, John, Hebrews, etc. His method precludes a presentation of any historical development. This is so much more surprising since Stauffer does away with the canon as normative for NT theology.[326] He is thus the first to follow Wrede's demand, but not for the same reason. Stauffer seeks to demonstrate that the "Christocentric theology of history" is built upon "the old biblical tradition"[327] and moves on in a straight line to the theology of post-NT Christianity.[328] One looks in vain for a justification of this procedure.[329] The beauty of the unified picture of the NT with prior Judaism and the later theology of Christianity appears at the expense of allowing the NT witness to stand by itself over against earlier or later developments.

The American scholar F. C. Grant wrote in his *Introduction to New Testament Thought* (1950) that this study does not pretend to be a NT theology,[330] although he affirms that "there *is* a New Testament theology, or perhaps several theologies, contiguous, partly overlapping—like the spheres or monads in cer-

323So praised by O. Cullmann, *Christ and Time* (London, 1962), p. 26 n. 9, as having "a lasting merit."

324Stendahl, *IDB*, I, 421.

325Schlier in *Dogmatic vs. Biblical Theology*, p. 98.

326Stauffer, *NT Theology*, pp. 44f., 73-79.

327P. 51.

328Pp. 235-257.

329Merk, *Biblische Theologie*, p. 253; W. G. Kümmel, "Review of E. Stauffer, *Die Theologie des NT*," *TLZ* 75 (1950), 421-426, esp. 425.

330F. C. Grant, *An Introduction to New Testament Thought* (Nashville, 1950), pp. 43-46.

tain pluralistic philosophies."[331] "New Testament theology was the theology of the growing Christian Church, as reflected in the New Testament, not a finished product, but a theology in process."[332] He argues that "a genetic organization of the theological data" of the NT is out of the question. The arrangement that is more serviceable is an arrangement of "areas of thought."[333] Accordingly, the task is "not so much of description as of interpretation."[334] In harmony with these methodological considerations Grant proceeds to develop the following "areas of thought": "Revelation and Scripture" (pp. 63-98), "The Doctrine of God" (pp. 99-143), "Miracles" (pp. 144-159), "The Doctrine of Man" (pp. 160-186), "The Doctrine of Christ" (pp. 187-245), "The Doctrine of Salvation" (pp. 246-267), "The Doctrine of the Church" (pp. 268-299), and "New Testament Ethics" (pp. 300-324). The basis for this presentation is that "there is a real unity in the New Testament—we must never lose sight of that," while it is clearly recognized that "diversity involves some of the basic ideas of New Testament theology."[335] Whether Grant is responsible for the "breaking apart of reconstruction and interpretation"[336] because he is said to identify the "descriptive method" with "interpretation"[337] remains an open issue.

The brief and popular study entitled *Introducing New Testament Theology* by A. M. Hunter of Scotland is designed to be a guide to NT theology for ministers and interested laymen. It reveals a more or less historical approach to NT theology based upon

[331]Pp. 26f.

[332]P. 60.

[333]P. 24.

[334]P. 27. Merk (*Biblische Theologie*, p. 265) misinterprets Grant in his claim that "interpretation" is to be defined as the "descriptive method."

[335]P. 30.

[336]P. 51.

[337]This is claimed by Merk, *Biblische Theologie*, p. 265.

"the fact of Christ"[338] which includes sections on "the kingdom of God and the ministry of Jesus," "the gospel of the kingdom," and "the resurrection," followed by "the first preachers of the fact,"[339] and concludes with "the interpreters of the fact" in the form of Paul, Peter, the author of Hebrews, and John.[340] This "brilliantly clear book"[341] is interested particularly in the unity of the NT theologians without overlooking their diversity,[342] an attempt not surprising for a scholar who wrote a book on *The Unity of the New Testament* (1944).[343]

The NT theologies of Alan Richardson (1958), F. Stagg (1962), and R. E. Knudsen (1964)[344] were followed on the Continent by a more rigorous "modern historical" approach in NT theology by W. G. Kümmel (1969), J. Jeremias (1971, 1975), and E. Lohse (1974).[345] Stephen C. Neill's *Jesus Through Many Eyes. Introduction to the Theology of the New Testament* (1976) is the most recent work in the "modern historical" direction of NT theology. Most of these NT theologies will receive more detailed attention in the following chapter.

In a class by itself is the four-volume work of Martin Albertz under the title *Message of the New Testa-*

[338]A. M. Hunter, *Introducing New Testament Theology* (London, 1957; 2nd ed., 1963), pp. 13-61.

[339]Pp. 63-85.

[340]Pp. 87-151.

[341]Harrington, *Path*, p. 128.

[342]Hunter, *Introducing NT Theology*, p. 7.

[343]A. M. Hunter, *The Unity of the New Testament* (London, 1943), Germ. trans. *Die Einheit des Neuen Testaments* (Munich, 1959).

[344]A. Richardson, *An Introduction to the Theology of the New Testament* (London, 1958); F. Stagg, *New Testament Theology* (Nashville, 1962); R. E. Knudsen, *Theology in the New Testament. A Basis for Christian Faith* (Chicago, 1964).

[345]W. G. Kümmel, *Die Theologie des Neuen Testament nach seinen Hauptzeugen: Jesus, Paulus, Johannes* (Göttingen, 1969; 2nd ed. 1972), Eng. trans. *The Theology of the New Testament According to Its Major Witnesses: Jesus-Paul-John* (Nashville, 1973); J. Jeremias, *Neutestamentliche Theologie*, 1. Teil (Gütersloh, 1971), Eng. trans. *New Testament Theology: The Proclamation of Jesus* (New York, 1971); E. Lohse, *Grundriss der neutestamentlichen Theologie* (Stuttgart, 1974).

ment (1946-57).[346] In 1230 pages the former student
of T. Zahn and A. von Harnack strikes out on his
own path. He suggests that the traditional critical
introduction to the NT and the traditional historical-
critical theology of the New Testament need to be
recast in radically new ways.[347] The first two volumes
attempt to rework the field of NT introduction along
the lines of form criticism and carry the subtitle
"Origin of the Message." The remaining two volumes
grow organically out of the first two and contain the
"Unfolding of the Message." Albertz was stimulated
by W. Michaelis "to bring to a fundamental criticism
the entire traditional (critical) theology from the time
that it placed man, even the pious one, in the center
of thinking."[348] He argues against R. Bultmann's program of demythologization by stating that Bultmann
"does not derive the concept of myth from the NT"
but from "the scholarship of the 19th century" and
notes that "the Pastoral Letters would have taught him
that there are no myths in the church, and Paul would
tell him that Christ is no myth for him."[349] That this
argument misses Bultmann's usage of myth does not
need to be stated.

Albertz claims that "NT theology is a child of the
time of Enlightenment."[350] He criticizes the philosophical approach of F. C. Baur, the method of "concepts-of-doctrine" (*Lehrbegriffe*) as used by B. Weiss,
the religio-psychological approaches of A. von Harnack
and A. Deissmann, the religio-historical method of W.
Bousset and others, and the attempt to interpret the

[346]M. Albertz, *Botschaft des Neuen Testamentes*, 1. Band: *Die
Entstehung der Botschaft*, 1. Halbband: *Die Entstehung des Evangeliums* (Zollikon-Zurich, 1946); 2. Halbband: *Die Entstehung des
apostolischen Schriftkanons* (Zollikon-Zurich, 1952); 2. Band: *Die
Entfaltung der Botschaft*, 1. Halbband: *Die Voraussetzungen der Botschaft. Der Inhalt der Botschaft* (Zollikon-Zurich, 1954); 2. Halbband:
Der Inhalt der Botschaft (Zollikon-Zurich, 1957).
  [347]I/2, 306.
  [348]II/2, 15.
  [349]I/1, 10f.
  [350]II/1, 15.

NT on the basis of a modern world view as is the case in E. Stauffer and R. Bultmann.[351] Thus the place of a NT theology must be taken by an "unfolding of the NT message." The schema for this unfolding is provided in 2 Corinthians 13:13, which is the source for the headings of the key sections: (1) "The Grace of the Lord Jesus Christ"; (2) "The Love of God"; and (3) "The Fellowship of the Holy Spirit."

In view of the fact that Albertz comes from the form critical school, it is not at all clear why he can hold on to form criticism which is also influenced by the *Zeitgeist*[352] and disclaim the validity of other branches of research which also reflect the *Zeitgeist*. Another inconsistency is revealed in his condemnation of the religio-historical approach and the fact that he does not wish to do without the religio-historical "Framework of the Message."[353] It is evident that Albertz uses a highly individualistic approach. But we agree with E. Fascher that "all this should not hinder us to admit that this work is filled with suggestions for future research, and the young generation can only be asked to come to grips with it."[354]

Now we need to return to the salvation-history approach to NT theology. We had seen that the earlier phase of the approach of *Heilsgeschichte* (salvation-history) was associated with J. Ch. K. von Hofmann, T. Zahn, and A. Schlatter. This line of approach is most vigorously pursued through two major studies by O. Cullmann.[355] The most recent Continental European

[351]II/1, 15-21. See also M. Albertz, "Die Krisis der sogenannten neutestamentlichen Theologie," *Zeichen der Zeit* 10 (1954), 370-376.

[352]See E. V. McKnight, *What is Form Criticism?* (Philadelphia, 1969); J. H. Hayes, ed., *Old Testament Form Criticism* (San Antonio, Tex., 1974).

[353]Albertz, *Die Entfaltung der Botschaft*, II/1, 22-64.

[354]E. Fascher, "Eine Neuordnung der neutestamentlichen Fachdisziplin?" *TLZ* 83 (1958), 618. See also Schnackenburg, *NT Theology Today*, pp. 38f.; Kraus, *Biblische Theologie*, p. 188 n. 87; Merk, *Biblische Theologie*, pp. 262f.; Harrington, *Path*, p. 117.

[355]O. Cullmann, *Christus und die Zeit* (Zollikon-Zurich, 1946), Eng. trans. *Christ and Time* (London, 1951); idem, *Heil als Geschichte: Heilsgeschichtliche Existenz im Neuen Testament* (Tübingen, 1965), Eng. trans. *Salvation in History* (New York, 1967).

NT theology by L. Goppelt, posthumously published in two volumes, also follows the salvation-history approach.[356] The well-known American evangelical scholar George E. Ladd had his *magnum opus* published in 1974 under the title *A Theology of the New Testament*, and C. K. Lehman, another evangelical scholar, published in the same year his *Biblical Theology, 2: New Testament*.[357] The works by Cullmann, Ladd, and Goppelt will be discussed in the next chapter on methodology.

An excellent description of the "Biblical Theology Movement" in America from the 1940s onward is provided by B. S. Childs.[358] His unique emphasis that it was distinctly American has been challenged by J. Barr who points out that "in Great Britain and on the Continent the same broad tendencies existed, although the setting was different."[359] The "Biblical Theology Movement" included such features as (1) opposition to philosophical systems, (2) contrast between Hebrew and Greek thought, (3) emphasis on the unity of the Testaments, (4) uniqueness of the Bible as against its environment, (5) reaction against the older "liberal" theology, and (6) revelation of God in history. Childs believes that "the end of the Biblical Theology Movement as a dominant force in American theology" came in 1963.[360] Thus there is a need for a new Biblical Theology. It must be clearly recognized that in the thinking of Childs "the enterprise of Biblical Theology is a different discipline

---

[356]L. Goppelt, *Theologie des Neuen Testaments*, 2 vols., ed. J. Roloff (Göttingen, 1975-76).

[357]G. E. Ladd, *A Theology of the New Testament* (Grand Rapids, Mich., 1974); C. K. Lehman, *Biblical Theology, 2: New Testament* (Scottdale, Pa., 1974).

[358]B. S. Childs, *Biblical Theology in Crisis* (Philadelphia, 1970), pp. 13-87.

[359]J. Barr, "Biblical Theology," *IDB Sup.* (Nashville, 1976), p. 105. See also J. Barr, *Old and New in Interpretation* (New York, 1966); idem, *The Bible in the Modern World* (New York, 1973).

[360]Childs, *Biblical Theology in Crisis*, p. 85.

from either OT or NT Theology."[361] This means that in his understanding there are legitimate fields of OT theology and NT theology. NT theology would be "chiefly a descriptive enterprise" which is different from Biblical theology.   Childs maintains "that the canon of the Christian church is the most appropriate context from which to do Biblical Theology."[362] This writer has dealt elsewhere with Childs' approach.[363] Since Childs is not directly dealing with NT theology, it seems unnecessary to describe his proposals for Biblical Theology here.

This historical survey has highlighted the origin and checkered history of NT theology.   Fundamental issues remain unresolved and are the subject of a continuing debate among scholars of various backgrounds and schools of thought.   We have attempted to highlight the major roots in the present debate on the nature, function, purpose, and limitations of NT theology.

[361]A private communication cited in Hasel, *OT Theology,* p. 50 n. 57.
[362]Childs, *Biblical Theology in Crisis,* p. 99.
[363]Hasel, *OT Theology,* pp. 49-55.

II. Methodology in NT Theology

The question of methodology is fundamental. It was raised in a unique way by J. P. Gabler in 1787;[1] his views were a powerful catalyst for future thought and remain so today. The cluster of issues connected with and surrounding NT theology (and Biblical theology) have been debated in the past and are being debated with unrelenting vigor in the present. The complexity of the issues is compounded by the fact that even those scholars who follow the same methodological approach to NT theology do not always agree, sometimes even on basic questions. Then there is a merging of methods. This fact makes it not only difficult but also precarious to assign a particular theologian to a given method. We shall proceed in letting the issues of methodology arise by surveying four

[1]Johann Phillip Gabler's inaugural lecture "Oratio de iusto discrimine theologiae biblicae et dogmaticae, regundisque recte utriusque finibus," delivered at the University of Altdorf, March 30, 1787, marked the beginning of a new phase in the study of Biblical theology through its claim that Biblical theology is historical in character [e genere historico] in that it sets forth what sacred writers thought about divine matters . . ." (in Gableri Opuscula Academica II [1831], pp. 183f.). Cf. R. Smend, "J. Ph. Gablers Begründung der biblischen Theologie," EvTh 22 (1962), 345ff. William Wrede's programmatic essay Über Aufgabe und Methode der sogenannten Neutestamentlichen Theologie (Göttingen, 1897), p. 8, Eng. trans. by R. Morgan, The Nature of New Testament Theology (SBT 2/25; London, 1973), p. 69, emphasizes again the "purely historical" character of NT (Biblical) theology.

major, current approaches to NT theology, each represented by more than one scholar's work.

A. The Thematic Approach

1. *Alan Richardson.* The presentation of NT theology by Alan Richardson under the title *An Introduction to New Testament Theology* (1958) has been hailed as "the greatest New Testament theology we have."[2]

Richardson grants us a glimpse into his understanding of NT theology in the Preface. He claims that the only way to know whether "the apostolic Church possessed a common theology and that it can be reconstructed from the New Testament literature" is "to frame an hypothesis concerning the underlying theology of the New Testament documents and then to test the hypothesis by reference to the text of those documents in the light of all available critical and historical knowledge."[3] This is understood to include "historical, critical, literary, philological, archaeological," and other methods. V. Taylor points directly to the issue at stake in this methodology, namely that Richardson's hypothesis "is nothing less than the claim that the events of the life, 'signs', passion and resurrection of Jesus, as attested by the apostolic witness, can account for the 'data' of the New Testament better than any other hypothesis current today."[4] The hypothesis which Richardson defends is "that Jesus Himself is the author of the brilliant re-interpretation of the Old Testament scheme of salvation ('Old Testament Theology') which is found in the New Testament, . . ."[5]   Thus one

[2]W. J. Harrington, *The Path of Biblical Theology* (Dublin, 1973), p. 186.

[3]A. Richardson, *An Introduction to the Theology of the New Testament* (London, 1958), p. 9.

[4]Vincent Taylor, "The Theology of the New Testament," *ET* 70 (1958/59), 168.

[5]Richardson, *An Introduction to the Theology of the NT*, p. 12.

expects a thoroughgoing historical study of the NT
data regarding the totality of NT faith in the historical
Jesus[6] of the kind known from the work of J. Jeremias.
This expectation is warranted from the approval of the
methods enumerated by him. This expectation, however, is frustrated.

Richardson chooses to structure his book in sixteen
chapters. Here we touch upon the matter of the
nature of NT theology and thus the methodological
issue. Although Richardson has informed us that "New
Testament theology, when written by Christians, will
necessarily begin with apostolic faith"[7] and claims in
the opening sentence of Chapter I, entitled "Faith and
Hearing," that "it is fitting to begin a consideration
of the theology of the New Testament with a study
of the fundamental concept of faith,"[8] he has not
explained why the subject of faith is more fitting for
beginning a NT theology than, let's say, "the proclamation of Jesus"[9] or "the kerygma of the primitive community and the Hellenistic community,"[10] without even
wishing to mention Bultmann's "the message of
Jesus."[11] One can hardly conceive that Richardson
wished to imply that a NT theology, written with a
different first chapter, is not "Christian." Is Richardson
attempting to present a "Christian" NT theology rather
than a non-Christian one? This is to raise the methodological issue of whether a NT theology in the
genuine sense can be written only by a believer. K.
Stendahl is known as a firm supporter of the descrip-

[6]Richardson (pp. 13f., 41-43, 135, 199, 362) engages in a running
polemic against R. Bultmann. See L. E. Keck, "Problems of New
Testament Theology," *Novum Testamentum* 7 (1964/65), 225f.

[7]Richardson, *An Introduction to the Theology of the NT*, p. 11.

[8]P. 19.

[9]E. Lohse, *Grundriss der neutestamentlichen Theologie* (Stuttgart,
1974), pp. 18ff.

[10]So H. Conzelmann, *An Outline of the Theology of the New Testament* (London, 1969), pp. 29ff.

[11]R. Bultmann, *Theology of the New Testament* (London, 1965),
I, 3ff.

tive approach to OT and NT theology.[12] He affirms that the

> descriptive task can be carried out by believer and agnostic alike. The believer has the advantage of automatic empathy with the believers in the text—but his faith threatens to have him modernize the material, if he does not exercise the canons of descriptive scholarship rigorously. The agnostic has the advantage of feeling no such temptation, but his power of empathy must be considerable, if he is to identify himself sufficiently with the believer of the first century.[13]

Richardson wholeheartedly disagrees with Stendahl's position: ". . . apart from faith the inward meaning of the NT is unintelligible."[14] "A proper understanding of Christian origins or of New Testament history is possible only through the insight of Christian faith."[15] Thus Richardson opts for a presupposition of faith for the writing of a NT theology. This means for him that "no pretense is made of remaining within the limits of purely descriptive science. . . ."[16] In view of this position it is hardly acceptable to describe Richardson's method with O. Merk as a descriptive method.[17] We believe we are close to the truth in suggesting that Richardson's method is the "confessional method" which is also employed in OT theology.[18]

A critical unresolved question regarding Richardson's confessional method relates to the issue of whether

[12]K. Stendahl, "Biblical Theology, Contemporary," *IDB*, I, 418-432; idem, "Method in the Study of Biblical Theology," *The Bible in Modern Scholarship*, ed. J. P. Hyatt (Nashville, 1965), pp. 196-208.

[13]Stendahl, *IDB*, I, 422.

[14]Richardson, *An Introduction to the Theology of the New Testament*, p. 19.

[15]P. 13.

[16]P. 12.

[17]O. Merk, *Biblische Theologie des Neuen Testaments in ihrer Anfangszeit* (Marburg, 1972), p. 266.

[18]See Th. C. Vriezen, *An Outline of OT Theology* (2nd ed.; Newton, Mass., 1970); G. A. F. Knight, *A Christian Theology of the Old Testament* (2nd ed.; London, 1964). See also R. de Vaux, "Peut-on écrire une 'théologie de l'AT'?" *Bible et Orient* (Paris, 1967), pp. 59-71.

a NT theology should be written from the framework of "Christian faith" or NT faith or *my* faith.[19] Since Richardson speaks of "Christian faith" in an undefined way, one is tempted to think of "Christian faith" as understood by an Anglican.[20] What claim to objectivity does such a confessional theology of the NT have? Does not an Anglican write a NT theology valid for fellow Anglicans with the same understanding of "Christian faith" and a Lutheran for Lutherans, etc.? It appears that a NT theology needs to maintain its independence over against confessional or creedal domination. This does not mean that the descriptive method is the long looked for panacea for NT theology. More on the issues relating to the descriptive method below.

Let us return to the issue of the structure of Richardson's NT theology. It is recognized by all that every historian or theologian is subjective in the selection of his material.[21] But we are wondering about the methodological structure of the following 16 chapters: Faith and Hearing; Knowledge and Revelation; The Power of God Unto Salvation; The Kingdom of God; The Holy Spirit; The Reinterpreted Messiahship; The Christology of the Apostolic Church; The Life of Christ; The Resurrection, Ascension and Victory of Christ; The Atonement Wrought By Christ; The Whole Christ; The Israel of God; The Apostolic and Priestly Ministry; Ministries Within the Church; The Theology of Baptism; and The Eucharistic Theology of the New Testament. This is a thematic structure. Are the order, number, and sequence of these chapters determined by "Christian faith" or the "Apostolic faith"? If "Jesus Himself is the real author of the theology of the New

[19]Hasel, *Old Testament Theology: Basic Issues in the Current Debate* (2nd ed.; Grand Rapids, Mich., 1975), pp. 39-42.

[20]Keck, "Problems of NT Theology," p. 237, speaks of Richardson's picture of Jesus as follows: "The Jesus who teaches everything Richardson attributes to him . . . is a Christian theologian, probably an Anglican."

[21]Stendahl, *IDB,* I, 422.

Testament,"[22] does the thematic structure derive from Him? Richardson's thematic structure as such is not the basic issue here, but rather (1) the lack of the relationship of the chapters to each other, (2) the omission of such important major NT themes as creation, man, law, ethics,[23] and (3) particularly the methodological justification for the thematic approach.[24] Richardson speaks of the "underlying theology of the New Testament documents" and "the content and character of the faith of the Apostolic Church" which should lead him to a presentation of the theology of these documents and the faith of the Apostolic Church. But this is not what the book presents. A NT theology written with a thematic structure should find the themes and motifs and their relationship to each other in the NT itself. Richardson did not seem to come to his subject from "within" but superimposed structures from without, even though he wisely refrained from the Theology-Anthropology-Soteriology (God-Man-Salvation) approach of dogmatic (systematic) theology used by earlier NT theologians.

2. *Karl H. Schelkle.* The Roman Catholic *Neutestamentler* Karl H. Schelkle from the University of Tübingen, Germany, began to publish in 1968 a four-volume *Theology of the New Testament.*[25] This ambitious project seeks to present "a unified New Testa-

---

[22]A. Richardson, *The Bible in the Age of Science* (London, 1961), p. 144.

[23]This is particularly noted by W. G. Kümmel, "Review of A. Richardson," *TLZ* 85 (1960), 922; Merk, *Biblische Theologie,* p. 266 n. 180.

[24]See esp. Keck, "Problems of NT Theology," pp. 221-225.

[25]K. H. Schelkle, *Theologie des Neuen Testaments I: Schöpfung: Welt-Zeit-Mensch* (Düsseldorf, 1968), Eng. trans. *Theology of the New Testament I: Creation: World-Time-Man* (Collegeville, Minn., 1971); *Theologie des Neuen Testaments II: Gott war in Christus* (Düsseldorf, 1973), Eng. trans. *Theology of the New Testament II: Salvation History-Revelation* (to be published); *Theology of the New Testament III: Morality* (Collegeville, Minn., 1973); *Theologie des Neuen Testaments IV: Reich-Kirche-Vollendung* (Düsseldorf, 1974), Eng. trans. *Theology of the New Testament IV: The Rule of God-Church-Eschatology* (to be published).

ment theology."[26] Schelkle's methodology does not "follow the historical development of the *Kergyma* and reflection as found within the structure of the New Testament itself." Instead, he pursues "more weighty words, concepts, and themes through the New Testament, and to describe in systematic summarization what is to be thought of their actual formation and meaning in the individual writings and groups of writings which comprise the New Testament."[27] Thus he follows a path which was already considered by J. P. Gabler,[28] suggested by A. Deissmann[29] and not ruled out even by W. Wrede who did not think, however, that this was a part of NT theology proper.[30]

Surprisingly, Schelkle waits until the opening section of his third volume to discuss his understanding of the methodology, nature, and purpose of NT theology.[31] "The theology of the New Testament . . . can be defined as 'word about God' on the basis of the word in which God reveals himself in the new covenant—which, indeed, assimilates to itself the old covenant—and which word is set down in the book

[26]*Theology of the NT*, III, p. v.

[27]I, p. v.

[28]Gabler in *Gableri Opuscula Academica* II (1831), 185f., 189f. Cf. Merk, *Biblische Theologie*, pp. 277, 279f.

[29]A. Deissmann, "Zur Methode der biblischen Theologie des Neuen Testaments," *ZThK* 3 (1893), 137-139; reprinted in *Das Problem der Theologie des Neuen Testaments*, ed. G. Strecker (Darmstadt, 1975), pp. 78f. (Hereafter cited as *PTNT*.)

[30]W. Wrede, *Über Aufgabe und Methode der sogenannten Neutestamentlichen Theologie* (Göttingen, 1897), reprinted in *PTNT*, p. 95 n. 18, Eng. trans. "The Task and Method of 'New Testament Theology'," in R. Morgan, *The Nature of New Testament Theology* (SBT 2/25; London, 1973), p. 186 n. 19: "Alongside 'New Testament theology', a special 'history of New Testament or early Christian concepts' would be a valuable and desirable supplement. This would investigate the historical origin or the most important concepts of the New Testament; it would discover the changes they have undergone and the historical reasons for them, and also illuminate their influence. The task has many points of contact with New Testament theology, but is quite different from it."

[31]This is a slightly modified version of his essay "Was bedeutet 'Theologie des Neuen Testaments'?" *Evangelienforschung*, ed. J. Bauer (Graz/Wien/Köln, 1968), pp. 299-312.

of the New Testament as attestation to this revelation."[32] On the basis of this definition one would
expect that NT theology is per definition restricted
to the canon of the NT writings. Indeed, Schelkle
affirms that the "source of the New Testament theology
is contained in the canon of the New Testament," but
he is quick to add, "the writings of the Fathers of the
Church, especially the earlier Fathers, are to be considered along with them."[33] Schelkle has not justified
this procedure. On the one hand he holds on to the
NT canon as the "source" for NT theology, thereby
separating himself from a purely or thoroughgoing
historical presentation along the lines of Wrede and
his followers, and on the other hand he wishes to
consider the early Fathers of the Church along with
the authors of the NT. This methodological procedure
raises the question to what degree the NT can stand
on its own feet and to what degree it is read through
the eyes of the early Fathers of the Church. Or to
put it differently, to what degree is Schelkle's method
permitting him to present "the more weighty words,
concepts, and themes"[34] as those of the NT itself?
Is his method not asking for a *religionsgeschichtliche*
(history-of-religions) approach of presenting "the more
weighty words, concepts, and themes" of early Christian literature as a whole?

Does Schelkle conceive of his NT theology as following the descriptive approach? His answer is explicit: "New Testament theology will not only describe the New Testament report but will interpret
it."[35] Here is a dual approach: description *and* interpretation. In this respect Schelkle differs from the
descriptive approach to NT theology as advocated by
K. Stendahl[36] who follows the tradition of Gabler-

[32]*Theology of the NT*, III, 3.
[33]P. 9.
[34]Pp. 10f.
[35]P. 17.
[36]Stendahl, *IDB*, I, 422.

Bauer-Wrede. Schelkle speaks of the descriptive aspect in terms of an attempt to "inquire after its content and the purposes of the forms of its declarations, which forms are perhaps unfamiliar to us."[37] The aspect of interpretation seeks to "relate the New Testament declarations to our modern questions and to our time."[38] It would be entirely wrong to read Schelkle's aspect of "interpretation" in terms of Bultmannian existentialist interpretation. Schelkle views NT theology as a preparation for dogmatic theology. Interpretation is that facet of NT theology which "makes clearly intelligible what is contained therein [NT] and continues and correlates what was begun therein."[39] Interpretation, then, involves a correlation of NT thoughts that need to be related to modern questions and to modern times.

Schelkle is highly sensitive to the issue of the unity of the NT and the unity of the Bible. "An exposition of the New Testament theology, though it cannot erase the differences in the separate writings, will nevertheless have the duty, and pursue the goal, of recognizing and displaying the unity of the New Testament within its very diversity."[40] Even though there are "distinct theologies of the Synoptics, of Paul, and of John, still it is *one* theology, *the* New Testament theology. . . . The New Testament writings as a group are bound together in unity by two very real facts: they all revolve about Jesus Christ, and they all have their origin in the Church."[41] Regarding the former fact Schelkle declares, "If Christ is really the Word of God (John 1:1), then he is not only part, but the very center of New Testament theology."[42] At this point we need to remind ourselves that Schelkle seeks

---

[37]Schelkle, *Theology of the NT*, III, 17.
[38]Ibid.
[39]Ibid.
[40]Pp. 10f.
[41]P. 8.
[42]P. 17.

to present "a unified New Testament theology."[43]
Schelkle's understanding of the unity of the NT is
the key to the thematic approach he adopts.

It is Schelkle's conviction that

> basically there are two possibilities which present
> themselves in the drafting of a New Testament theology.
> One possibility is to treat the epochs of the New Tes-
> tament proclamation according to their leading figures,
> each in a separate section; Synoptics, Primitive Congre-
> gation, Paul, John, Late Apostolic Writings. . . . The
> other possibility is to pursue ideas and themes of the
> New Testament proclamation through to the end of
> the New Testament, and to treat the areas of faith and
> life comprehensively.[44]

Schelkle opts for the second one. (One may question
whether there are really only two possibilities.) The
thematic approach leads him to organize his NT
theology along four major themes, each of which is
treated in a separate volume: I. Creation (World,
Time, Man); II. Revelation in History and in Salvation History (Jesus Christ and the Redemption; God,
Spirit, Trinity); III. Christian Life (NT Morality);
IV. God's Dominion, Church, Consummation. It has
been observed that this organization follows "the traditional dogmatic loci."[45] It is difficult to escape that
conclusion entirely. Schelkle leaves himself open to the
charge that he superimposes upon the NT a schema
from the outside. Although he seems to anticipate
this criticism, he has not cleared himself entirely.[46]

The thematic approach has the advantage of letting
the unity of the NT appear.[47] It may be that very

[43]P. v.
[44]P. 21.
[45]P. Stuhlmacher, *Schriftauslegung auf dem Wege zur biblischen
Theologie* (Göttingen, 1975), p. 130.
[46]Schelkle, *Theology of the NT*, III, 15: "An arrangement and
systematization of New Testament theology cannot be imposed upon
the New Testament from without but must be extracted from the New
Testament itself. To apply modern systematic schemata to the New
Testament is to do violence to the latter."
[47]P. 21.

interest in the unity of the NT that has caused Schelkle to opt for this approach.[48] However that may be, one of the most novel aspects of the thematic approach as practiced by Schelkle is the longitudinal investigation of NT ideas and themes in their chronological development in the NT witnesses. He is also to be praised for the tracing of these ideas and themes back to the OT.[49] To highlight these connections between the Testaments[50] is to contribute to Biblical theology which is rent apart since the separate treatments of G. L. Bauer at the end of the eighteenth century.

B. The Existentialist Approach

1. *Rudolf Bultmann.* It has been indicated previously that Bultmann's heritage lies in the "purely historical" direction of research and that he is deeply rooted in the history-of-religions school.[51] This means first of all that his historical roots are deeply grounded in the historical-critical method of research.[52] The second historical root is found in Bultmann's association with dialectical theology in the 1920s, particularly K. Barth and F. Gogarten. Out of this arose a powerful catalyst in his raising the theological question. Bultmann was not

[48]It is no surprise that Schelkle is charged with a lack of appreciation for the NT's diversity. See G. Haufe, "Review of 'K. H. Schelkle, *Theologie des NT I*,'" *ThLZ* 94 (1969), 909f.

[49]So rightly Merk, *Biblische Theologie,* p. 269; Harrington, *Path,* p. 139; Stuhlmacher, *Schriftauslegung,* p. 137.

[50]From a different perspective the continuity between the Testaments is also emphasized by F. F. Bruce, *New Testament Development of Old Testament Themes* (3rd ed.; Grand Rapids, Mich., 1973); M. Burrows, *An Outline of Biblical Theology* (Philadelphia, 1946); and J. Blenkinsopp, *A Sketchbook of Biblical Theology* (London, 1968).

[51]Here Bultmann's well-known book *Das Urchristentum im Rahmen der antiken Religionen* (Zurich, 1949), Eng. trans. *Primitive Christianity in Its Contemporary Setting* (Edinburgh, 1956) has its place.

[52]Rightly emphasized by his student G. Bornkamm, "Die Theologie Rudolf Bultmanns," *Geschichte und Glaube* I (Munich, 1968), pp. 157f.

satisfied with the historical issue, i.e., "the act of thinking."[53] He and others before him (e.g., A. Schlatter)
believed that the NT writings "have something to
say to the present."[54] This presupposition is rooted
in his understanding of history which is in broad con-
tours already spelled out in the Introduction of his
concise book, entitled *Jesus*, written in 1926,[55] which
builds on his famous *History of the Synoptic Tradition*
(1921).[56] Bultmann "aimed to avoid everything beyond history and to find a position for myself *within*
history. . . . For the essential of history is in reality
nothing *super*historical, but is event in time."[57] Bultmann's understanding of history and of human existence has led him to incorporate into his system
Heideggerian existentialism[58] on the basis of which he
is the most adamant proponent of an "existentialist
interpretation." Bultmann combines "historical reconstruction" with "existentialist interpretation."[59]

"Existentialist interpretation" is closely bound up
and interrelated with his program of demythologization.[60] The literature and scope of Bultmann's program
of demythologizing the NT are so complex and

[53]Bultmann, *Theology of the NT*, II, 250f.

[54]P. 251.

[55]R. Bultmann, *Jesus* (Berlin, 1926), pp. 7-18, Eng. trans. *Jesus and the Word* (London, 1934; 2nd ed., 1958), pp. 11-19.

[56]R. Bultmann, *Die Geschichte der synoptischen Tradition* (Göttingen, 1921), Eng. trans. *The History of the Synoptic Tradition* (New York, 1963; 2nd ed. 1976).

[57]Bultmann, *Jesus and the Word*, p. 14.

[58]The importance of Heidegger's analysis of existence and Bultmann's own philosophy of history comes to expression in Bultmann's Gifford Lectures of 1955 published under the title *History and Eschatology: The Presence of Eternity* (New York, 1957; 2nd ed., 1962).

[59]R. Bultmann, "Foreword," in J. Macquarrie, *An Existentialist Theology* (Harper Torchbook ed.; New York, 1965), p. vii, states, ". . . the hermeneutic principle which underlies my interpretation of the New Testament arises out of the existential analysis of man's being, given by Martin Heidegger in his work, *Being and Time*."

[60]See Chap. I, footnotes 256f., 261. See on this subject also J. Macquarrie, *The Scope of Demythologizing. Bultmann and His Critics* (New York, 1960); R. Marle, *Introduction to Hermeneutics* (New York, 1967), pp. 32-66.

voluminous[61] that we limit ourselves, at the risk of a one-sided presentation, to but a few representative remarks taken from Bultmann's original essay of 1941 entitled "New Testament and Mythology" and his more recent *Jesus Christ and Mythology* (1958). Bultmann defines: "Demythologizing is an hermeneutic method, that is, a method of interpretation, of exegesis."[62] Demythologizing as a method of interpretation is needed because "the cosmology of the New Testament is essentially mythical in character. The world is viewed as a three-storied structure, with the earth in the center, the heaven above, and the underworld beneath."[63] This view of the world, as assumed to be correct, "is incredible to modern man, for he is convinced that the mythical view of the world is obsolete."[64] Thus there are only two directions to follow in Bultmann's understanding, namely either one expects modern man to accept the Gospel message and with it the "mythical view of the world" or "theology must undertake the task of stripping the Kerygma from its mythical framework, of 'demythologizing' it."[65] This does not mean for Bultmann that one should subtract from the kerygma or eliminate from it.[66] "Our task to-day is to use criticism to interpret it,"[67] namely "existentially."[68]

Bultmann's concept of "reconstruction" and "interpretation" is basic for an understanding of his *Theology of the New Testament*. He declares:

[61]An excellent review of ca. 500 publications on Bultmann's hermeneutic and theology is provided by the post-Bultmannian G. Bornkamm, "Die Theologie Bultmanns in der neueren Diskussion," *Theologische Rundschau* 29 (1963), 33-141, reprinted in Bornkamm, *Geschichte und Glaube I*, pp. 173-275.

[62]R. Bultmann, *Jesus Christ and Mythology* (London, 1960; New York, 1958), p. 45.

[63]R. Bultmann, "New Testament and Mythology," *Kerygma and Myth,* ed. H. W. Bartsch (New York, 1961), p. 1.

[64]P. 3.

[65]Ibid.

[66]P. 9.

[67]P. 12.

[68]P. 10.

The presentation of New Testament theology offered in this book stands, on the one hand, within the tradition of the historical-critical and the history-of-religions schools and seeks, on the other hand, to avoid their mistake which consists of the tearing apart of the act of thinking from the act of living and hence a failure to recognize the intent of theological utterances.[69]

"Reconstruction" of the writings of the NT thus follows the canons of the historical-critical method and the history-of-religions school but not to reconstruct a picture of early Christianity as a phenomenon of the historical past. "Reconstruction stands in the service of the interpretation of the New Testament writings under the presupposition that they have something to say to us."[70] "Interpretation" means to explicate "the theological thoughts of the New Testament in their connection with the 'act of living'—i.e. as explication of believing self-understanding." In Bultmann's view this means that "the task of a presentation of New Testament theology" is "to make clear this believing self-understanding in its reference to the kerygma."[71] Bultmann explains here that the coordination of "reconstruction" and "interpretation" is the key for the understanding of his NT theology. We have chosen to deal with Bultmann's NT theology under the heading of "Existentialist Approach" because his presentation, as we hope to have indicated, belongs to those NT theologies which are conditioned by a particular philosophical system,[72] namely the existentialism of the early Heidegger.[73]

On the basis of this background one can gain an appreciation of the structure of Bultmann's *Theology of the New Testament*. Part I is entitled "Presupposi-

[69]Bultmann, *Theology of the NT*, II, 250f.

[70]P. 251.

[71]Ibid.

[72]N. A. Dahl, "Die Theologie des Neuen Testaments," *Theologische Rundschau* 22 (1954), 25.

[73]See J. M. Robinson and John B. Cobb, Jr., *The Later Heidegger and Theology*, "New Frontiers in Theology I" (New York, 1963).

tions and Motifs of New Testament Theology" and contains chapters on "The Message of Jesus,"[74] "The Kerygma of the Earliest Church,"[75] and "The Kerygma of the Hellenistic Church Aside from Paul."[76] Part II takes us to the center of Bultmann's presentation with "The Theology of Paul"[77] with chapters on "Man Prior to the Revelation of Faith"[78] in which he treats anthropological concepts, including body, life, mind, conscience, heart, flesh, sin, world; and on "Man Under Faith"[79] which is divided into sections on the righteousness of God, grace, faith, and freedom. Independent of Pauline theology is Part III with "The Theology of the Gospel of John and the Johannine Epistles"[80] with chapters on "Orientation," "Johannine Dualism," "The 'Krisis' of the World," and "Faith." The concluding Part IV is entitled "The Development toward the Ancient Church,"[81] which is divided into church order, doctrine, development, and Christian living.

This methodological procedure of presenting NT theology reveals immediately its debt to the program of W. Wrede[82] and more directly of W. Bousset's *Kyrios Christos*[83] whose division he follows with the headings "The Kerygma of the Earliest Church," "The Kerygma of the Hellenistic Church," "The Theology of Paul," and "The Theology of John" as exponents of the kerygma of the Hellenistic church.

Bultmann opens his NT theology with the following provocative sentence: "*The message of Jesus* is a pre-

[74]Bultmann, *Theology of the NT*, I, 3-32.
[75]Pp. 33-62.
[76]Pp. 63-183.
[77]Pp. 185-352.
[78]Pp. 190-269.
[79]Pp. 270-352.
[80]Vol. II, 3-92. In the German original this still is Part III.
[81]Pp. 95-236.
[82]See above, n. 1.
[83]W. Bousset, *Kyrios Christos. Geschichte des Christusglaubens von den Anfängen des Christentums bis Irenaeus* (Göttingen, 1913; 6th ed.; Darmstadt, 1967), Eng. trans. *Kyrios Christos* (Nashville, 1970).

supposition for the theology of the New Testament rather than a part of that theology itself."[84] Probably no one has stated the opposite to this sentence and its implications more emphatically than Stephen Neill in his recent NT theology: "Every theology of the New Testament must be a theology of Jesus—or it is nothing at all."[85] It has been noted quite correctly[86] that Bultmann's key sentence corresponds to the demand of F. C. Baur as well as Baur's concept of the presentation of the message of Jesus.[87] Bultmann's form critical studies of the Synoptics[88] and his book on *Jesus* from 1926 form the basis of the presentation of Jesus' message. In other words the message of Jesus is *reconstructed* with critical methodologies from the kerygma about Jesus Christ, the crucified and risen One.

The critical reaction to Bultmann's theology of which his NT theology is an epoch-making climax has come from many quarters. Bultmann's views on the historical Jesus and the kerygmatic Christ are the basis of the current debate on this aspect of NT theology. In the previous chapter we described the dissatisfaction with Bultmann's views among his own students such as E. Käsemann, G. Bornkamm, H. Braun, J. M. Robinson, E. Fuchs, and G. Ebeling,[89] who are customarily called "post-Bultmannians." They may be considered to belong to the center of Bultmann's critics. These engaged in the "new quest" of the historical Jesus to explore the question of continuity between the historical Jesus and the kerygmatic Christ.[90]

[84]Bultmann, *Theology of the NT,* I, 3 (italics his).

[85]S. Neill, *Jesus Through Many Eyes. Introduction to the Theology of the New Testament* (Philadelphia, 1976), p. 10.

[86]O. Merk, *Biblische Theologie,* p. 254.

[87]See F. C. Baur, *Vorlesungen über Neutestamentliche Theologie,* ed. F. F. Baur (Leipzig, 1864), pp. 45-127.

[88]See above, n. 56.

[89]Representative literature is cited in footnotes 257, 272-276 in Chapter I above.

[90]See the critique by N. Perrin, *Rediscovering the Teaching of Jesus* (2nd. ed.; New York, 1976), pp. 233f.

There are also "right wing critics"[91] such as K. Barth, J. Schniewind, J. Jeremias, E. Ellwein, E. Kinder, W. Künneth, H. Diem, H. Thielicke, and P. Althaus.[92] The critics of Lutheran orthodoxy accuse Bultmann of denying the objective factualness of such redemptive events as the incarnation, atonement, resurrection, ascension, and second coming. Norman Perrin, who distinguishes between "historical knowledge," "historic knowledge," and "faith-knowledge," points out that

> the attack upon Bultmann's position from the right seeks to establish closer links than Bultmann will allow between historical knowledge and faith-knowledge. . . . On the right we have the presupposition that the Incarnation or the Biblical concept of God active in history, or the traditional view of Christianity as related to certain revelational events in history, or the like— that this demands a real and close relationship between historical knowledge and faith-knowledge, and that justice must be done to this in our discussion of the question of the historical Jesus.[93]

It is evident that here is a parting of the ways between Bultmann's existentialist hermeneutic of the correlation

[91]R. H. Fuller, *The New Testament in Current Study* (New York, 1962), p. 16.

[92]K. Barth, "Rudolf Bultmann—An Attempt to Understand Him," *Kerygma and Myth II,* ed. H. W. Bartsch (London, 1962), pp. 83-132; J. Schniewind, "A Reply to Bultmann," *Kerygma and Myth I,* ed. H. W. Bartsch (New York, 1961), pp. 45-101; J. Jeremias, *The Problem of the Historical Jesus* (Philadelphia, 1964); E. Ellwein, "R. Bultmann's Interpretation of the Kerygma," *Kerygma and History,* eds. C. E. Braaten and R. A. Harrisville (New York, 1962), pp. 25-54; E. Kinder, "Historical Criticism and Demythologizing," *ibid.,* pp. 55-85; W. Künneth, "Bultmann's Philosophy and the Reality of Salvation," *ibid.,* pp. 86-119; H. Diem, "The Earthly Jesus and the Christ of Faith," *ibid.,* pp. 197-211; H. Thielicke, "The Restatement of New Testament Mythology," *Kerygma and Myth I,* pp. 138-174; P. Althaus, *Faith and Fact in the Kerygma Today* (Philadelphia, 1959). It should be noted that F. Gogarten, *Demythologizing and History* (London, 1955) has come to the defense of Bultmann against the "right wing critics."

[93]Perrin, *Rediscovering the Teaching of Jesus,* p. 239.

of reconstruction and interpretation and that of the "right wing critics."

Among Bultmann's "left wing critics" are the Swiss "liberal" theologian Fritz Buri, the German existentialist philosopher Karl Jaspers, and the American theologian Schubert M. Ogden.[94] Buri suggests that Bultmann has not gone far enough in his program of demythologizing. He has left the act of God as a remnant of mythology. The act of God in Jesus Christ needs to be "dekerygmatized." There is an inconsistency in Bultmann's proposal in that he properly understands Christian faith as a transition from inauthentic to authentic existence, but then maintains inconsistently with the former a necessary link with the historical Jesus in this process. Jaspers faults Bultmann for introducing an objective factor into an existential movement where it has no place in maintaining a link with the historical Jesus. Ogden faults Bultmann, because "he completely nullifies his own constructive proposal for a solution to the contemporary theological problem"[95] in that he distinguishes inconsistently between "possibility in principle" and "possibility in fact."[96] Ogden maintains that a possibility in principle is always a possibility in fact which means the abandonment of the particularity of Christian faith.[97] Bultmann replied by questioning whether the charge of "inconsistency" is not "the legitimate and necessary character of what the New Testament calls the stumbling block."[98] The point the "left wing critics"

[94] F. Buri, "Entmythologisierung oder Entkerygmatizierung?" *Kerygma und Mythos II*, ed. H. W. Bartsch (Hamburg, 1954), pp. 85ff.; idem, "Theologie der Existenz," *Kerygma und Mythos III*, ed. H. W. Bartsch (Hamburg, 1955), pp. 81ff.; K. Jaspers, *R. Bultmann. Die Frage der Entmythologisierung* (Munich, 1954); idem, *Philosophical Faith and Revelation* (New York, 1967), pp. 287, 324f.; idem and R. Bultmann, *Myth and Christianity* (New York, 1958); S. M. Ogden, *Christ without Myth* (New York, 1961).

[95] Ogden, *Christ without Myth*, p. 215.

[96] Pp. 111ff.

[97] Pp. 143, 151, 156, 160.

[98] R. Bultmann, "Review of S. M. Ogden, *Christ Without Myth*," *Journal of Religion* 42 (1962), 226.

attempted to drive home consists of the conviction that, even if we may speak of God or the transcendent in a meaningful way, "the essential relativity of all historical events means that we cannot think in terms of a knowledge of Jesus that is different *in kind* from knowledge we may have of other historical persons."[99] This means that Jesus is but a supreme example capable of being imitated (Buri, Jaspers) or the "decisive manifestation" of what is known also elsewhere (Ogden).

Bultmann's presentation of Pauline theology is rightly understood as the center of his NT theology. He considers Paul to be "the founder of Christian theology."[100] This means that "in relation to the preaching of Jesus, the theology of Paul is a new structure, and that indicates nothing else than that Paul has his place within Hellenistic Christianity."[101] This distinction seems to reflect why Bultmann's NT theology employs largely the descriptive method in dealing with the topics of Part I of his work while in Parts II and III with the presentation of Pauline and Johannine theology the anthropological interpretation is used.[102] Concerning Paul, Bultmann summarizes: "Paul's theology can best be treated as his doctrine of man: first, of man prior to the revelation of faith, and second, of man under faith, for in this way the anthropological and soteriological orientation of Paul's theology is brought out."[103] Paul's own conversion is interpreted in existentialist categories of the early Heidegger as a surrender of "his previous understanding of himself; i.e. he surrendered what had till then been the norm and meaning of his life. . . . His was not a conversion of repentance; . . . it was obedient submission to the judgment of God, made known in the cross of Christ, upon all human accomplishment and

[99]Perrin, *Rediscovering the Teaching of Jesus,* p. 239 (italics his).
[100]Bultmann, *Theology of the NT,* I, 191.
[101]P. 189.
[102]Stendahl, *IDB,* I, 420f.; C. E. Cox, "R. Bultmann: Theology of the New Testament," *Restoration Quarterly* 17 (1974), 157.
[103]Bultmann, *Theology of the NT,* I, 191.

boasting. It is as such that his conversion is reflected in his theology."[104] Bultmann considers "Paul's theology to be at the same time anthropology."[105] The method employed to explicate this predetermined point of view is a terminological analysis of such Pauline terms as body, soul, spirit, world, law, death, righteousness, grace, faith, and freedom.

Reactions to this approach of an anthropological or existentialist interpretation of Paul vary. M. Barth describes the end result of Bultmann's methods in presenting Pauline theology as follows: "Bultmann describes Paul as the apostle of true self-understanding and existence, in short, as an apostle of true existence. Paul is made into an existentialist among the apostles. But Paul calls himself without tiring an apostle of Jesus Christ."[106] Barth believes that even if the same letters considered by Bultmann as inauthentic (Eph., Col., 2 Thess., 1-2 Tim., Titus) were included in the *Corpus Paulinum*, then there would still not come about a revision of the presentation of Pauline theology by Bultmann because he engages in "content-criticism" (*Sachkritik*)[107] on the basis of which Pauline statements on the Holy Spirit, resurrection, second Adam,

[104]P. 188.

[105]Bultmann, *Theologie des NT*, p. 187. The Eng. trans. "Paul's theology can best be treated as his doctrine of man" in *Theology of the NT*, I, 191, is imprecise.

[106]M. Barth, "Die Methode von Bultmanns 'Theologie des Neuen Testaments'," *Theologische Zeitschrift* 11 (1955), 15.

[107]See R. Bultmann, *Glauben und Verstehen I* (4th ed.; Göttingen, 1961), pp. 38-64; idem, "The Problem of a Theological Exegesis," *The Beginnings of Dialectical Theology*, ed. J. M. Robinson (Richmond, Va., 1968), I, 236-256; idem, "Is Exegesis without Presuppositions Possible?" *Existence and Faith: Shorter Writings of Rudolf Bultmann*, ed. S. M. Ogden (New York, 1960), pp. 289-296. Bultmann's notion of "content-criticism" is discussed by J. M. Robinson, "Hermeneutic Since Barth," *The New Hermeneutic*, "New Frontiers in Theology II," eds. J. M. Robinson and J. B. Cobb, Jr. (New York, 1964), pp. 31-34; W. Schmithals, *Die Theologie Rudolf Bultmanns: Eine Einführung* (2nd ed.; Tübingen, 1967), p. 251; W. G. Doty, *Contemporary New Testament Interpretation* (Englewood Cliffs, N.J., 1972), pp. 21f.

original sin, and knowledge are eliminated.[108]   This procedure goes hand in hand with Bultmann's concept of pre-understanding[109] and interpretation: "There is no bare interpretation of 'what is there,' but in some way . . . the interpretation of the text always goes hand in hand with the exegete's interpretation of himself."[110] The hermeneutical circle seems to imply more subjectivity than should be granted.[111] Barth concludes: "It is likely that only a method of research and presentation is adequate for Paul if the witness of the apostle concerning Christ (and not his philosophy of life) is placed in the center of the questioning and description."[112] Barth wishes to put the Christological standpoint into the center of the stage which is occupied by anthropology in Bultmann's system.

This is not unrelated to the attempt of the Catholic student of Bultmann H. Schlier, who has perhaps moved furthest from his teacher.[113] Schlier says, "To my mind, the theology of the New Testament, when dealing with St. Paul, will develop his theology as a function of the Event, in whose basic traits he sees comprehended the history and existence of mankind. This is the resurrection of Jesus Christ, the crucified Lord, who has been exalted in view of his coming, so that his being raised up was an eschatological or final act."[114] In contrast to Bultmann, Schlier argues for a presentation of the theology of the Synoptics side by side with the theologies of Paul and John.[115] Instead of making Pauline theology the basis of NT

[108]Barth, "Die Methode," p. 15.

[109]Bultmann, *Existence and Faith*, pp. 289-296.

[110]Bultmann, *The Beginnings of Dialectical Theology*, I, 242.

[111]See the critique by E. Betti, *Die Hermeneutik als Allgemeine Methodik der Geisteswissenschaften* (Tübingen, 1967).

[112]Barth, "Die Methode," pp. 15f.

[113]H. Schlier, "Über Sinn und Aufgabe einer Theologie des Neuen Testaments," *Biblische Zeitschrift* 1 (1957), 6-23, reprinted in *PTNT*, pp. 323-344, Eng. trans. in *Dogmatic vs. Biblical Theology*, ed. H. Vorgrimler (Baltimore, 1964), pp. 87-113.

[114]Schlier, *Dogmatic vs. Biblical Theology*, p. 90.

[115]P. 99.

theology (so Bultmann), Schlier proposes to make the early Christian confessional formulae the basis of NT theology, because "they are the primary utterance of the revelation of Jesus Christ as it voiced itself."[116] Schlier, says E. Käsemann, "turned his [Bultmann's] ideas down side up—or, as it is usually put, upside down."[117]

Bultmann's former student H. Braun[118] raised the question of the possibility of a NT theology, because the NT is no more than a series of disparate statements about central theological subjects. He explicates his view by discussing such subjects as Christology, soteriology, law, eschatology, and the doctrine of the sacraments. Braun's thesis is as follows: "The authors of the New Testament make statements dealing with man's salvation and with his relation to God which cannot be brought into harmony with one another, and which prove by their disparateness that their subject matter is not what they state, *expressis verbis*, in mutual contradiction."[119] The solution to these problems is a more radical anthropological interpretation of God. "At any rate, God would not be understood as the one existing for himself, as a species which would only be comprehensible under this word. God then means much rather the whence of my being agitated."[120] Braun has brought to a consistent conclusion his anthropological interpretation of the appearance of Jesus and the NT in his book *Jesus*.[121] L. Goppelt assesses Braun's

[116]Ibid.

[117]E. Käsemann, "The Problem of a New Testament Theology," *NTS* 19 (1973), 240.

[118]H. Braun, "Die Problematik einer Theologie des Neuen Testaments," *ZThK* Beiheft 2 (1961), 3-18, reprinted in H. Braun, *Gesammelte Studien zum Neuen Testament und seiner Umwelt* (Tübingen, 1962), pp. 325-341, and in *PTNT*, pp. 405-424, Eng. trans. "The Problem of a New Testament Theology," *The Bultmann School of Biblical Interpretation: New Directions?*, ed. R. W. Funk (New York, 1965), pp. 169-183.

[119]Braun, "The Problem of a NT Theology," p. 169.

[120]Pp. 182ff.

[121]H. Braun, *Jesus. Der Mann aus Nazareth und seine Zeit* (Stuttgart/Berlin, 1969).

anthropocentricity in his essay and book as "a following through to the end the path of historicism in which NT theology is given up; . . . in terms of the history of research it signals the end of an epoch."[122] Even in the eyes of the post-Bultmannian Käsemann "this [Braun's] kind of mysticism means bankruptcy and a protest should be raised in the name of intellectual honesty, when humanism is in this fashion taken over by Christianity."[123]

No scholar belonging to the post-Bultmannian school has as yet produced a NT theology. This does not mean that interest in this is dead. J. M. Robinson has turned to the subject in a provoking essay[124] which was discussed in the previous chapter. Robinson seeks to build on the "new hermeneutic" and its presuppositions in linguistic philosophy and to exchange Bultmann's anthropological interpretation for a move "into the language that can be interpreted in terms of alternatives in the modern world, extending them 'theologically,' 'ontologically,' 'cosmologically,' 'politically,' etc. . . ."[125] Robinson wants to stay with the correlation of "reconstruction" and "interpretation" or, as he calls it, the "historical and the normative."[126] Over against Robinson are some theses of E. Käsemann, who does not speak of the twofold aspect of "reconstruction" and "interpretation" in the Bultmann tradition. He explains that "New Testament theology is . . . of necessity a historical discipline. . . ."[127] "In regard to method, the different aspects and perspectives of eschatology provide guidelines for New Testament theology. In regard to content, they provide the backcloth for its

[122]L. Goppelt, *Theologie des Neuen Testaments,* ed. J. Roloff (Göttingen, 1975), I, 38. See also his review of Braun's book *Jesus* in *ThLZ* 95 (1970), 744-747.

[123]Käsemann, "The Problem of a New Testament Theology," p. 241.

[124]See Chapter I, footnote 3.

[125]Robinson, "The Future of NT Theology," p. 22.

[126]P. 20.

[127]Käsemann, "The Problem of a NT Theology," p. 242.

main themes in their successive stages of development."[128] Käsemann does not go into detail regarding the actual working out of a New Testament theology.

Norman Perrin has shifted more and more into the camp of the post-Bultmannians and away from his teacher J. Jeremias.[129] Perrin criticizes Bultmann for not achieving a theology of the New Testament at all, but only a theology of Paul and John. "It is simply not true that everything before Paul and John is preparation for them, and everything after them is a falling away from their achievements."[130] Perrin, however, has finally come to agree with Bultmann (and with Conzelmann) that Jesus is "the presupposition of the New Testament."[131] The concern of a NT theology is thus not the historical Jesus, i.e., the "memory-image of Jesus," but the post-resurrection "faith-image of Jesus,"[132] i.e., the historic Christ. This means that Perrin cannot follow Jeremias, Kümmel, Goppelt, Neill, and others who begin their presentation of NT theology with the historical Jesus. Nor does he follow Bultmann's "crude hermeneutical method"[133] of demythologizing. What Bultmann designated as Jewish apocalyptic mythology is Jewish apocalyptic symbolism. Perrin follows here particularly Paul Ricoeur's[134] and

[128]P. 244.

[129]This is evident in his recent publications; note especially his *Rediscovering the Teachings of Jesus* (2nd ed.; New York, 1976); N. Perrin, *The New Testament, An Introduction* (New York, 1974); idem, *A Modern Pilgrimage in New Testament Christology* (New York, 1974); idem, *Jesus and the Language of the Kingdom* (New York, 1976).

[130]N. Perrin, "Jesus and the Theology of the New Testament," unpublished paper read at the Catholic Biblical Association (Denver, Colo., Aug. 18-21, 1975), p. 6.

[131]Perrin, *The NT: An Introduction*, pp. 5, 277-302.

[132]Perrin, *Rediscovering the Teaching of Jesus*, pp. 243-248. Independent of Perrin the American Van A. Harvey developed in his book *The Historian and the Believer* (New York, 1966), pp. 265-281, the designation "perspective image," which is equal to Perrin's "faith image," a designation for the historic Christ.

[133]Perrin, "Jesus and the Theology of the NT," p. 14.

[134]P. Ricoeur, *The Symbolism of Evil* (Boston, 1960); see now "Paul Ricoeur on Biblical Hermeneutics," *Semeia* 4 (1975), 1-148.

P. Wheelwright's[135] theories of symbol.[136] A genuinely
post-Bultmannian NT theology is based in Perrin's
view on the philosophical work on the nature and function of signs and symbols. Perrin has already indicated
that he understands "Kingdom of God" on the lips
of Jesus as a symbol which functions by evoking a
myth, the myth of God active within the history of
his people on their behalf.[137] Perrin's thesis is that
"the theology of the New Testament may be discerned as we follow the function of the Jesus figure,
the Jesus material, the Jesus story, within the different
theological systems represented by early Christian
apocalyptic writings and by the synoptic Gospels and
Acts."[138] Perrin feels that "a similar approach to the
theological systems represented by Paul, John, and the
literature of emergent Catholicism" can be taken.[139]
The unifying factor "is the *symbolic* figure of Jesus,
who is the constant in all the different theological
systems developed in the New Testament."[140] Would
Perrin reach a radically different "interpretation" than
that of Bultmann? His own prediction was that he too
would probably reach a position close to Bultmann's
as far as the interpretation of the message of Jesus
into the twentieth century was concerned but "on the
basis of an understanding and interpretation of Jesus'
use of symbolic language, not on the basis of a hermeneutics of demythologizing. . . ."[141] If Bultmann
built his hermeneutic on demythologizing myth, then
Perrin built his hermeneutic on deciphering symbol.
If Bultmann's NT theology is to be characterized by

[135]P. Wheelwright, *Metaphor and Reality* (Bloomington, 1962).

[136]N. Perrin, "Eschatology and Hermeneutics: Reflections on
Method in the Interpretation of the New Testament," *JBL* 93
(1974), 3-14.

[137]This is elucidated in detail in Perrin's recent work *Jesus and
the Language of the Kingdom.*

[138]Perrin, "Jesus and the Theology of the NT," p. 26.

[139]P. 26.

[140]P. 15.

[141]P. 14.

demythologizing myth, then Perrin's proposed post-Bultmannian NT theology could be expected to engage in deciphering symbol. Whether or not the usage of linguistic philosophy in NT theology will become as much a battlefield as existentialist philosophy remains to be seen.

2. *Hans Conzelmann.* Conzelmann is the only disciple of Bultmann to have published a NT theology; his work is entitled *An Outline of the Theology of the New Testament* and was published in 1967.[142] In fact, this is the first Protestant NT theology to appear in Germany since the publication of Bultmann's own NT theology. Although it is generally agreed that in content he makes no significant advance on Bultmann,[143] in methodology there are some distinct changes which become already apparent, at least to some degree, in the structure of his work. An "Introduction"[144] deals with the problem of a theology of the New Testament, the Hellenistic and Judaistic environment. This is followed by Part I titled "The Kerygma of the Primitive Community and the Hellenistic Community"[145] and Part II, "The Synoptic Kerygma."[146] Conzelmann deals

[142]H. Conzelmann, *Grundriss der Theologie des Neuen Testaments* (Munich, 1967), Eng. trans. from 2nd ed. of 1963 *An Outline of the Theology of the New Testament* (New York, 1969).

[143]See the reactions by W. G. Kümmel, "Die exegetische Erforschung des NT in diesem Jahrhundert," *Das Neue Testament im 20. Jahrhundert* (Stuttgart, 1970), pp. 123f.; G. F. Hasel, "Review of H. Conzelmann, *Grundriss der Theologie des NT,*" *AUSS* 8 (1970), 86-89; P. Stuhlmacher, "Neues vom Neuen Testament," *Pastoraltheologie* 58 (1969), 424f.; H. Küng, *Menschwerdung Gottes* (Freiburg, 1970), p. 588; E. Güttgemanns, "Literatur zur Neutestamentlichen Theologie," *Verkündigung und Forschung* 15 (1970), 47-50; M. Bouttier, "Théologie et Philosophie du NT," *Etudes Théologiques et Religieuses* 45 (1970), 188-194, esp. 189f.; W. J. Harrington, "New Testament Theology. Two Recent Approaches," *BTB* 1 (1970), 173-184; Merk, *Biblische Theologie,* pp. 258f.; Käsemann, "The Problem of a NT Theology," p. 241; Robinson, "The Future of NT Theology," pp. 19f.

[144]Conzelmann, *An Outline of NT Theology,* pp. 1-25.

[145]Pp. 29-93.

[146]Pp. 97-152.

with the "Theology of Paul" in Part III,[147] but contrary
to Bultmann Part IV treats "The Development After
Paul,"[148] and then comes the theology of John.[149]

The structure of Conzelmann's NT theology as compared with that of Bultmann, of which he says that
it "will remain basic for a long time yet, and the outline presented here betrays its indebtedness to him in
a number of places,"[150] reveals three major changes
which have a distinct methodological significance:
(1) "The message of Jesus," which is for Bultmann
"a presupposition for the theology of the New Testament rather than a part of that theology itself,"[151] is
totally omitted by Conzelmann. He insists "that the
'historical Jesus' is not a theme of New Testament
theology" in which he agrees with Bultmann but disagrees with him in not considering it even as a presupposition of NT theology. He does so on the basis
of "methodological consistency and as a result of the
exegetical basis to my approach."[152] "The basic problem
of New Testament theology is not, how did the
proclaimer, Jesus of Nazareth, become the proclaimed
Messiah, Son of God, Lord? It is rather, why did
faith maintain the identity of the Exalted One with
Jesus of Nazareth after the resurrection appear-
ances?"[153] (2) Conzelmann reverses the sequence of
the last two parts as compared with Bultmann's work.
Several reasons are advanced for this: (a) To avoid
a value judgment that the movement towards the
"early church" was a retrogression; (b) the special
association of the Pauline literature with the post-
Pauline literature and the existence of a school of
Paul; and (c) the fact that the "apostolic" and "post-
apostolic" ages "are not so much a presupposition as

[147]Pp. 155-286.
[148]Pp. 289-317.
[149]Pp. 321-358.
[150]P. xv.
[151]Bultmann, *Theology of the NT*, I, 3.
[152]Conzelmann, *An Outline of NT Theology*, p. xvii.
[153]P. xviii.

an ingredient of New Testament theology."[154] This means that Conzelmann seeks to be consistent in his presentation of NT theology by elimination or reclassifying presuppositions of NT theology. If he strives for consistency, then what rationale has his first part which reconstructs the kerygma of the Jewish and Hellenistic communities? (3) Conzelmann advances most markedly beyond Bultmann in his inclusion of the content of the Synoptic gospels as being part of the concept of NT theology. This is the direct result of redaction critical studies done in Gospel research[155] of which Conzelmann was a pioneer himself.[156] Unfortunately "his historical scepticism almost negates the result."[157]

Aside from these changes as reflected by the structure or plan of Conzelmann's NT theology there are additional key issues that bear directly on methodology in NT theology. Conzelmann does to a degree what Schlier said needed to be done,[158] that is, he seeks on the basis of the method of *Traditionsgeschichte* (tradition history) to reconstruct "the original *texts* of the faith, the oldest formulations of the creed."[159] In contrast to Schlier's approach Conzelmann assumes an early Christian creed and refuses to make any connection between it and the Synoptics. This makes it possible for him to return to the Bultmannian position, "that is, to regard the confessional formulae as the objectification of the Christian self-understanding, which in the subsequent process of interpretation is

[154]P. xvi.

[155]See especially J. Rohde, *Die redaktionsgeschichtliche Methode* (Hamburg, 1966), Eng. trans. *Rediscovering the Teaching of the Evangelists* (Philadelphia, 1969); N. Perrin, *What is Redaction Criticism?* (London, 1970).

[156]See H. Conzelmann, *Die Mitte der Zeit* (Tübingen, 1953), Eng. trans. *The Theology of St. Luke* (London, 1960).

[157]Harrington, "New Testament Theology," p. 183.

[158]Schlier, "A Theology of the NT," pp. 99-101.

[159]Conzelmann, *An Outline of NT Theology*, p. xv. See also H. Conzelmann, *Theologie als Schriftauslegung. Aufsätze zum NT* (Munich, 1974), pp. 106-119, 131-151.

partly elucidated, partly made more uniform, and partly distorted."[160] Objections to the reconstruction of an early Christian creed come from several quarters. E. Güttgemanns speaks of the reconstruction of the creed as "a hazardous enterprise that is too risky in view of the fragmentary nature of early Christian literature and the poorly documented early Christian history which is hidden in primitive historical darkness (F. Overbeck), especially when this reconstruction is made into the foundation of the unity of the kerygmata."[161] A similar reservation is voiced by Käsemann: "In my view an early Christian creed is already excluded by the variety of the existing formulae. It is not until the post-Pauline period, and even there rather seldom, that we can truly say that the New Testament authors see their task as the explication of the confession."[162] The issue at stake is whether the confessional formulae are considered as objectifications of the self-understanding of faith or whether Christology replaces the self-understanding of faith as the focal point. Schlier seeks a broader basis by including the Synoptics in the definitive tradition and thinks in so doing primarily of the proclamation of the incarnation, passion, and resurrection.[163]

In the previous lines we have observed how Conzelmann is able to return to Bultmann's position despite his different starting point. On the whole, it remains true also for Conzelmann that theology does not speak objectively about God and world; theology is anthropology. Faith brings about a new self-understanding. Harrington states, "All this is Heidegger, through the medium of Bultmann; it is not Paul, or John — or Jesus."[164] In any case, Conzelmann shares Bultmann's existentialist inter-

---

[160]Käsemann, "The Problem of a NT Theology," p. 241.

[161]Güttgemanns, "Literatur zur Neutestamentlichen Theologie," p. 49.

[162]Käsemann, "The Problem of a NT Theology," p. 241.

[163]Schlier, "A Theology of the NT," pp. 101f.

[164]Harrington, *The Path of Biblical Theology*, p. 197; idem, "New Testament Theology," p. 184.

pretation. But is he as heavily oriented to interpretation as was Bultmann?

Conzelmann reveals a shift in the correlation of reconstruction and interpretation. This shift is one towards reconstruction, i.e., the historical rather than the normative. Over against Bultmann's time, in which there was a need for strong emphasis on "interpretation of the meaning of what was said and the *message* of the texts," Conzelmann feels that the "perspectives have shifted."[165] Today there is "a new tendency towards historical positivism and relativism. The upward trend in which biblical scholarship delighted for decades itself proved to be a piece of escapism — into the historical."[166] Conzelmann seeks to counter this tendency towards historical positivism and relativism by a tactic opposed to Bultmann, who emphasized "interpretation," i.e., what the reconstruction means for modern man as translated through the philosophical medium of existentialism. Conzelmann lays stress "on historical reconstruction, i.e., the presentation of the thought-world of the New Testament as conditioned by its time."[167] This shift toward the historical is a significant one for Conzelmann, who remains fully committed to the Bultmannian correlation of "reconstruction" and "interpretation."[168] Conzelmann seems to have the support of Käsemann, who considers NT theology to be "a historical discipline."[169] These shifts in the Bultmannian camp reveal that NT theology is in a state of flux even among those known to favor the existentialist approach.

It should not be overlooked that the existentialist approaches of both Bultmann and Conzelmann fail to represent the views of the NT as a whole. The existentialist approach can only deal with such sections of the NT as are amenable to existentialist interpretation.

---

[165]Conzelmann, *An Outline of NT Theology,* p. xiii (italics his).
[166]Ibid.
[167]P. xiv.
[168]Robinson, "The Future of NT Theology," p. 19.
[169]Käsemann, "The Problem of a NT Theology," p. 242.

Those sections of the NT which do not lend themselves to this approach are undergoing "content-criticism" or are left out of consideration altogether. The existentialist approaches of Bultmann and Conzelmann appear to consider such NT documents as Hebrews, 1-2 Peter, James, Jude, and Revelation as stepchildren unworthy of attention. This raises other questions regarding the adequacy of the existentialist approach.

C. The Historical Approach

1. *Werner G. Kümmel.* There could be no sharper contrast to Conzelmann's thesis that "the basic problem of New Testament theology is not, how did the proclaimer, Jesus of Nazareth, become the proclaimed Messiah, Son of God, Lord"[170] than the NT theology of Kümmel published two years later (1969).[171] Kümmel does not belong to the Bultmann School; instead, he represents the "modern historical" direction of research and seeks to do precisely what Conzelmann believed is not the basic problem of NT theology.

Kümmel sets forth his task in concise words: "I shall attempt to set forth the preaching of Jesus, the theology of Paul against the background of the primitive community, and the message of Christ in the gospel of John, in their essential features, and, on the basis of this presentation, to inquire about the unity which is exhibited in these forms of proclamation."[172] The structure of his tome reflects this task.[173] Chapter I treats "The Procla-

[170]Conzelmann, *An Outline of NT Theology,* p. xviii.

[171]W. G. Kümmel, *Die Theologie des Neuen Testaments nach seinen Hauptzeugen:Jesus-Paulus-Johannes* (Göttingen, 1969; 2nd ed., 1972), Eng. trans. *The Theology of the New Testament According to its Major Witnesses: Jesus-Paul-John* (Nashville, 1973).

[172]Kümmel, *Theology of the NT,* p. 18.

[173]See the reactions by M. Hengel, "Theorie und Praxis im Neuen Testament?" *Evangelische Kommentare* 3 (1970), 744-745, esp. 744; Güttgemanns, "Literatur zur Neutestamentlichen Theologie," pp. 44-46; Küng, *Menschwerdung Gottes,* pp. 588, 591; Merk, *Biblische Theologie,* pp. 259-261; Lohse, *Grundriss der neutestamentliche Theologie,* p. 12.

mation of Jesus According to the First Three Gospels"[174] in which Jesus' message is consciously placed at the beginning of NT theology in order to show how the Proclaimer became the proclaimed One. Chapter II turns to "The Faith of the Primitive Christian Community"[175] which sees things in a new light on account of the resurrection event. "The Theology of Paul" in Chapter III[176] stands at the transition from the Palestinian apostolic community to the later Gentile Christian community. Paul is "the first theologian of Gentile Christianity" but between him and the person and preaching of the earthly Jesus there is not only a historical but also a substantive relationship.[177]

Kümmel differs radically in his answer to the question of "Paul and Jesus"[178] in which Bultmann[179] (and Conzelmann) see a hiatus along the line of W. Wrede.[180] Kümmel maintains that Paul is a sound witness and interpreter of Jesus. This does not, of course, mean that there are no differences between them, but they are not, at the core, only peripheral. It is concluded that "Jesus and Paul are witnesses to the same historical truth, but Paul only points backward and forward to the salvation brought by Jesus and expected from Jesus."[181] The theology of the Johannine writings is treated in Chapter IV entitled "The Johannine Message of Christ in the Fourth Gospel and in the Epistles."[182]

[174]Kümmel, *Theology of the NT*, pp. 22-95.

[175]Pp. 96-136.

[176]Pp. 137-254.

[177]Pp. 244-254.

[178]See H. Ridderbos, *Paul and Jesus* (Grand Rapids, Mich., 1957); E. E. Ellis, *Paul and His Recent Interpreters* (Grand Rapids, Mich., 1961), pp. 26-34; H. Ridderbos, *Paul. An Outline of His Theology* (Grand Rapids, Mich., 1975), pp. 13-43. Also A. Schweitzer, *Paul and His Interpreters* (New York, 1964), pp. 244f.

[179]R. Bultmann, "Jesus and Paul," *Existence and Faith*, pp. 183-201.

[180]W. Wrede, *Paulus* (Tübingen, 1904) (reprinted in K. H. Rengstorf and U. Luck, *Das Paulusbild in der neueren deutschen Forschung* [Tübingen, 1964], pp. 1ff.), Eng. trans. *Paul* (London, 1908).

[181]Kümmel, *Theology of the NT*, p. 254.

[182]Pp. 255-321.

The Johannine writings present the activity and the preaching of Jesus Christ "deliberately and consistently from the perspective of the belief of the community of the late period of primitive Christianity."[183] John "strictly joins not only the person of Jesus but also the salvation wrought by Jesus to God's historical saving action in Jesus Christ, and thereby proclaims Jesus and this salvation as the eschatological salvation event."[184] In the final chapter Kümmel asks about the unity of the message of Jesus, Paul and John with the title "Jesus-Paul-John: The Heart of the New Testament."[185] Kümmel affirms that there is development of thought and that there is not a straight-line continuation in every aspect of thought, but the major witnesses of the NT sound forth from them

> one message in common, that in Jesus God, the Lord of the world, has come to us. But this coming of God can become a personal reality for us only if we so allow ourselves to be grasped by God's love that has come to us in Jesus Christ that we become new persons, who let our "light so shine before men that they may see your good works and glorify your Father who is in heaven" (Matt. 5:16).[186]

Kümmel gives us the first NT theology in this century in which the demand of A. Deissmann[187] — and in a somewhat different way of G. L. Bauer[188] — comes to the forefront, namely the matter of the unity of the NT. Although Kümmel is unable to answer the question of the unity of the whole NT because his NT theology is limited to the major witness of Jesus, Paul, and John, he is followed in his procedure by E. Lohse, who concludes his *Outline of New Testament Theology* (1974)

[183]P. 321.
[184]Ibid.
[185]Pp. 322-333.
[186]P. 333.
[187]A. Deissmann, "Zur Methode der biblischen Theologie des Neuen Testaments," *PTNT*, p. 79.
[188]Merk, *Biblische Theologie,* p. 260.

also with a chapter on "The Unity of the New Testament."[189]

Is Kümmel committed to the correlation of "reconstruction" and "interpretation" as we have met it in the existential approach to NT theology? Kümmel responds: "The scientific concern with the understanding of the New Testament must, precisely when it is pursued in the context of the church and from the presupposition of faith, take account of the fact that we also *can* come to a believing hearing of the message of the New Testament only in *one* way: namely, by seeking to make the utterances of the ancient authors of the New Testament understandable, just as their contemporary readers and/or hearers could and had to understand them."[190] While for Bultmann and Conzelmann "interpretation" is separate from reconstruction and to be achieved by means of existentialism, Kümmel unites reconstruction and interpretation so that the latter is allied to the former, because "a great deal depends on whether one pursues such research as one uninvolved and in conscious detachment, or as one inwardly involved and hence as one who hears with ultimate openness."[191] It appears to be evident that Kümmel is primarily interested in providing a moderate critical reconstruction which often comes close to the positions of O. Cullmann and largely relinquishes interpretation.[192]

2. *Joachim Jeremias.* The foremost representative of the "positive-historical" direction of research is the internationally known scholar of the University of Göttingen, J. Jeremias. He became one of the foremost critics of Bultmann's approach of making NT theology a "kerygmatic theology"[193] and developed an "intensive

---

[189]Lohse, *Grundriss der neutestamentlichen Theologie*, pp. 161-164.
[190]Kümmel, *Theology of the NT*, p. 16.
[191]Ibid. See also Merk, *Biblische Theologie*, pp. 260f.
[192]Goppelt, *Theologie des NT*, I, 44.
[193]A critical assessment is provided by J. S. Stewart, "The Christ of Faith," *The New Testament in Historical and Contemporary Perspective. Essays in Memory of G. H. C. Macgregor* (Oxford, 1965), pp. 261-280.

historical anticriticism"[194] of which E. Käsemann noted
that the formerly "pietistic" direction has become historically oriented and the formerly "purely historical"
direction is engaged in theology.[195] The research of
Jeremias seeks to serve historical truth and to protect
the Word from docetic evaporation.[196] He had already
gained international recognition for his work on the
parables and his studies on the eucharistic words of Jesus
and the Aramaic background of the *logia* of Jesus.[197] In
all of this he was interested in the *ipsissima vox Jesu*
(very voice of Jesus),[198] in order to allow the man of
our time to hear the voice of Jesus as the contemporaries
of Jesus heard that voice.[199] An understanding of this
setting in the contemporary scholarly scene is vital for
an appreciation and evaluation of the *magnum opus* of
Jeremias.

In 1971 Jeremias published simultaneously in German
and English the first volume of his *New Testament Theology: The Proclamation of Jesus*,[200] of which it has been

[194]Goppelt, *Theologie des NT*, I, 43.

[195]E. Käsemann, *Exegetische Versuche und Besinnungen* (Göttingen,
1964), II, 32-41.

[196]J. Jeremias, "The Present Position in the Controversy Concerning the Problem of the Historical Jesus," *ET* 59 (1958), 333ff.; idem,
The Problem of the Historical Jesus (Philadelphia, 1964).

[197]J. Jeremias, *The Parables of Jesus* (3rd ed.; London, 1972);
idem, *The Eucharistic Words of Jesus* (2nd ed.; London, 1966);
idem, *Abba. Studien zur neutestamentlichen Theologie und Zeit-
geschichte* (Göttingen, 1966); idem, *The Central Message of the
New Testament* (New York, 1965).

[198]Jeremias writes in *The Parables of Jesus*, p. 9, the following: "It
is to be hoped that the reader will perceive that the aim of the
critical analysis contained in the second part of this book is nothing
less than a return, as well grounded as possible, to the very words of
Jesus himself. Only the Son of Man and his word can invest our
message with full authority."

[199]Jeremias, *The Parables of Jesus*, p. 114: "Our faith is to return
to the actual living voice of Jesus. How great the gain if we succeed
in rediscovering here and there behind the veil the features of the
Son of Man! To meet with him can alone give power to our preaching."

[200]J. Jeremias, *Neutestamentliche Theologie I. Teil: Die Verkündigung Jesu* (Gütersloh, 1971; 2nd ed. 1973), Eng. trans. *New Testament Theology: The Proclamation of Jesus* (New York, 1971).

said already that it "may prove to be the most important book written about the New Testament in the last fifty years."[201] It may be said without hesitation that in this work of Jeremias there is no correlation between "reconstruction" and "interpretation" of the kind known from Bultmann and his school. "Interpretation" is at best the systematizing of the proclamation of Jesus as gained through reconstruction of his words by means of a critical methodology.[202] This means that in all essentials we have here an approach close to the "descriptive NT theology" in the Stendahl tradition.[203]

Chapter I carries the title "How Reliable Is the Tradition of the Sayings of Jesus?"[204] It is concerned with the problem of the historical Jesus, the very subject considered by Bultmann to be a presupposition of NT theology and declared to be no part of NT theology at all by Conzelmann. Jeremias is interested in investigating "whether our sources are sufficient to enable us to bring out the basic ideas of the preaching of Jesus with some degree of probability,"[205] which means the historical reconstruction of "the pre-Easter tradition."[206] This is to be achieved by means of (1) the "comparative method" ("religionsvergleichende Methode")[207] which employs primarily the "criterion of dissimilarity" on the basis of which "a saying or a theme" can be tested to derive "either from Judaism or from the early church";[208] and (2) the "examination of *language and style*" ("*sprachlich-stilistische* Tatbestände").[209] These two

[201]S. Neill, *Jesus Through Many Eyes. Introduction to the Theology of the New Testament* (Philadelphia, 1976), p. 169.

[202]Harrington, *Path*, p. 201, misses the real intent of the methodology of Jeremias' *NT Theology* in his evaluation that it "is a badly needed corrective to the scepticism of the existentialist view."

[203]Stendahl, *IDB*, I, 422.

[204]Jeremias, *NT Theology*, pp. 1-41. It should be noted that this title is not framed in the form of a question in the German original.

[205]P. 1.

[206]P. 3.

[207]P. 2.

[208]Ibid.

[209]P. 3.

methods produce fairly certain results and permit a reconstruction of the *ipsissima vox Jesu*.[210] With regard to the Synoptics "it is the inauthenticity, and not the authenticity, of the sayings of Jesus that must be demonstrated."[211]

Chapter II treats "The Mission of Jesus"[212] with the subheadings of "Jesus and John the Baptist," "The Call of Jesus," "Handing on the Revelation," "Abbā as an Address to God," and "Yes to the Mission." In each case he follows the method of inquiring for the sources, the content, and the significance or meaning of the respective item. This pattern is not followed in Chapters III and IV which deal with the proclamation of Jesus under the headings "The Dawn of the Time of Salvation"[213] and "The Period of Grace"[214] respectively. Jeremias concludes, "The central theme of the public proclamation of Jesus was the kingly reign of God."[215] Chapter V describes the personal appeal of Jesus' message which leads to the formation of "The New People of God"[216] as a remnant community of faith which worships God without end. Jeremias demonstrates his methodology in Chapter VI, "Jesus' Testimony to His Mission,"[217] the German title of which is more precise with "Das Hoheitsbewusstsein Jesu," in which Jesus is shown to have understood himself to be "the bringer of salvation."[218] Jeremias argues that the emphatic use of *egō* is without parallel in the world of Jesus and thus supports an implicit christology.[219] "Son of man is the only title used by Jesus of himself whose authenticity is to be taken

[210]Pp. 29-37. See also J. Jeremias, *The Prayers of Jesus* (SBT 2/6; London, 1967), pp. 108-115.
[211]Jeremias, *NT Theology*, p. 37.
[212]Pp. 42-75.
[213]Pp. 76-121.
[214]Pp. 122-158.
[215]P. 96.
[216]Pp. 159-249.
[217]Pp. 250-299.
[218]Pp. 250-257.
[219]Pp. 254f.

seriously."[220] It goes back to Daniel 7:13. He argues against his own student's conclusion that this title has its background in Canaanite mythology by pointing out that "in view of the enormous time lapse between the texts of Ras Shamra and the book of Daniel this is hardly conceivable."[221] Jesus' understanding of his passion is reconstructed. "Jesus saw his imminent suffering clearly and announced it beforehand. . . . Jesus had considered the question of the necessity of his death and had found the answer to this question in scripture, primarily in Isaiah 53, the chapter about the suffering servant, but also in other passages such as Zechariah 13:7."[222] The most important allusions to Jesus' suffering are the eucharistic words.[223]

In the final chapter, "The Earliest Tradition and the Earliest Interpretation,"[224] Jeremias moves beyond the proclamation of Jesus in his attempt to relate the proclamation of Jesus with Easter, namely the resurrection. The second German edition contains a brief but significant concluding addition in which Jeremias reveals his understanding of the relationship of Jesus' proclamation to the church's witness:

> Both entities, the proclamation of Jesus and the witness of the faith of the church, the pre-Easter and post-Easter message, belong insolubly together. . . . They relate to each other as call to response. The gracious offer of salvation in the form of the words and deeds of Jesus, his death on the cross and his exaltation, is the call of God to the world; the witness of the church in its formal as well as material manifoldedness, the choir of countless tongues which sing praises to his name and which confess him before the world, is the response which is wrought by the Spirit to the call.[225]

[220]P. 258.
[221]P. 268 n. 1.
[222]P. 286.
[223]Pp. 288-292.
[224]Pp. 300-311.
[225]Jeremias, *Neutestamentliche Theologie,* I, 295.

The last sentences sum up in superb language the concern of Jeremias: "The call stands above the response, because Jesus is the Kyrios and the Kyrios stands above his messengers. The Kyrios above is the beginning and end, the center and measure of all Christian theology."[226]

This first part of the NT Theology of Jeremias brings together in a masterly way everything Jeremias has been known for. A recent reviewer summed it up by saying, "Few other NT scholars could have written the book."[227] Jeremias appears again as a conservative critic who insists that there is a connection between all major NT themes and the proclamation of Jesus. The post-Easter church responded to the call of Jesus but did not engage in the kind of creativity ascribed to it by those who see no, or virtually no, connection between the kerygma of the church and the historical Jesus. O. Merk points out that in the work of Jeremias the differentiation between the individual evangelists recedes into the background in favor of the reconstruction of the form and message of Jesus. In this respect Jeremias is said to be close to G. L. Bauer.[228] It remains to be seen to what extent the expected second volume of Jeremias' NT theology deals with the theology of the evangelists. In terms of the comparative method employed by Jeremias it is lamented by L. Goppelt, who himself attempts to demonstrate links between the historical Jesus and the proclamation of the church, that the principle of analogy as regards the Jewish surroundings makes Jesus into a purely Jewish phenomenon.[229] The "criterion of dissimilarity" which Jeremias adopts from N. Perrin for the demonstration of authenticity has its own problems.[230] A more basic methodological issue

[226]Ibid.

[227]C. E. Carlston, "Review of J. Jeremias, *New Testament Theology: The Proclamation of Jesus,*" *JBL* 91 (1972), 260-262, esp. 261.

[228]Merk, *Biblische Theologie,* p. 262.

[229]Goppelt, *Theologie des NT,* I, 44.

[230]H. Koester, "The Historical Jesus: Some Comments and Thoughts on Norman Perrin's *Rediscovering the Teaching of Jesus,*" *Christology and a Modern Pilgrimage,* ed. H. D. Betz (Philadelphia, 1971), pp. 123-136.

relates to the tantalizing silence on the part of Jeremias as regards the justification for presenting the proclamation of Jesus as a part of NT theology. In view of the situation of the debate on this methodological issue (e.g. Bultmann, Conzelmann, Perrin) one wonders why Jeremias has not in even one word intimated a justification for his methodological procedure or indicated that he will do so in a subsequent volume. Is it entirely self-evident that the proclamation of Jesus constitutes the foundation and basis for NT theology?

D. The Salvation History (Heilsgeschichte) Approach

1. *Oscar Cullmann.* The well-known professor emeritus at the University of Basel and the Sorbonne in Paris, O. Cullmann, has not written a book with the title NT Theology.[231] He needs to be included in a discussion of methodology in the discipline of NT theology because he is the foremost representative of the salvation history[232] approach to the NT in this century. Cullmann's basic prolegomenon of NT "salvation history" appeared first in 1946 under the title *Christ and Time*,[233] which was followed by his in-depth study *Salvation in History*, published first in 1965.[234] These works have created a lively debate.[235]

[231]K. Fröhlich, "Die Mitte des Neuen Testaments. Oscar Cullmanns Beitrag zur Theologie der Gegenwart," *Oikonomia: Heilsgeschichte als Thema der Theologie. Festschrift für O. Cullmann* (Stuttgart, 1967), pp. 203-219, esp. 213, has pointed out that other scholars give the title "Theology of the New Testament" to the kind of book which Cullmann published under the title *Die Christology des Neuen Testaments* (Tübingen, 1957), Eng. trans. *The Christology of the Testament* (2nd ed.; Philadelphia, 1967).

[232]This writer prefers the translation "salvation history" for *Heilsgeschichte* and "salvation historical" for "heilsgeschichtlich" instead of "redemptive history" in order to avoid the impression that history itself has redemptive power.

[233]O. Cullmann, *Christus und die Zeit. Die urchristliche Zeit und Geschichtsauffassung* (Zurich, 1946; 3rd ed., 1962), Eng. trans. *Christ and Time* (London, 1951; 2nd ed., 1962).

[234]O. Cullmann, *Heil als Geschichte: Heilsgeschichtliche Existenz im Neuen Testament* (Tübingen, 1965; 2nd ed., 1967), Eng. trans. *Salvation in History* (New York, 1967).

[235]See especially Cullmann's own reaction to such critics as R. Bult-

In his earlier study Cullmann attempted to give a basic outline of NT salvation history through a reconstruction of the early Christian understanding of time and its interpretation as a filled time within the tension of "already" and "not yet." Christ is "the center of time" or the "mid-point" of time,[236] which is to be understood as a linear conception of time. It is, however, not "a straight line, but a *fluctuating line* which can show wide variation."[237] It must be clearly understood that Cullmann's salvation history approach is not to be equated either with earlier approaches under this name by scholars in the seventeenth to the nineteenth centuries or those who use the term "in the bad sense of 'positive', 'pious', 'churchy' or 'uncritical'."[238] For Cullmann the salvation history approach means a "striving for nothing less than an answer to the old question 'What is Christianity?' "[239]

It shall be our purpose to provide a brief survey of the content of Cullmann's *magnum opus, Salvation in History,* before we ask how he understands salvation

---

mann, E. Fuchs, F. Buri, J. Körner, H. Conzelmann, K. G. Steck, and J. Barr in *Christ and Time* (2nd ed.), pp. xv-xxxi. Among the more important recent treatments of Cullmann's views are: Stendahl, *IDB,* I, 420f.; Fröhlich, "Die Mitte des NT," pp. 203-219; D. Braun, "Heil als Geschichte," *EvTh* 27 (1967), 57-76; Kraus, *Biblische Theologie,* pp. 185-188; Bouttier, "Théologie et Philosophie du NT," pp. 188f.; E. Güttgemanns, "Literatur zur Neutestamentlichen Theologie. Randglossen zu ausgewählten Neuerscheinungen," *Verkündigung und Forschung* 12 (1967), 38-87, esp. 44-49; Harrington, "New Testament Theology," pp. 184-189; idem, *Path,* pp. 197-201; G. Klein, "Bibel und Heilsgeschichte. Die Fragwürdigkeit einer Idee," *ZNW* 62 (1971), 1-47; J. T. Clemons, "Critics and Criticism of Salvation History," *Religion in Life* 41 (1972), 89-100; G. E. Ladd, "The Search for Perspective," *Interpretation* 25 (1971), 41-62; K. Schubert, "Geschichte und Heilsgeschichte," *Kairos* 15 (1973), 89-101; I. G. Nicol, "Event and Interpretation. O. Cullmann's Conception of Salvation History," *Theology* 77 (1974), 14-21.

[236]Cullmann, *Christ and Time,* pp. 121-174.
[237]Cullmann, *Salvation in History,* p. 15 (italics his).
[238]P. 11.
[239]P. 19.

history to function. Part I contains the "Prolegomena."[240] It surveys research on second-century gnosticism, eschatology in the twentieth century, hermeneutics as it relates to salvation history, and it provides a definition of salvation history. Part II carries the title "The Genesis of the Salvation Historical Approach."[241] Its content treats event and interpretation, the faith of the biblical witnesses, the constant and contingency, and the consolidation of salvation-historical excerpts in the NT. "Phenomenological Characteristics"[242] are treated in Part III with emphases on history and myth, salvation history and history, and the tension of the "already" and the "not yet." With Part IV we reach the heart of the book in its treatment of "The Main New Testament Types"[243] of salvation history, namely the beginnings of salvation history with Jesus,[244] the intermediate period of salvation history,[245] and the Gospel of John[246] and salvation history.[247] Finally, Part V provides "A Survey of Systematic Theology and the History of Dogma: Salvation History and the Post-Biblical Period."[248] This survey reveals at once that Cullmann seeks to vindicate salvation history as the essential framework of the NT witnesses and offers a challenge to the existentialist approach to NT theology as manifested by R. Bultmann and his followers.

Within the confines of our purpose it will be impossible to deal adequately with the rich and fruitful stimuli provided by Cullmann. We attempt to highlight briefly the nature of salvation history as understood by Cullmann before we address methodological issues. Cullmann does not understand salvation history "as a

[240]Pp. 19-83.
[241]Pp. 84-135.
[242]Pp. 136-185.
[243]Pp. 186-291.
[244]Pp. 187-236.
[245]Pp. 236-248.
[246]Pp. 248-268.
[247]Pp. 268-291.
[248]Pp. 292-338.

history *alongside* history . . .; it unfolds in history, and
in this sense belongs to it."[249] An integral aspect of Biblical salvation history is that certain "historically con-
trollable" events are "open to historical investigation . . .
events belonging to secular history which are placed
in a definite connection not disclosed by history itself."[250] "Events belonging to secular history" receive a
salvation-historical interpretation. Cullmann's dependence on G. von Rad's views are freely acknowledged,[251]
a view which has distinct problems.[252] With regard to
the movement of event and interpretation Cullmann
writes, "Salvation history does not arise by a simple
adding up of events recognized in faith as saving events.
It is rather the case that *corrections* of the interpretations of past saving events *are undertaken in the light
of* new events."[253] The process of event and interpretation is a complex one. "The act of interpretation . . . is
regarded as belonging to salvation history itself."[254]
Cullmann sums up his view of these complex issues by
emphasizing three distinct aspects: ". . . first, the naked
event [*nackte Ereignis*] to which the prophet must be
an eye-witness and which is conceived by non-believers
as well, who are unable to see any revelation in it; second, the revelation of a divine plan being disclosed in
the event to the prophet with which he aligns himself in
faith; third, the creation of an association with earlier
salvation-historical revelations imparted to other prophets in the reinterpretation of these revelations."[255] Jesus
"includes himself in the event happening at the place
in which he stands. But the new revelation was consistent in his proclaiming this as the decisive locus of all
salvation history."[256] It may be stated with all fairness

[249]P. 153.
[250]Pp. 139f.
[251]Pp. 54, 88.
[252]Hasel, *OT Theology*, pp. 57-75.
[253]Cullmann, *Salvation in History*, p. 88 (italics his).
[254]P. 89.
[255]P. 90.
[256]P. 117.

that Cullmann's view of revelation as given in both event and interpretation contains ambiguities.[257]

It has been noted that Cullmann adopts von Rad's position, which is understood to go "along the lines of salvation history,"[258] namely, "the progressive reinterpretation of Israel's old traditions is continually awakened by new events in the present."[259] While Cullmann speaks of the "naked event" (nackte Ereignis),[260] von Rad denies its existence: "There are no *bruta facta* at all; we have history only in the form of interpretation, only in reflection."[261] It is crucial to von Rad's argumentation that in the historical-critical picture of Israel's history no premises of faith or revelation are taken into account since the historical-critical method works without a God-hypothesis.[262] Israel, however, "could only understand her history as a road along which she travelled under Yahweh's guidance. For Israel, history existed only where Yahweh has revealed himself through act and word."[263] Von Rad rejects the either-or choice of considering the kerygmatic picture as unhistorical and the historical-critical picture as historical. He contends that "the kerygmatic picture too . . . is founded in actual history and has not been invented." Nevertheless, he speaks of the early "historical experiences" of primeval history in terms of "historical poetry," "legend," "saga," and "poetic stories"[264] containing "anachronisms."[265] The

257See esp. Nicol, "Event and Interpretation," pp. 18-21.

258Cullmann, *Salvation in History*, p. 54.

259Ibid.

260P. 90.

261This point is made by G. von Rad, "Antwort auf Conzelmann's Fragen," *EvTh* 24 (1964), 393, in a dispute with H. Conzelmann, "Fragen an Gerhard von Rad," *EvTh* 24 (1964), 113-125.

262G. von Rad, *Old Testament Theology* (Edinburgh, 1965), II, 417.

263G. von Rad, "Offene Fragen im Umkreis einer Theologie des AT," *ThLZ* 88 (1963), 409. The problem of the relationship of word and event, word and acts, etc., is the subject of an essay by G. F. Hasel, "The Problem of History in OT Theology," *AUSS* 8 (1970), 32-46.

264Von Rad, *OT Theology*, I, 108f.

265Vol. II, 421f.

important thing for von Rad is not that the historical kernel is overlaid with "fiction" but that the experience of the horizon of the later narrator's own faith as read into the saga is "historical"[266] and results in a great enrichment of the saga's theological content. All of this is part and parcel of the method of the history-of-traditions. He states, "The process by which the salvation-historical perspective originated is no longer completely comprehensible everywhere in the Old Testament. In the first place, the historical occasions for the origins and further development of the oldest traditions cannot always be told with certainty, especially when oral traditions or oral kerygmata are often involved, which were then set down in liturgical confessional formulas. . . . It is only in the great historical conceptions . . . that we are able to become better acquainted with the origin of the salvation-historical interpretations and reinterpretations."[267] Cullmann's indebtedness to von Rad's traditio-historical method which he reworks into his salvation-historical approach with the constant interpretation of the so-called "naked event" and later reinterpretation of the "salvation-historical tradition"[268] raises the question whether or not Cullmann's approach is really able to overcome the problems related to the whole issues of history and history of tradition with its two pictures of history, namely that established by the historical-critical method and that presented by the kerygma of the Biblical witnesses.[269] Cullmann expressed his opinion regarding the criticism of von Rad by W. Eichrodt and F. Hesse that the *kerygma* is put in place of the "real history" by suggesting that "in reality, a greater agreement exists between these three scholars than perhaps they themselves think."[270]

It has become clear in the meantime that this is not

[266]P. 421.
[267]Cullmann, *Salvation in History*, p. 89.
[268]P. 90.
[269]See Hasel, *OT Theology*, pp. 57-75.
[270]Cullmann, *Salvation in History*, p. 54.

the case.[271] Cullmann points out emphatically that "the thing that distinguishes history from salvation history is the role played by revelation in salvation history, both in the experiencing of events and facts, and in the appropriation of the accounts and their interpretation ('kerygma') through faith. Here events are experienced as divine revelation, and likewise the accounts and interpretations are ascribed to divine revelation."[272] Revelation is the distinguishing criterion, so that "the historical saving process is the centre of all history, including primeval and eschatological history."[273] Revelation is active in sorting out of the total historical process "the selection of events" included in salvation history which "is determined in the *plan of God*."[274] In all of this salvation history is the overarching category into which are incorporated several Biblical schema. Typology "presupposes a salvation-historical point of view."[275] The schema of "promise and fulfillment" is related to salvation history in that "fulfillment within the biblical framework is never complete. Salvation history continues to develop. Although God remains true to his promise, it is fulfilled in a way hard to survey in detail and in a manner not at the disposal of human knowledge once for all."[276] It is to Cullmann's credit to have presented a carefully thought out view of "salvation history as representing the essence of the New Testament message. . . ."[277] He does so in conversation with the leading minds in the theological scene and addresses himself to the leading critics of salvation history.[278]

[271]F. Hesse, *Abschied von der Heilsgeschichte* (Zurich, 1971). Note also J. Barr, "Story and History in Biblical Theology," *Journal of Religion* 56 (1976), 1ff.

[272]Cullmann, *Salvation in History*, pp. 151f.

[273]P. 148.

[274]P. 154.

[275]P. 133.

[276]P. 124.

[277]P. 150.

[278]For example, K. G. Steck, *Die Idee der Heilsgeschichte. Hofmann-Schlatter-Cullmann* (Zurich, 1959); G. Klein, "Offenbarung als Geschichte? Marginalien zu einem theologischen Programm," *Monatsschrift für Pastoraltheologie* (1962), 65ff.; G. Fohrer, "Prophetie und Geschichte," *ThLZ* 24 (1964), 481ff., etc.

In the year 1962 K. Stendahl suggested that in *Christ and Time* Cullmann "recaptured the mood of thought of the NT writers and stays within it long enough to work out its implications for different aspects of NT thought."[279] Stendahl has a positive stance toward the methodological issue for NT theology as raised by Cullmann. He suggests that Cullmann's approach remains "descriptive." O. Merk notes that it is a "reconstruction" of the early Christian understanding of time.[280] Cullmann does not engage in "interpretation," i.e., the transforming or translating of the NT religious understanding of salvation history into a framework suitable for modern man.[281] Does Cullmann consider such an "interpretation" or "'what it means' today to be arbitrary or dehistoricizing? Cullmann provides now a partial answer. He is convinced along with Bultmann that a decision is being called for by the NT: "The divine event, together with its interpretation revealed to the prophets and apostles . . . extends a claim to me about which I must make a decision . . . to align my existence with that concrete history revealed to me, with that sequence of events."[282] "If the decision of faith intended *in the New Testament* asks us to align ourselves with that *sequence of events,* then the sequence may not be demythologized, de-historicized, or deobjectified."[283] In contrast to Bultmann's demythologizing in which eschatology is reinterpreted existentially by divesting it of its temporality, i.e., by collapsing the richness of the NT kerygma to a "punctual eschatology" in the here and now, we have the alternative of Cullmann who argues that the salvation-historical tension between the "already" and the "not yet" is the key to the understanding of the NT. "The whole theology of the New Testament, including Jesus' preaching, is qualified by

279Stendahl, *IDB,* I, 421.
280Merk, *Biblische Theologie,* p. 253.
281Robinson, "The Future of NT Theology," p. 19.
282Cullmann, *Salvation in History,* p. 69.
283P. 70 (italics his).

this tension."[284] Man today lives in the extension of the "intermediate period of salvation-history," an "intermediate stage between two poles, the poles of the biblical period and the end time."[285] Cullmann reminds us, "What is crucial for salvation-historical theology is the relationship to the present."[286] It appears that the descriptive task is for Cullmann the crucial one. He refuses to have the NT salvation history translated into the present by existentialism, Platonism,[287] or any other system.

2. *George E. Ladd.* Professor G. E. Ladd is one of the best-known evangelical scholars on the North American continent[288] whose scholarship has been recognized by peers of other theological schools of thought. He is one of two Americans to have provided a full-scale NT theology after a silence of American scholars on the subject for about seven decades.[289] Ladd's *magnum opus* is entitled *A Theology of the New Testament* (1974) and belongs squarely to the salvation-history approach in NT theology.

[284]P. 172.
[285]P. 293.
[286]P. 308 n. 2.
[287]P. 204.
[288]The following works and studies are particularly important: G. E. Ladd, *Crucial Questions About the Kingdom of God* (Grand Rapids, Mich., 1952); idem, *The Blessed Hope* (7th ed.; Grand Rapids, Mich., 1973); idem, *Jesus and the Kingdom. The Eschatology of Biblical Realism* (2nd ed.; Waco, Tex., 1970); idem, *The New Testament and Criticism* (Grand Rapids, Mich., 1967); idem, "Why Not Prophetic-Apocalyptic?" *JBL* 81 (1962), 230-238; idem, "History and Theology in Biblical Exegesis," *Interpretation* 20 (1966), 54-64; idem, "The Problem of History in Contemporary NT Interpretation," *Studia Evangelica* 5 (1968), 88-100; idem, "The Search for Perspective," *Interpretation* 25 (1971), 41-62.
[289]In 1906 G. B. Stevens of Yale University published the second edition of his *The Theology of the New Testament* (1st ed.; Edinburgh, 1901). The books by F. Stagg, *New Testament Theology* (Nashville, 1962) and R. E. Knudsen, *Theology in the New Testament. A Basis for Christian Faith* (Chicago/Los Angeles, Calif., 1964) are written for laypersons and do not pretend to be mature NT theologies. The other full-scale work was written by another scholar of the evangelical-conservative tradition, namely C. K. Lehman, *Biblical Theology 2: New Testament* (Scottdale, Pa., 1974).

The intention of Ladd's tome is "to introduce seminary students to the discipline of New Testament
theology."[290] Ladd does not make a distinction between
Biblical theology and NT theology as advanced by
B. S. Childs,[291] because Ladd defines history and historical method on the basis of different presuppositions.
"Any man's presuppositions distinctly influence his approach."[292] The truthfulness of the Biblical story is the
issue at stake. "Presuppositions about the nature of
history have continued to interject themselves into the
reconstruction of the biblical message. . . . For scholars
who feel bound by secularistic historical method, history
has no room for divine men. Therefore, back of the
Jesus of the Gospels must be hidden an historical
Jesus."[293] The presupposition of history as a closed
continuum of horizontal causes and effects is unable
to deal with the reality expressed in Scripture. Therefore, any approach adequate to the content of the Bible
must be in harmony with presuppositions taken from
it and be in harmony with the total reality expressed
in the Bible. "Since biblical theology is concerned with
the self-revelation of God and with the redemption of
men, the very idea of revelation and redemption involves certain presuppositions that are everywhere implicit and often explicit in the Bible. These presuppositions are God, man, and sin."[294] These presuppositions
imply that "Biblical history" is not to be reconstructed
in the same way in which historians reconstruct "history." Although the Bible represents God as acting
through "ordinary" historical events, "God has been
redemptively active in one stream of history in a way
in which he is not active in general history; it [the
Bible] also is conscious that at given points God has

[290]G. E. Ladd, *A Theology of the New Testament* (Grand Rapids,
Mich., 1974), p. 5.
[291]See above, pp. 70f.
[292]Ladd, *Theology of the NT*, p. 5.
[293]P. 26.
[294]Ibid.

acted in history in ways that transcend ordinary historical experience."[295] The most vivid illustration of the divine act in history is the resurrection of Jesus Christ. "From the point of view of scientific historical criticism, the resurrection cannot be 'historical,' for it is an event uncaused by any other historical event and it is without analogy. God, and God alone, is the cause of the resurrection. . . . Indeed, its very offense to scientific historical criticism is a kind of negative support for its supernatural character."[296] The real issue here is a theological one. "Revelatory events are not produced by history but through the Lord of history, who stands above history, acts within history for the redemption of historical creatures."[297] The activity of God in unique events of history is a part of salvation history.

Ladd's view of salvation history is unlike that of Cullmann in that he does not link it to tradition history. Salvation history, which Ladd designates imprecisely as "redemptive history" or "holy history,"[298] is made up of a series of events in which God revealed himself as nowhere else. Here he follows C. F. H. Henry. In his description of salvation history as a "stream of revelatory history"[299] Ladd does not follow Cullmann's concepts of "reinterpretation" of earlier interpretations or "corrections" of earlier salvation-historical interpretations, but employs the language of G. E. Wright[300] in stating that the NT stands in this stream of salvation history and that "New Testament theology . . . consists primarily of the recital of what God has done in Jesus of Nazareth."[301] The substance of Christian proclamation is likewise "the recital of God's acts in history."[302]

[295]P. 29.
[296]P. 30. See also G. E. Ladd, *I Believe in the Resurrection of Jesus* (Grand Rapids, Mich., 1975).
[297]Ladd, *Theology of the NT*, p. 30.
[298]P. 28.
[299]P. 27.
[300]G. E. Wright, *God Who Acts. Biblical Theology as Recital* (SBT 8; 8th ed.; London, 1966).
[301]Ladd, *Theology of the NT*, p. 28.
[302]Ibid.

Is the method of New Testament theology a "retelling" or "reciting" of what is reported in the documents of the NT? Is "recital" the most legitimate form of theological discourse on the New Testament? Does it mean that the theologian or preacher just "recites" what the NT has told without "translating" or "decoding" or "interpreting" it theologically for modern man? Ladd explains as follows: "Biblical theology has the task of expounding the theology in the Bible in its own historical setting, and its own forms, categories, and thought forms."[303] He goes on to be more specific: "New Testament theology must be primarily a descriptive discipline."[304] Here he follows K. Stendahl but qualifies Stendahl's definition by the adverb "primarily," which seems to mean "not exclusively." There seems to be a kind of tension in Ladd's description of methodology for NT theology because of the qualifier "primarily" and other statements that remain unexplained such as the following: "It [Biblical theology] is basically a description and interpretation of the divine activity within the scene of human history that seeks man's redemption."[305] Does Ladd really mean that aside from engaging in "description," i.e., the descriptive task, the NT (or Biblical) theologian also needs to engage in "interpretation," i.e., the theological task of making the message of the NT meaningful? Just as the adverb "primarily" is tantalizing in its intent, so another adverb is tantalizing as Ladd contines to define more closely. Biblical theology "is not initially concerned with the final meaning of the teachings of the Bible or their relevance for today. This is the task of systematic theology."[306] If Biblical and thus NT theology is not "primarily" and not "initially" involved in interpreting the Bible's meaning for today, then it is so "secondarily" and "ultimately."

[303]P. 25.
[304]P. 5. "Biblical theology is primarily a descriptive discipline" (p. 25).
[305]P. 26.
[306]P. 25.

What does this mean with regard to the notion of "recital"? How is it to be accomplished? These crucial methodological issues beg for further attention. On the other hand, it appears that the "descriptive" task involves for Ladd at the same time interpretation.[307]

Ladd has structured his NT theology into six major parts, each of which is subdivided into chapters. Each of these chapters plus many subsections contain valuable bibliographies of the most recent literature in the English language. Part I treats "The Synoptic Gospels."[308] It opens with the instructive chapter on the history and nature of NT theology. (This general introduction to the discipline of NT theology should actually be placed as a separate introductory section before the first part.) Unfortunately Ladd does not provide us with the theology of Matthew, Mark, and Luke as one should expect but provides a thematic cross-section of which eight chapters deal with aspects of the kingdom as preached by Jesus, and five with aspects of christological concepts. This whole first part is somewhat abruptly introduced by a chapter on John the Baptist. It is surprising that there is no equivalent chapter on Jesus himself.

Part II treats "The Fourth Gospel."[309] It opens with a chapter on critical problems which states Ladd's aim: "To discover to what degree it is similar or dissimilar to . . . the Synoptics."[310] This is admirably achieved in chapters on Johannine dualism, Christology, eternal life, the Christian life, the Holy Spirit, and eschatology. It is not at all clear why Ladd can claim that "the Gospels record the works and words of Jesus"[311] and treat in Part I the Synoptics as historically reliable sources of

[307]For example, the meaning of imminence (p. 210), the meaning of the resurrection of Jesus (p. 318), the meaning of the ascension of Jesus (p. 334), the meaning of Paul's conversion (p. 361), the meaning of Paul's view of revelation (p. 391), etc.

[308]Pp. 13-210.

[309]Pp. 213-308.

[310]P. 222.

[311]P. 28.

the life of Jesus[312] only to maintain later that "it is obviously not the intent of the Synoptic Gospels to give a report of the *ipsissima verba* [very words] of Jesus. . . ."[313] Should the Synoptics, if the latter judgment of Ladd is correct, not also be treated theologically as the Gospel of John? On what basis should the Synoptics be treated differently?

Part III is concerned with the theology of the book of Acts under the title "The Primitive Church."[314] The first chapter defends the essential historical reliability of the book of Acts in which he is now supported with greater erudition by W. W. Gasque.[315] Chapters on the resurrection, eschatological kerygma, and the church summarize the theology of Acts.

The theology of Paul as gained from Part IV[316] forms next to the theology of the Gospel of John one of the high points in Ladd's NT theology. Paul was a man of the Jewish, Hellenistic, and Christian worlds.[317] "Paul was prepared as a Jewish theologian to think through, under the guidance of the Holy Spirit, the implications of the fact that the crucified Jesus of Nazareth was indeed the Messiah, the resurrected and ascended Son of God. This led him to many conclusions radically different from those that he had held. . . ."[318] This meant "a radical modification of Paul's view of *Heilsgeschichte,* which is a radical departure from Judaism."[319] Since salvation history involves a unifying concept, Ladd considers the center of Pauline theology along with W. D. Davies as "the realization of the coming new age of redemption by the work of Christ. . . . The unifying

[312]P. 177: "Other evidences strengthen the view that the gospel tradition is historically sound . . . [and] that the church possessed a sound memory in reporting the words and deeds of Jesus."
[313]P. 221.
[314]Pp. 311-356.
[315]W. W. Gasque, *A History of the Criticism of the Acts of the Apostles* (Grand Rapids, Mich., 1976).
[316]Ladd, *Theology of the NT,* pp. 359-568.
[317]P. 360.
[318]P. 361.
[319]P. 369.

center is . . . the redemptive work of Christ as the center of redemptive history [*Heilsgeschichte*]."[320] This is not unlike the view of H. N. Ridderbos as expounded in his monumental *Paul: An Outline of His Theology*.[321] Ladd uses all thirteen canonical letters of Paul (as does Ridderbos) in his elucidation of Pauline theology.[322] He makes the point that we can speak of Pauline *theology*. "Is 'theology' only a descriptive discipline of what early Christians believed, or has God been pleased to use Paul as the outstanding individual instrument in the early church to communicate to men authoritative, redemptive truth?" What Paul says is theologically normative: "There can be little doubt about how Paul would answer this question, for his letters reflect a sense of authority in the light of which Paul's entire thought must be read."[323] This leaves the distinct impression that Ladd understands the descriptive tasks to be on the whole normative for modern man.[324] Interpretation of the "final meaning of the teachings of the Bible or

[320]P. 374.

[321]H. Ridderbos, *Paul: An Outline of His Theology* (Grand Rapids, Mich., 1975), p. 39: "The governing motif of Paul's preaching is the saving activity of God in the advent and the work, particularly in the death and the resurrection of Christ. This activity is on the one hand the fulfillment of the work of God in the history of the nation Israel, the fulfillment therefore also of the Scriptures; on the other hand it reaches to the ultimate consummation of the parousia of Christ and the coming of the kingdom of God. It is this great redemptive-historical [*heilsgeschichtlich*] framework within which . . . all of its subordinate parts receive their place and organically cohere."

[322]Ladd, *Theology of the NT*, pp. 376-379.

[323]P. 379.

[324]Ladd, *Jesus and the Kingdom*, p. xiii: "Biblical Realism designates the effort to understand the New Testament writings from within the mind of their authors, to stand where the biblical writers stand, rather than to force the biblical message into modern thought forms. . . . However, this interpretative effort [to interpret the Bible in terms which are meaningful to the modern man] must not result in structuring the biblical message in a modern framework that is alien to the Bible and which therefore distorts the biblical perspective."

their relevance for today . . . is the task of systematic theology."[325]

Part V carries the heading "The General Epistles"[326] and summarizes the theology of Hebrews, James, 1 Peter, 2 Peter, Jude and the Johannine Epistles. It is not clear why the Johannine Epistles and the Gospel of John are not treated together under the theology of John, since they are considered to derive from the same author. Likewise 1-2 Peter and the so-called Petrine speech(es) in Acts could have been organized into a theology of Peter. Or in a manner similar to G. B. Stevens the general epistles aside from those of John could have been incorporated into Part III, "The Primitive Church." Unfortunately Ladd provides no rationale for his structure. This applies again for his last section, Part VI, "The Apocalypse."[327]

Ladd's salvation history approach has certain methodological weaknesses which have been pointed out repeatedly and need not be rehearsed again. His approach lends itself to a conceptual unity which is, however, not realized. His NT theology, on the other hand, treats every NT document, even the theologies of the stepchildren of the discipline of NT theology, viz., Hebrews, James, Jude, 1-2 Peter, etc. The salvation history approach has also led him to explicate the links of the NT and its theology with that of the OT. Ladd is best in his description of the constituent concepts of Johannine and Pauline theology by means of tracing key words, titles, expressions, phrases, and the like with great perception. He does so in a way not unlike a mini-dictionary. In this respect he has provided something like a "Biblical concept theology,"[328] that is, a treatment of distinct Biblical concepts as expressed by

---

[325]Ladd, *Theology of the NT*, p. 25.

[326]Pp. 571-616.

[327]Pp. 619-632.

[328]To my knowledge this designation was coined by D. H. Kelsey, *The Uses of Scripture in Recent Theology* (Philadelphia, 1975), pp. 24, 29f., 37f.

extensive word studies, which are incorporated into and are expressive of salvation history.

3. *Leonhard Goppelt.* Professor Goppelt, before his sudden death in 1973, taught at the University of Munich (and before that at Hamburg). For a whole decade he had worked incessantly on a NT theology which was published posthumously in two volumes in 1975 and 1976 respectively by his student J. Roloff. Goppelt was already widely known from several studies,[329] but his *Theology of the New Testament* deserves also to be translated into the English language.

Goppelt provides in his NT theology the most detailed and informative section on "History and Problems of the Discipline" of all NT theologies written to the present day.[330] In it he outlines the various positions, particularly since about 1900, and sees himself following the broad salvation-history approaches of G. von Rad and O. Cullmann. He points out, however, against Cullmann that the NT does not know "salvation history as the plan of a universal history, but only the correlation of promise and fulfillment. For example, the salvation-historical views of Romans 4 and 5 cannot be united into one total picture; they designate each one for itself that faith or Christ is (respectively) fulfilled promise."[331] Goppelt limits his definition of salvation history primarily to the schema of promise and fulfillment. Salvation history is not a history that is separated from regular history "neither through its miracle-like nature nor through demonstrable continuity. Salvation history is much more a sequence of historical processes which are ultimately characterized and connected with

[329]L. Goppelt, *Typos. Die typologische Deutung des Alten Testaments im Neuen* (Gütersloh, 1939; 3rd ed.; Darmstadt, 1969); idem, *Die apostolische und nachapostolische Zeit* (2nd ed.; Göttingen, 1966), Eng. trans. *The Apostolic and Post-Apostolic Times* (Philadelphia, 1962).

[330]L. Goppelt, *Theologie des Neuen Testaments. Erster Teil: Jesu Wirken in seiner theologischen Bedeutung* (Göttingen, 1975), pp. 19-51.

[331]P. 49. See also L. Goppelt, "Paulus und die Heilsgeschichte," *Christologie und Ethik* (Göttingen, 1968), pp. 202ff.

each other and that through it the final self-demonstra-
tion of God in Jesus is prepared and that Jesus takes
his stand with them."[332] Goppelt does not place unique
emphasis on salvation history at the exclusion of the
historical-critical method. He seeks "to bring into a
critical dialogue the principles of the historical-critical
method of biblical research, i.e., criticism, analogy, and
correlation, with the self-understanding of the NT."[333]
In terms of methodology the "critical dialogue" takes
both the historical, namely the traditio-historical and
the religio-historical, connections and the salvation-historical ones seriously. In terms of the relationship between Jesus and John the Baptist this means that one is
"relative" and the other is "exclusive." "The traditio-
historical and religio-historical connection between
Jesus and John the Baptist is *relative*, the salvation-
historical one exclusive."[334] This dialogue of a confronta-
tion of the NT testimonies concerning John the Baptist
with the historical situation attempts to clarify the immediate background of Jesus and in conjunction with
religio-historical investigation leads to a presentation of
the self-understanding of Jesus.

Goppelt defines the goal of NT theology as an attempt
"to derive from the single writing or groups of writings
[of the NT] materially ordered and connected pictures
of the work of Jesus or the proclamation and teaching
of the early church."[335] Beyond it NT theology "mirrors
more distinctly the positions of modern theologians with
their respective total understanding and their presuppositions than is possible in interpretations of particular
pericopes."[336] Goppelt does not limit himself to reconstruction or the descriptive task. Modern man and
modern society are not to be confronted merely with
the "letter" of the NT witness. "Both parties, the NT

[332]Goppelt, *Theologie des NT*, I, 82.
[333]P. 50.
[334]P. 82.
[335]P. 17.
[336]Ibid.

and the man of today, have to be brought into a critical dialogue with each other."[337] Even though such a "critical dialogue" is primarily the task of systematic theology, a presentation of the manifold scholarly attempts at interpretation and their presuppositions "enable the reader to participate in the dialogue of research and make it possible to form his own opinion."[338]

Each of Goppelt's two volumes is devoted to one main part. Vol. I carries the subtitle "The Theological Meanings of Jesus' Activity" and is totally devoted to the content as indicated in the title. The first chapter discusses the historical and theological issues related to the question of the starting-point of NT theology. Exegetical study has shown that "the starting-point of NT theology is the Easter-kerygma which according to early Christian tradition was responsible for the formation of Christian churches and the continued influence of Jesus."[339] The foundation of NT theology was nevertheless the reporting of the earthly activity of Jesus, so that NT theology on the basis of its own structure has to ask for the earthly Jesus. In contrast to the "old quest" the "historical Jesus" is not to be had; "NT theology, however, asks for Jesus as he has shown himself in his earthly days to his followers, and this is also the Jesus who has had a historic[340] influence."[341] Aside from the NT's own structure the lack of analogies from contemporary personalities for the continued influence of Jesus "provide historical reasons that make it proper to begin a presentation of NT theology with the activity and path of Jesus."[342] In order to do this Goppelt develops his "own tradition-critical analysis" on the basis of which the Synoptic Gospels provide material for "the presentation of Jesus, the theology of the

---

[337]P. 18.
[338]P. 17.
[339]P. 56.
[340]The adjectives *geschichtlich* and *historisch* are translated "historic" and "historical" respectively.
[341]P. 58.
[342]P. 62.

early Christian Church, and finally the theology of the Evangelists."[343] Contrary to critical opinion the Gospel of John also "provides tradition-critical information for the earthly activity of Jesus."[344] After a brief discussion of "the historical framework" of Jesus' activity[345] and "the salvation-historical starting-point of John the Baptist"[346] Goppelt devotes eight chapters to the proclamation of Jesus.

Chapter II begins with "The Coming of the Rulership of God"[347] because the center of Jesus' preaching is the kingdom of God.[348] Goppelt's normal procedure is to describe briefly the terminology concept and its correlates in the gospels. Then he provides a succinct survey of its background in the OT, Judaism, and Hellenism, and also discusses the history of research. Finally he elucidates his own understanding of the NT data in contrast or agreement with other opinions. This is not only extremely informative but also highly stimulating and calls for constant interaction of thought.

The subject of "conversion" as a demand of Jesus and a gift of the divine rulership is treated in Chapters III and IV.[349] Chapter V, "Jesus' Saving Activity as Expression of Eschatological Renewal," is concerned with miracles as part of Jesus' activity.[350] The Messianic self-consciousness is the subject of Chapter VI. "The Self-Understanding of Jesus"[351] demonstrates that Jesus used of himself at least the designation "Son of Man." The goal of Jesus' activity is dealt with in Chapter VII, "Jesus and the Church."[352] The last chapter is concerned

[343]P. 65.
[344]P. 67.
[345]Pp. 70-83.
[346]Pp. 83-93.
[347]Pp. 94-127.
[348]Pp. 94, 101.
[349]Pp. 128-188.
[350]Pp. 189-206.
[351]Pp. 207-253.
[352]Pp. 254-270.

with "Jesus' End" which includes passion, death, resurrection, and ascension.[353]

The second volume of Goppelt's NT theology was published in 1976 and carries the subtitle "Manifoldness and Unity of the Apostolic Witnesses to Christ." It contains the post-Pentecost development as the earliest church understood it in three major parts: Part II, "The Early Church (The Church Among Israel)," contains chapters on "Jesus' Discipleship as Church" and "The Beginnings of Christology."[354] The theological principle at work is "the dialogical correlation between the formulation of the Jesus-tradition and the explication of the Easter-kerygma . . . in the proclamation and teaching of the early church. . . ."[355] This dialogical correlation principle is the answer to the development of the earliest Christology (contra H. Koester).[356] Part III, "Paul and Hellenistic Christianity,"[357] begins with an introduction on the problem of Hellenistic Christianity and a chapter on the presuppositions of Pauline theology. It centers on Pauline theology, particularly on Christology, the event of proclamation, righteousness, and the church. The center of Pauline theology is the concept of righteousness which is neither a Christ mysticism (W. Wrede, A. Schweitzer), nor a purely forensic concept (R. Bultmann, H. Conzelmann), nor primarily the subjective aspect of the nature of God (A. Schlatter, E. Käsemann, P. Stuhlmacher). Goppelt combines a forensic emphasis, namely "God puts man in the right relationship with himself" with a subjective one whereby "man lives in this relationship."

Part IV, "The Theology of the Post-Pauline Writ-

[353]Pp. 271-299.

[354]L. Goppelt, *Theologie des Neuen Testaments. Zweiter Teil: Vielfalt und Einheit des apostolischen Christuszeugnisses* (Göttingen, 1976), pp. 325-355.

[355]P. 353.

[356]P. 354. See H. Koester and J. M. Robinson, *Trajectories through Early Christianity* (Philadelphia, 1971).

[357]Goppelt, *Theologie des NT*, pp. 356-479.

ings,"[358] is structurally inchoate. The first chapter treats both the theology of 1 Peter under the title "The Responsibility of Christians in Society according to 1 Peter" and the theology of Revelation under the heading "Christians in the Post-Christian Society of the Endtime According to John's Revelation." The second chapter pairs the theology of James, i.e., a theology of the empire, with the theology of Matthew under the title "The Meaning of the Appearance of Jesus in Matthew." Chapter III is devoted to the theology of Hebrews followed by Luke, the theologian of salvation history. The separation of the treatments of the theology of the gospel of Luke from that of Acts is unique. The concluding chapter is on Johannine theology and is not fully developed. The editor informs us that Part IV of Goppelt's theology was put together from a manuscript used for lectures and a tape-recording from his lectures in the summer of 1973. This may account for some of its unusual structural design. One misses treatments of the theology of Mark, the so-called Deutero-Pauline letters, including Ephesians, the Pastoral Epistles, and 2 Peter and Jude. Did they not fit into the salvation history approach as understood by Goppelt or did other matters cause him not to include them in his work?

Concluding Remarks

Our survey of four major approaches to NT theology has highlighted the fact that there is no agreement among the leading practitioners of NT theology as regards the issue of methodology. The complexity of the issues relates to the most basic aspects of methodology. Let us point to some of these in concluding this chapter.

1. The thematic approach goes hand in hand with the cross-section method in which one or more major themes are treated longitudinally. Students of the NT

[358]Pp. 480-643.

have come to take seriously that there is inevitably a subjective element in all historical research. The particular subjectivity of the thematic approach is the question of selectivity. The NT theologian engaged in a cross-section method along a single major theme or many simpler themes has to be guided by a principle of selection. Closely aligned to the former is a principle of congeniality. The principle of selection leads a NT theologian to choose a key theme of the NT or both the NT and the OT such as the covenant or the kingdom of God, the Christological principle, etc. The principle of congeniality relates all the other themes, motifs, or concepts congenial to the major theme. But it is here already that distinct limitations of this approach make themselves felt. First, on what objective basis does the principle of selection function? Is it functioning as in the case of Schelkle on the basis of the traditional God-Man-Salvation arrangements of dogmatics? If so, then issues may be introduced to which the NT may give only the most incidental answer or answers elicited to questions in which the NT has no interest. Second, the principle of congeniality can only function in relation to the major theme or themes chosen. This implies that other themes, motifs, or concepts which are important in the NT are neglected or forced into a mold not of their own. Third, if the principle of selection is used in a way not related to a major theme, on what basis other than a subjective one (the problem of Richardson) can some themes be included and others omitted? Can the world of NT thought or belief be systematized in this way? Is any theme sufficiently comprehensive to include within it all varieties of NT (or Biblical) thought? The richness of the diversified nature of the Biblical materials requires an approach that is commensurate to the materials with which it deals.

2. We have seen that one of the major methodological problems of NT theology is the question of the place of Jesus in NT theology. Is "the message of Jesus . . . a presupposition for the theology of the New Testament

rather than a part of that theology itself," to use the
famous words of Bultmann? This judgment has been
supported as we noted by Conzelmann in Germany and
most recently by Perrin in the United States. On the
other hand it is most strongly opposed by Jeremias,
Kümmel, Goppelt, and Neill among others. They seek
to demonstrate historically that the Proclaimer (Jesus)
became the Proclaimed (Christ). This whole issue is
among other things primarily a problem of the
modern understanding of history and its method.
By definition the historical-critical method functions
on the basis of the principles of correlation, analogy,
and criticism (E. Troeltsch) within a closed continuum
of natural causes and effects in which there is no room
for a God-hypothesis or supernatural causes. Thus history and faith are considered as opposites and one is
not to support the other. The historical-critical method
of Gospel research is severely restricted. O. A. Piper
states, "There is no satisfactory method by which the
Gospel records can be brought into agreement with
the modern idealistic or positivistic views of history."[359]
Long ago M. Kähler wrote an important essay in which
he addressed himself to the difference between the
"historical Jesus" and the "historic Christ" of the Bible.[360] It is said that "the *historische* Jesus is the creation of the historical-critical method — a *Holzweg*, a
road that leads nowhere. . . . The rejection of the biblical
portrait of Jesus in favor of a hypothetical historical
Jesus, and the effort to trace the stages between the
two, is not the result of open-minded inductive study
of our sources, but of philosophical presuppositions
about the nature of history."[361] Although this may be
true, it does not settle the question for those who accept such presuppositions as valid. It remains one of the

[359]O. A. Piper, "Christology and History," *Theology Today* 19
(1962), 333.
    [360]M. Kähler, *The So-Called Historical Jesus and the Historic Bib-
lical Christ,* trans. by O. E. Braaten (Philadelphia, 1964).
    [361]Ladd, *Theology of the NT,* p. 179.

key methodological issues of critical Biblical scholarship. Does Christian faith really go back to Jesus himself or is it a construct of the early Church? This question will exercise NT theologians for some time to come.

3. The methodological issue concerns the question whether there is such a thing as NT theology or whether the historical study of the NT and its world is not rather to be called, as W. Wrede suggested in 1897, "A History of Primitive Christian Religion." This problem is with us with full force. H. Koester and J. M. Robinson are the strongest supporters of a return to the history-of-religions approach.[362] Just as dialectical theology in the post-World War I period brought with itself a revival of theology over against religion, so the 1970s are marked by an attempt to shift back to religion from theology. A key aspect in this issue is the question of a NT theology being limited to the canonical writings. From the historical point of view the writings of the New Testament are but a part of the total literature produced by early Christians and the question is what validity and significance is there in the canonical NT writings. The issue is on the one hand whether the NT is the production of the church or whether the church is the production of the NT, and on the other whether the inclusion of documents in the canon is investing particular authority to these documents by the church or whether the church included particular documents in the canon because of her recognition of authority inherent in these documents. Even if B. S. Childs' call for a new Biblical theology within the context of the Christian canon[363] is not heeded[364] for a variety of reasons, then one can easily agree with N. Perrin that "the fact remains that the New Testament is an entity, which as an entity, has played and does play an enormous

---

[362]See above, n. 356.

[363]B. S. Childs, *Biblical Theology in Crisis* (Philadelphia, 1970), pp. 91-148.

[364]J. Barr, "Biblical Theology," *IDB Sup.* (Nashville, 1976), pp. 110f.

role in Christian history, and I am not prepared to dissolve it into something else without much stronger grounds than the historical ambiguities of the process of the formation of the canon. . . . A history of the religion of early Christianity would be most welcome, but from the standpoint of the Christian communities a theology of the New Testament is an urgent need."[365] Is a NT theology a descriptive discipline or a theological one? This brings us to the final issue of central methodological concern.

4. One of the most fundamental methodological problems for NT theology is the issue of historical reconstruction and theological interpretation. Bultmann's program of demythologization is part and parcel of the process of stripping the kernel from its shell and translating the kerygma with the aid of existentialist philosophy for modern man. The main weight is placed in Bultmann's case upon existentialist interpretation. J. M. Robinson is ready to point out that "of course a Jesus, Paul, or John could never have understood the terminology of demythologizing or existentialism."[366] Bultmann's most faithful follower H. Conzelmann expresses the recent trend and the weight of his own direction, namely "historical reconstruction, i.e. the presentation of the thought-world of the New Testament as conditioned by its time."[367] The matter of historical reconstruction is closely bound up with what K. Stendahl calls the "descriptive method"[368] with its rigorous distinction between "what it meant" and "what it means." There are several ways[369] in which the historical and descriptive approach of "what it meant" — that this is

[365]Perrin, "Jesus and the Theology of the NT," p. 3.

[366]Robinson, "The Future of New Testament Theology," p. 20.

[367]Conzelmann, *An Outline of NT Theology*, p. xiv.

[368]Stendahl, *IDB*, I, 418-432; idem, "Method in the Study of Biblical Theology," *The Bible in Modern Scholarship*, ed. J. P. Hyatt (Nashville, 1965), pp. 196-209.

[369]These are succinctly stated by D. H. Kelsey, *The Uses of Scripture in Recent Theology*, pp. 202f. n. 18, but formulated in a slightly different way.

also interpretation should always be remembered — is related to the theological and interpretative approach of "what it means." First, it may be decided that the descriptive approach that seeks to determine "what it meant" by whatever methods of inquiry this is established is considered to be identical with "what it means." Second, it may be decided that "what it meant" contains propositions, ideas, etc. that are to be decoded and translated systematically and explicated and that this is "what it means," even though those explications may never have occurred to the original authors and might have been rejected by them. Third, it may be decided that "what it meant" is an archaic way of speaking, dependent upon its own culture and time, which needs to be redescribed in contemporary ways of speaking of the same phenomena and that this redescription is "what it means." "This assumes that the theologian has access to the phenomena independent of scripture and 'what it meant,' so that he can check the archaic description and have a basis for his own."[370] Fourth, it may be decided that "what it meant" refers to the way in which early Christians used Biblical texts and that "what it means" is simply the way these are used by modern Christians. In this case there is a genetic relationship. D. H. Kelsey notes, "None of these decisions can itself be either validated or invalidated by exegetical study of the text, for what is at issue is precisely how exegetical study is related to doing theology.[371] If this is the case, then one must ask on what grounds one makes a theological judgment in favor of one over the other of these or other ways of relating "what it meant" to "what it means."

Criticisms of the distinction between "what it meant" and "what it means," i.e., between reconstruction and interpretation or what is historical and objective and what is theological and normative have been advanced

[370]**P.** 203.
[371]Ibid.

by several people. For example, B. S. Childs[372] objects against the descriptive method on account of its limiting nature. The descriptive task cannot be seen as a neutral stage leading to later genuine theological interpretation. The text, says Childs, is "a witness beyond itself to the divine purpose of God." There must be "the movement from the level of the witness to the reality itself."[373] Stendahl concedes that the descriptive task is "able to describe scriptural texts as aiming beyond themselves, . . . in their intention and their function through the ages. . . . "[374] But Stendahl denies that the explication of this reality is a part of the task of the Biblical theologian. Childs, however, insists that "what the text 'meant' is determined in large measure by its relation to the one to whom it is directed." He argues that "when seen from the context of the canon both the question of what the text meant and what it means are inseparably linked and both belong to the task of the interpretation of the Bible as Scripture."[375] A. Dulles makes a similar point when he speaks of the "uneasiness at the radical separation . . . between what the Bible meant and what it means." Whereas Stendahl gives normative value to the task of what the Bible means, Dulles maintains that that normative value must be given also to what the Bible meant. If this is the case, then Stendahl's dichotomy is seriously impaired because "the possibility of an 'objective' or non-committed descriptive approach, and thus . . . one of the most attractive features of Stendahl's position" is done away with.[376] Similar points are made by R. A. F. MacKenzie,

---

[372]"Interpretation in Faith: The Theological Responsibility of an OT Commentary," *Interpretation* 18 (1964), 432-449.

[373]Pp. 437, 440, 444.

[374]*The Bible in Modern Scholarship*, p. 203 n. 13.

[375]*Biblical Theology in Crisis*, p. 141.

[376]"Response to Krister Stendahl's Method in the Study of Biblical Theology," *The Bible in Modern Scholarship*, pp. 210f. Stendahl, of course, maintains that there is no "absolute objectivity" to be had (*IDB*, I, 422: *The Bible in Modern Scholarship*, p. 202). He is completely right in emphasizing that the relativity of human objectivity

C. Spicq, and R. de Vaux.[377] How can the non-normative descriptive method with its limiting historical emphasis lead us to the totality of the theological reality contained in the text? By definition and presupposition the descriptive historical method is limited to such an extent that the total theological reality of the text does not come fully to expression. Does NT theology need to be restricted to be nothing more than a "first chapter" of historical theology? Can NT theology also have normative value on the basis of the recognition that what the Bible meant is normative in itself? Can NT theology draw its very principles of presentation and organization from the documents that make up the NT rather than from the ecclesiastic creeds, or scholastic tradition or modern philosophy? Would it not be one of the tasks of NT (and OT) theology to come to grips with the nature of the Biblical texts as aiming beyond themselves, as theological and ontological in their intention and function through the ages, without defining in advance the nature of Biblical reality?

---

does not give us an excuse to "excel in bias," but neither, we insist, does it give us the possibility of doing purely descriptive work.

[377]R. A. F. MacKenzie, "The Concept of Biblical Theology," *Theology Today*, 4 (1956), 131-135, esp. 134: "Coldly scientific — in the sense of rationalistic — objectivity is quite incapable of even perceiving, let alone exploiting, the religious values of Scripture. There must be first the commitment, the recognition by faith of the divine origin and authority of the book; the the believer can properly and profitably apply all the most conscientious techniques of the subordinate sciences, without in the least infringing on their due autonomy or being disloyal to the scientific ideal." C. Spicq as quoted in J. Harvey, "The New Diachronic Theology of the OT (1960-1970)," *BTB* 1 (1971), 18f.; R. de Vaux, "Method in the Study of Early Hebrew History," in *The Bible in Modern Scholarship*, pp. 15-17; "Peut-on écrire une 'théologie de l'AT'?" *Bible et Orient* (Paris, 1967), pp. 59-71.

III. The Center and Unity in NT Theology

A. The Issue

One of the most hotly debated issues in NT studies is the question of the center and unity of the NT.[1] This

[1]The following studies are particularly significant: A. M. Hunter, *The Unity of the New Testament* (London, 1943); idem, *Die Einheit des Neuen Testaments* (Munich, 1952); E. Käsemann, "Begründet der neutestamentliche Kanon die Einheit der Kirche?" *EvTh* 11 (1951/52), 13-21; reprinted in *Das Neue Testament als Kanon*, ed. E. Käsemann (Göttingen, 1970), pp. 124-133; B. Reicke, "Einheitlichkeit oder verschiedene 'Lehrbegriffe' in der neutestamentlichen Theologie," *Theologische Zeitschrift* 9 (1953), 401-415; H. H. Rowley, *The Unity of the Bible* (4th ed.; London, 1968); G. E. Ladd, "Eschatology and the Unity of New Testament Theology," *Expository Times* 68 (1956/57), 268-273; W. Künneth, "Zur Frage nach der Mitte der Schrift," *Dank an P. Althaus*, eds. W. Künneth and W. Joest (Gütersloh, 1957), pp. 121-140; H. Braun, "Die Problematik einer Theologie des Neuen Testaments," *ZThK* Beiheft 2 (Sept., 1961), 3-18, Eng. trans. "The Problem of a New Testament Theology," *Journal for Theology and Church* 1 (1965), 169-185; F. Mussner, "Die Mitte des Evangeliums in neutestamentlicher Sicht," *Catholica* 15 (1961), 271-292; R. Schnackenburg, *New Testament Theology Today* (London, 1963), pp. 22f.; K. Fröhlich, "Die Mitte des Neuen Testaments: O. Cullmanns Beitrag zur Theologie der Gegenwart," *Oikonomia. Heilsgeschichte als Thema der Theologie. Festschrift für O. Cullmann* (Hamburg-Bergstedt, 1967), pp. 203-219; K. Haacker, "Einheit und Vielfalt in der Theologie des Neuen Testaments," *Themelios* 4 (1968), 27-44; A. Kümmel, "Mitte des Neuen Testaments," *L'Evangile, Hier et Aujourd'hui. Melanges offerts au F.-J. Leenhardt* (Geneva, 1968), pp. 71-85; A. Stock, *Einheit des Neuen Testaments* (Zurich, 1969); R. Smend, *Die Mitte des Alten Testaments* (Zurich, 1970); I. Lönning, *"Kanon im Kanon." Zum dogmatischen Grundlagenproblem des neutestamentlichen Kanons* (Oslo/Munich, 1972);

question is in many respects at the very heart of the current debate on the nature of NT theology. The problem of the center of the NT relates to the question of presenting a NT theology on the basis of a single or multiple center, no matter how it is defined. The problem of the unity of the NT cannot be divorced from that of the center because the latter is customarily conceived of as the key to the unity of the NT itself. It is ultimately the question whether one can find *one* theology of the NT or whether the NT yields such a manifold diversity of theologies that no unity can be discerned.

It is not necessary to survey the development of this issue during the last two centuries, in which rather divergent presentations of Biblical theology were brought forth.[2] The problem of the center of the OT in the current debate on OT theology is not unrelated to the issues in NT theology.[3] The question that is raised in a unique way since the 1950s is to what degree the NT is homogeneous, if at all.[4] We should remind ourselves, however, that J. P. Gabler already in 1787 had called for the task of distinguishing, on the basis of his own criteria, between "the different authors and the particular forms of speech which were used by each in ac-

A. T. Nikolainen, "Om planläggningens problem i en totalframställning av Nya testamentets teologi," *Svensk Exegetisk Arsbok* 37/38 (1972/73), 310-319; H. Riesenfeld, "Reflections on the Unity of the New Testament," *Religion* 3 (1973), 35-51; U. Luz, "Theologia crucis als Mitte der Theologie im Neuen Testament," *EvTh* 34 (1974), 116-141; E. Lohse, "Die Einheit des Neuen Testaments als theologisches Problem. Überlegungen zur Aufgabe einer Theologie des Neuen Testaments," *EvTh* 35 (1975), 139-154; W. Schrage, "Die Frage nach der Mitte und dem Kanon im Kanon des Neuen Testament in der neueren Diskussion," *Rechtfertigung. Festschrift für E. Käsemann,* eds. J. Friedrich, W. Pöhlmann, and P. Stuhlmacher (Tübingen/ Göttingen, 1976), pp. 415-442.

2See above, Chapter I, and particularly Smend, *Die Mitte des AT*, pp. 7, 27-46.

3G. F. Hasel, "The Problem of the Center in the OT Theology Debate," *ZAW* 86 (1974), 65-82; idem, *OT Theology*, pp. 77-103.

4P. Grech, "Contemporary Methodological Problems in New Testament Theology," *BTB* 2 (1972), 264f.

cordance with his time and place. . . . One has to collect
carefully the conceptions of the individual authors and
to order them each according to their place. . . . From
the time of the new forms of doctrine [of the NT] one
must collect the conceptions of Jesus, Paul, Peter, John
and James."[5] The collection of these "conceptions" of
the different NT authors is to go behind the conceptions
in the minds of the NT writers to find a uniformity on
the basis of which that which is central can be distinguished from that which is peripheral. This approach
calls for "content criticism" (Sachkritik) which is at the
forefront of the current issue. K. Haacker notes that this
involves two presuppositions in the method proposed
by Gabler: (1) The possibility to distinguish by means
of human reason between the divine and the human,
the transcendent and the historical and relative. The
authority of Scripture for interpretation has been replaced by reason as the actual source of revelation because it decides what revelation is. (2) It is proper to
ask for the "conceptions" of the individual authors,
which leads to an eclectic synthesis without any dogmatic authority.[6] The aftermath of these and associated
presuppositions appear to be among the root causes for
the contemporary emphases on diversity and disparity
in the NT. E. Lohse has put it in the following terms:
"Historical-critical exegesis of the NT writings forces
us to conclude that they . . . do not develop a unified
teaching but offer different theological presentations."[7]
E. Käsemann has repeatedly emphasized that the NT
contains "a manifoldedness of divergent conceptions"[8]
and that in the NT "by and large there is no internal
coherence. The tensions everywhere evident amount at

[5]J. P. Gabler, "Oratio de iusto discrimine theologiae biblicae et
dogmaticae," Gableri Opuscula Academica II (Ulm, 1831), p. 187.
German trans. in O. Merk, Biblische Theologie des Neuen Testaments
in ihrer Anfangszeit (Marburg, 1972), pp. 285f.

[6]Haacker, "Einheit und Vielfalt in der Theologie des NT," pp. 30f.

[7]Lohse, "Die Einheit des NT theologisches Problem," p. 148.

[8]E. Käsemann, Exegetische Versuche und Besinnungen II (Göttingen, 1964), pp. 27, 205.

times to contradictions,"[9] namely "irreconcilable theological contradictions."[10] A. Stock reminds us that the emphasis on contradictions and diversity in the NT is the result of the methodological tendency of historical criticism.[11] "The problem [of divergences] becomes particularly acute through the resistance of Scripture to this criticism on the basis of its own claim for canonical authority. This authority implies a unity no matter how it is understood."[12] Different scholars have maintained that there is a unity in diversity, but such unity is conceived of along different lines and gained with contradictory approaches.

It is imperative to make a twofold distinction with regard to the center of the NT. (1) The question of the center and unity of the NT itself, i.e., the issue as to whether there is something that appears as the undergirding aspect on the basis of which unity can be discerned in spite of all diversity, and (2) the question of the center as an organizing principle for NT theology on the one hand and as a criterion for "content criticism" which affirms in one form or another a "canon within the canon." The latter implies such antitheses as "authority/disintegration," "totality/selection," and "objectivity/subjectivity."[13]

Is it necessary to have a center for the presentation of the NT? This question is not easily answered. J. Barr speaks of a "plurality of 'centres'" which make many different organizations possible.[14] For the organization and structure of a NT theology no one of the centers does "necessarily have to claim exclusive rights as

[9]E. Käsemann, "The Problem of a New Testament Theology," *NTS* 19 (1973), 242; idem, *Exegetische Versuche und Besinnungen I* (2nd ed.; Göttingen, 1960), p. 218: the manifoldness "is in the NT so large that we have not only significant tensions but that we have to recognize irreconcilable theological contradictions."

[10]Käsemann, *Exegetische Versuche und Besinnungen I*, p. 218.

[11]Stock, *Einheit des NT*, pp. 9f.

[12]P. 10.

[13]Lönning, *"Kanon im Kanon,"* pp. 214-272.

[14]J. Barr, "Trends and Prospects in Biblical Theology," *Journal of Theological Studies* 25 (1974), 272.

against any other possibility. . . . To me, biblical theology, at least at some levels, partakes of the nature of an art, rather than that of a science."[15] This is an implicit admission that the "objectivity/subjectivity" problem shifts heavily to the side of subjectivity in both the selection of a proposed center among various possible centers and in the fact that the discipline of NT theology is conceived as an "art." Ultimately the question concerning the most adequate center of the NT remains as well as the question whether a center is needed for the presentation of a NT theology.

B. The Quest for the Center of the NT

1. *Anthropology.* R. Bultmann and his student H. Braun have both opted for anthropology as the center of the NT.[16] Bultmann's critical reconstruction of the NT serves existential interpretation.[17] He is guided by the "presupposition that they [NT writings] have something to say to the present."[18] Accordingly, the task of a presentation of NT theology means for Bultmann "to make clear this believing self-understanding in its reference to the kerygma. . . . This clarification takes place directly in the analysis of the theology of Paul and John."[19] Bultmann asserts, "Every assertion about God is simultaneously an assertion about man and vice versa. For this reason and in this sense Paul's theology is, at the same time, anthropology. . . . Therefore, Paul's theology can best be treated as his doctrine of man."[20] Likewise Johannine theology is best treated anthropologically.

Is the anthropological center of the theologies of Paul

[15]Ibid.

[16]See above, Chapter II, pp. 82-94.

[17]R. Bultmann, *Theology of the New Testament* (London, 1965), II, 251: "The reconstruction stands in the service of the interpretation of the New Testament writings. . . ."

[18]Ibid.

[19]Ibid.

[20]Bultmann, *Theology of the NT,* I, 191.

and John adequate for the structuring of a NT theology? Bultmann thinks so. But we must be reminded that he resorted to "content criticism" as M. Barth indicated[21] when it came to such Pauline statements as the Holy Spirit, resurrection, second Adam, original sin, and knowledge. They did not fit the anthropological center. Bultmann's center made him unable to deal with Romans 9-11.[22] E. Lohse notes that the center of kerygmatic anthropology forced Bultmann to push into the background such NT writings as the Synoptics, Acts, Catholic Epistles, and Revelation.[23] Is kerygmatic anthropology as a center of the NT proving too restrictive and too narrow? Is it not a category determined by existential interpretation, a predetermined means that leads in its own way to "a canon within the canon"?

H. Braun, one of Bultmann's students, has addressed himself several times to the question of the unity of the NT. Historical-critical exegesis divides the NT into a manifoldness of aspects and layers so that "the New Testament . . . has in its most central pieces neither a unity of expression (*Aussage-Einheit*) with reference to factual events nor a unity of doctrine (*Lehreinheit*) with reference to the articles of faith."[24] He discusses such NT concepts as law, eschatology, church and office, christology, soteriology, and sacraments[25] and concludes that they are "disparate teachings."[26] He summarizes:

> The New Testament conceals within itself disparate ideas; we have made them clear for ourselves in terms of christology, soteriology, attitude towards Torah, eschatology, and doctrine of the sacraments. These

[21]M. Barth, "Die Methode von Bultmann's 'Theologie des Neuen Testaments'," *Theologische Zeitschrift* 11 (1955), 15.

[22]H.-J. Kraus, *Die Biblische Theologie* (Neukirchen-Vluyn, 1970), p. 191.

[23]Lohse, "Die Einheit des NT als theologisches Problem," p. 150.

[24]H. Braun, "Hebt die neutestamentlich-exegetische Forschung den Kanon auf?" *Gesammelte Studien zum Neuen Testament und seiner Umwelt* (Tübingen, 1962), p. 314.

[25]Pp. 314-319.

[26]P. 320.

diversities refer, for their part, to a still deeper problem within the New Testaments statements, God as palpable and given and God as not palpable and not given.[27]

Braun appears as one scholar who has pushed the diversity of the NT to the extremes of total disparity. Nevertheless, he himself raises the question whether these disparate teachings and diverse layers negate an "inner center from which essential parts even if not the whole [of the NT] can be grasped."[28] Braun answers in the affirmative: "Unity is found in the three large blocks of the proclamation of Jesus, Paul, and in the Fourth Gospel . . . in the way in which man is seen in his position before God."[29] The "mutual contradiction"[30] of the authors of the NT is in Braun's view overcome through a theological anthropology. "Anthropology is . . . the constant; christology is the variable."[31] "I can speak of God only where I speak of man, and hence anthropologically. I can speak of God only where my 'I ought' is counterpointed by 'I may,' and hence soteriologically. . . . God would then be a definite type of relation with one's fellow man (*Mitmenschlichkeit*)."[32]

Braun's "inner center" of the NT is theological anthropology. That this "inner center" is not able to include all writings or blocks of writings from the NT is recognized by Braun himself, who therefore affirms the principle of "a canon within the canon."[33] A. Stock points out that "the unity of the NT encompasses for Braun as much as the message of the 'I may' and 'you ought' can be heard by him in a pure form."[34] He notes that here too subjectivity is the key in Braun's center of theological anthropology.

R. Bultmann affirmed that his intention has been most

[27]Braun, "The Problem of a NT Theology," p. 182.
[28]Braun, *Gesammelte Studien*, p. 320.
[29]Ibid.
[30]Braun, "The Problem of a NT Theology," p. 169.
[31]Braun, *Gesammelte Studien*, p. 272.
[32]Braun, "The Problem of a NT Theology," p. 183.
[33]Braun, *Gesammelte Studien*, pp. 227, 229-232.
[34]Stock, *Einheit des NT*, p. 32.

consistently carried on by Braun, whose concept of unity
with the constant of the self-understanding of the believer is explicitly accepted by him.[35] In contrast to
Bultmann's acceptance several post-Bultmannians have
indicated their opposition. E. Käsemann speaks bluntly
of Braun's "inner center" of theological anthropology as
a "kind of mysticism [which] means bankruptcy, and a
protest should be raised in the name of intellectual honesty when humanism is in this fashion taken over by
Christianity."[36] E. Lohse charges Braun with "radical
reductionism."[37] Whereas Bultmann's NT theology "presents anthropology," by Braun theology "is dissolved
into anthropology."[38] Lohse points that if the NT lacks
a unified Christology, then it should be noted that it
also lacks a unified anthropology.[39] G. Ebeling objects
to Braun's principle of unity because it even lacks anything Christian. Indeed Braun's theological anthropology is the attempt to define the nature of Christianity
without speaking about God and Jesus Christ. Ebeling
counters that God is not "an unintelligible cipher"[40] and
"Christology is indeed variable in the way it is expressed
(in its How) but not in the fact that it is expressed
(in its That). There is no choice — and this is for the
sake of the self-understanding of faith — between . . .
christological and non-christological kerygma."[41] "The
constant of the self-understanding of faith," affirms
Ebeling, is not anthropology, but "that the faith is
faith in Jesus Christ, that is, faith which is directed
to the christological kerygma, and which accepts this

[35]R. Bultmann, "The Primitive Christian Kerygma and the Historical Jesus," *The Historical Jesus and the Kergymatic Christ,* eds.
C. E. Braaten and R. A. Harrisville (Nashville, 1964), pp. 35f.

[36]Käsemann, "The Problem of a NT Theology," p. 241.

[37]E. Lohse, *Grundriss der neutestamentlichen Theologie* (Stuttgart,
1974), p. 13.

[38]Lohse, "Die Einheit des NT als theologisches Problem," p. 152;
idem, *Grundriss der ntl. Theologie,* p. 13.

[39]Lohse, *Grundriss der ntl. Theologie,* pp. 13f., 163.

[40]G. Ebeling, *Theology and Proclamation* (Philadelphia, 1966), p.
76.

[41]P. 48.

kerygma in its own confession."[42] These critical contributions to the issue of a center of the NT as maintained by Braun and supported by Bultmann reveal
the fundamental issues. Both "kerygmatic anthropology"
(Bultmann) and "theological anthropology" (Braun)
are found wanting when it comes to the question of
the center of the NT.

2. *Salvation History.* Our discussion of the salvation
history approach as represented by O. Cullmann, G. E.
Ladd, and L. Goppelt has indicated that under the same
name a variety of presentations of different theological
roots and aims can come to expression.[43] The scholar
who has engaged himself most comprehensively with
salvation history *(Heilsgeschichte)* in this century is O.
Cullmann. He objects vehemently against those who
find a "sadistic joy in emphasizing disparity and who
show anger against those who attempt to demonstrate
a line of connection at a given point."[44] Cullmann seems
to be seconded in his attempt to highlight salvation
history by F. C. Grant, who states that the NT's "history
is 'history of salvation' (*Heilsgeschichte*)."[45] Grant also
objects to today's "danger . . . that we may overemphasize the diversity by ignoring the unity."[46] "There
is a real unity in the New Testament presentation of
the Christian religion under all its diversity, in its view
of God, of his revelation, of salvation, of the finality
and absoluteness of Christ."[47] While Grant recognizes
unity in diversity and affirms salvation history, he differs from Cullmann as do others[48] in refraining from

[42]Ibid.

[43]See above, Chapter II, pp. 111-132.

[44]O. Cullmann, *Christologie des Neues Testaments,* p. 67.

[45]F. C. Grant, *An Introduction to New Testament Thought* (Nashville, 1950), p. 41.

[46]P. 42.

[47]P. 29.

[48]G. E. Ladd, *A Theology of the New Testament* (Grand Rapids,
Mich., 1974); L. Goppelt, *Theologie des Neuen Testaments,* 2 vols.
(Göttingen, 1975-76); A. M. Hunter, *Introducing New Testament
Theology* (2nd ed.; London, 1963).

employing salvation history as a unifying center of the NT.

In his book *Christ and Time* Cullmann outlined his understanding of Christ as the center of time as depicted by Jesus, Paul, and John.[49] For Cullmann Christ is the center of time but not of the NT. Already in the 1950s Cullmann confesses that "from different angles I always come up again to the same conclusions, namely, that the real center of early Christian faith and thought is redemptive [salvation] history *(Heilsgeschichte)*."[50] What this means is explicated in his *Christology of the New Testament* (2nd ed., 1967) in which he suggests that the NT is disinterested in the questions of nature and being but only in "functional Christology."[51] Cullmann's *magnum opus* under the title *Salvation in History* (1967) attempts "to rescue the term 'salvation history' from being abused."[52] It seeks to provide the evidence that the main NT types of salvation history rest in Jesus, Primitive Christianity, Paul, and the Fourth Gospel.[53] This means that the "salvation-historical perspective" applies for "all areas of early Christian faith, thought, and activity."[54]

It should be noted that "salvation history" is in Cullmann's thought the basis on which the canon of Scripture, both OT and NT, depends.[55] "It seems to be impossible to justify the canon apart from salvation history and it is not by accident that its justification is inevitably questioned whenever salvation history is rejected."[56] The "inmost essence of the Bible itself" is "salvation history" so that "both the idea of a canon

[49]O. Cullmann, *Christ and Time* (3rd ed.; London, 1962), p. xx.

[50]O. Cullmann, *The Early Church* (Philadelphia, 1956), p. xxi.

[51]O. Cullmann, *Christology of the NT* (Philadelphia, 1959), pp. 326f.

[52]Cullmann, *Christ and Time,* p. xxiv.

[53]O. Cullmann, *Salvation in History* (New York, 1967), pp. 186-291.

[54]P. 15.

[55]P. 55.

[56]P. 294.

and the manner of its realization are *a crucial part* of the salvation history of the Bible."[57]

Cullmann comes to speak of the problem of "the canon within the canon," i.e., the problem of a norm or criterion within the Bible with which a material selection can be undertaken. His objection to the Lutheran problem of a "canon within the canon" is explicit. "Any selection of a criterion is bound to be subjective and arbitrary. If we take seriously at all the thought of a canon comprising both Testaments, then we must say that it can only be salvation history which constitutes the unity of Scripture . . . , because it can include all these books."[58]

Cullmann must be given credit for taking seriously the total canon of the Bible. He refuses, at least in principle, to give in to the temptation of a selective principle. He seeks to avoid "a canon within the canon" as a concentration on a particular part of the whole by which the whole is to be judged. Cullmann's concern not only for the whole NT but even for the whole of Scripture appears second to none among continental NT scholars.

Reactions to Cullmann's "center" or "essence" of the Bible come from various quarters. C. F. Evans feels that the defect of "salvation history" in Cullmann's thought "is that it presupposes a kind of canal of sacred event or divine action flowing within the bounds of the world's history, with the consequent doubtful definitions and demarcations which go with determining where the canal is to be found."[59] R. Bultmann's early reaction to Cullmann's concept of *Heilsgeschichte* was that "he turns the theology of the New Testament into a Christian philosophy of history."[60] This can indeed be said

[57]Ibid. (italics his).

[58]P. 298.

[59]C. F. Evans, *Is 'Holy Scripture' Christian?* (London, 1971), p. 59.

[60]R. Bultmann, "History of Salvation and History," *Existence and Faith* (Cleveland/New York, 1960), p. 233; idem, "Heilsgeschichte und Geschichte. Zu O. Cullmann, *Christus und die Zeit,*" *PTNT*, p. 301.

of E. Stauffer's *New Testament Theology,* which takes as
its principle of arrangement the motif of salvation history.[61] Other scholars[62] followed Bultmann's charge
that Cullmann turned "salvation history" into a "Christian philosophy of history." To this Bultmann added
that neither Jesus, Paul, nor John thought about an ongoing process of salvation but that Christ was for the
latter the end of time and not its center.[63] In this Bultmann has been seconded by E. Fuchs and W. Kreck,[64]
who see Christ as the end of history. Cullmann has responded that "salvation history" is not a "Christian
philosophy of history" superimposed from the outside
upon the NT.[65] He is inadvertently supported by E.
Käsemann on the point that Christ is not the end of
history in the theology of Paul: "Paul cannot and will
not speak of an end of history that has already taken
place, but he does regard the time of the end as having
dawned."[66] Thus Cullmann's basic thesis that "salvation
history" is the principle of the unity of the NT, even
of the Bible, seems to remain unshaken.

It was Bultmann's student H. Conzelmann who produced his redaction critical study of the Gospel of Luke
under the title *Die Mitte der Zeit (The Center of Time),*[67]
which was borrowed from Cullmann. He attempted to
show that Luke is the theologian of salvation history.
Conzelmann supported what Bultmann had stated earlier, namely that "it is a gross overstatement to say that
the entire New Testament presupposes a unified con-

[61]See above, Chapter I, p. 41.

[62]For example, K. G. Steck, *Die Idee der Heilsgeschichte: Hofmann-Schlatter-Cullmann* (Zurich, 1959).

[63]Bultmann, "History of Salvation and History," p. 237; *PTNT,*
p. 306.

[64]E. Fuchs, "Christus das Ende der Geschichte," *Zur Frage nach
dem historischen Jesus* (Tübingen, 1960), pp. 79ff.; W. Kreck, *Die
Zukunft des Gekommenen* (1961).

[65]Cullmann, *Christ and Time,* pp. xviii-xxi; idem, *Salvation in History,* pp. 44-47, 56f., 62f.

[66]E. Käsemann, "On the Topic of Primitive Christian Apocalyptic,"
Journal for Theology and Church 6 (1969), 129.

[67]H. Conzelmann, *Die Mitte der Zeit* (Tübingen, 1953), Eng. trans.
The Theology of St. Luke (London, 1961).

ception of the history of salvation."[68] In Cullmann's view Conzelmann "wished to make clear that the whole construction is not the view of the New Testament but that of Luke — or better said, that it is a Lucan distortion. With his salvation history Luke abandoned the essence of Jesus' eschatology. . . . This he accomplished with his salvation-historical scheme of 'periods'. . . ."[69] Research into the Lucan theology continues. At present the contrast between Luke and Jesus and Luke and Paul is no longer seen along the lines depicted by Conzelmann. Recent assessments indicated that Luke has not " 'de-eschatologized' the gospel tradition without qualification"[70] and Luke's salvation history "includes within it the hope for an imminent end."[71] While Conzelmann emphasizes salvation history as the basic theme of Luke-Acts, others emphasize for Luke-Acts either salvation (I. H. Marshall), or ecclesiology (J. Jervell), or orthodoxy (C. H. Talbert).[72] In this instance, the attack upon Cullmann's thesis has not been as successful as Bultmannians thought at first. H.-J. Kraus defends Cullmann's view of *Heilsgeschichte* against the issues raised by K. G. Steck.[73]

[68]Bultmann, "History of Salvation and History," p. 235; *PTNT*, p. 303.

[69]Cullmann, *Salvation in History*, p. 46. Conzelmann *(An Outline of the Theology of the NT*, pp. 149-152) has lately affirmed that Luke's theology is no departure from primitive Christianity.

[70]A. J. Hultgren, "Interpreting the Gospel of Luke," *Interpretation* 30 (1976), 364; cf. S. Brown, *Apostasy and Perseverance in the Theology of Luke* (Rome, 1969); I. H. Marshall, *Luke: Historian and Theologian* (London, 1970); J. Jervell, *Luke and the People of God* (Minneapolis, 1972); C. H. Talbert, *Literary Patterns, Theological Themes and the Genre of Luke-Acts* (Missoula, 1974); E. Franklin, *Christ the Lord: A Study in the Purpose and Theology of Luke-Acts* (London, 1975); S. G. Wilson, *The Gentiles and the Gentile Mission in Luke-Acts* (Cambridge, 1973); H. Flender, *St. Luke, Theologian of Redemptive History* (London, 1967); W. G. Kümmel, "Current Theological Accusations against Luke," *Andover Newton Quarterly* 16 (1975), 131-145; C. H. Talbert, "Shifting Sands: The Recent Study of the Gospel of Luke," *Interpretation* 30 (1976), 381-395.

[71]Talbert, "Shifting Sands," p. 387.

[72]See above, n. 70.

[73]Kraus, *Die biblische Theologie*, pp. 352-355.

It has already been noted that Cullmann is a rare continental NT scholar who attempted to find a unifying theme for the entire Bible of both Testaments. He demonstrated that salvation history, aside from the question of how it is conceived, is an important Biblical concept. The question, however, remains whether it is indeed *the* unifying theme. Cullmann still needs to prove that all the documents of the OT testify to and have as their basic theme salvation history. The same applies for the NT documents. Even though salvation history itself is subject to a variety of definitions, it is to be conceded that it is a basic NT concept. The question remains, should it serve as an organizing principle for a NT theology? E. Stauffer attempted it and ended up with a philosophy of history. This does not necessarily mean that every such attempt will end in the same way. It is indeed possible to affirm that the perspective of salvation history is a basic concept in the Bible[74] without transforming it into *the* unifying center and employing it as *the* organizing principle for a NT theology.

3. *Covenant, Love, and Other Proposals.* The covenant concept of the Bible has come into the forefront of Biblical studies in recent years.[75] One of this century's giants of OT theology employed the covenant concept as the systematic principle of the organization of the OT. W. Eichrodt opted for a systematic cross-section treatment of the OT on the basis of the covenant concept.[76] Several scholars have suggested that the covenant can also serve as the unifying principle for the

[74]E. Käsemann, *Perspectives on Paul* (Philadelphia, 1971), p. 63: "I would even say it is impossible to understand the Bible in general or Paul in particular without the perspective of salvation history." This judgment does not lead Käsemann to make it into a unifying center which he sees in the Pauline message of justification.

[75]See especially D. J. McCarthy, *Old Testament Covenant, A Survey of Current Opinions* (Richmond, 1972); E. Kutsch, *Verheissung und Gesetz* (Berlin/New York, 1973).

[76]W. Eichrodt, *Theology of the Old Testament,* 2 vols. (Philadelphia, 1965-67).

NT. O. Loretz[77] has favored it and F. C. Fensham has outlined a covenant-based theology in a programmatic essay.[78] The fact is that not all parts of the NT are directly or even indirectly related to the covenant. Therefore, the covenant concept can at best lead to a cross-section method[79] of NT theology, because it is not sufficiently comprehensive to include within it the full richness and all the variety of NT thought.[80] It seems that it is impossible to do justice to the (Biblical and) NT testimonies by a unilinear approach, whether it be through such themes, concepts, or motifs as rulership of God,[81] kingdom of God,[82] rule of God and communion between God and Man,[83] or promise.[84] We may venture to add that even as central a concept as the resurrection[85] will not do justice to the richness

---

[77]O. Loretz, *Die Wahrheit der Bibel* (Freiburg, 1964).

[78]F. C. Fensham, "Covenant, Promise and Expectation in the Bible," *Theologische Zeitschrift* 23 (1967), 305-322. The covenant theme in the NT has also been stressed by D. R. Hillers, *Covenant: The History of a Biblical Idea* (Baltimore, 1969), pp. 178-188.

[79]See Hasel, *OT Theology: Basic Issues in the Current Debate,* pp. 43-46.

[80]So V. Warnach, *Agape. Die Liebe als Grundmotiv der neutestamentlichen Theologie* (Düsseldorf, 1951); C. Spicq, "Nouvelles réflexions sur la théologie biblique," *Revue des Sciences Philosophiques et Theologiques* 42 (1958), 212f.

[81]H. Seebass, "Der Beitrag des AT zum Entwurf einer biblischen Theologie," *Wort und Dienst* 8 (1965), 20-49, esp. 30ff.

[82]G. Klein, " 'Reich Gottes' als biblischer Zentralbegriff," *EvTh* 30 (1970), 642-670, suggests this as the center for both Testaments.

[83]G. Fohrer, "Der Mittelpunkt einer Theologie des Alten Testaments," *Theologische Zeitschrift* 24 (1968), 161ff., argues that his dual concept does justice to both OT and NT.

[84]W. C. Kaiser, "The Centre of Old Testament Theology: The Promise," *Themelios* 10 (1974), 1-10, considers "promise" as "a universal key to the Scriptures which is sufficient to encompass the great variety of Biblical books, themes and concepts" (p. 9).

[85]W. Künneth, *Ostergedanken* (Lahr, 1963), p. 18; idem, "Zur Frage nach der Mitte der Schrift," p. 130, suggests that the center and unity of the NT (and the OT as well) is the resurrection of Jesus Christ. For an exposition of Künneth's resurrection center, see M. Kwiran, *The Resurrection of the Dead. Exegesis of 1 Cor 15 in German Protestant Theology from F. C. Baur to W. Künneth* (Basel, 1972), pp. 335-357. Among other scholars holding to the resurrection as the center of the NT are R. Baumann, *Mitte und Norm des Christlichen. Eine Auslegung von 1 Kor 1, 1-3, 4* (Münster, 1968);

of NT thought when it comes to the writing of a NT theology. In touching upon the resurrection theme in the NT we are already in the realm of Christology to which we must give attention now.

4. *Christology.* Under the heading "Christology" we may discuss a variety of proposals regarding the center of the NT which are in some way or another related to Jesus Christ. B. Reicke's suggestion takes us into the early part of the 1950s and may be a suitable starting point for the proposals of a christological center. He suggests that "in the Christ-event . . . [there is] the material unity of the New Testament."[86] All NT writings refer to the same Jesus Christ and point to the same event connected with him, even though one can recognize that "in the Synoptics, John, and Paul and in part among other writers of NT books Jesus is presented in differing christological aspects."[87] F. C. Grant expresses his view similarly by affirming that the NT "is genuinely Christocentric."[88] P. Robertson sees in the "Christological theme" the factor which can "unify the whole of New Testament theology. . . ."[89] Many Protestant and Catholic scholars recognize in Jesus Christ the center of the NT.[90] A. L. Moore is a strong supporter of salvation

J. Guillet, "Die Mitte der Botschaft: Jesus Tod und Auferstehung," *Internationale Katholische Zeitschrift* 2 (1973), 225-238; and F. Courth, "Die historische Jesus als Auslegungsnorm des Glaubens?" *Münchener theologische Zeitschrift* 25 (1974), 301-316, esp. 306f.

[86]Reicke, "Einheitlichkeit oder verschriedene 'Lehrbegriffe' in der ntl. Theologie?" p. 405.

[87]P. 406.

[88]Grant, *Introduction to NT Thought,* p. 56.

[89]P. Robertson, "The Outlook for Biblical Theology," *Toward a Theology of the Future,* eds. D. P. Wells and C. H. Pinnock (Carol Stream, Ill., 1971), pp. 65-91, esp. 80.

[90]For example, H. Schlier, *Besinnung auf des Neue Testament* (Freiburg, 1964), p. 69; H. U. von Balthasar, "Einigung in Christus," *Freiburger Zeitschrift für Philosophie und Theologie* 15 (1968), 171-189, esp. 187; A. Vögtle, "Kirche und Schriftprinzip nach dem Neuen Testament," *Bibel und Leben* 12 (1971), 153-162, esp. 157; K. H. Schelkle, *Theologie des Neuen Testaments,* III, 17; H. von Campenhausen, *Die Entstehung der christlichen Bibel* (Tübingen, 1968), p. 378; W. Marxsen, *Der "Frühkatholizismus" im Neuen Testament* (Neukirchen-Vluyn, 1958), p. 67; Ladd, *A Theology of the NT,* p.

history as the basic conception of the NT, but emphasizes that "from the centre, Jesus Christ, the line of
salvation-history runs backward through the covenant
to creation and beyond, and forwards through the
church and its mission to the Parousia and beyond."[91]
Without denying the salvation-historical concept of the
NT, the "Christological unity" is the key to the NT.[92]
It can be said that G. E. Ladd is committed to salvation
history as much as is Cullmann, but in opposition to
the latter Ladd refuses against his earlier opinion to let
the salvation-historical or eschatological structure[93] provide the synthesis for an organization of NT theology.
He believes that a NT theology written from the point
of view of a single organizing principle can be done so
only on the basis of "great loss." "There is great richness
in the variety of New Testament theology which must
not be sacrificed."[94]

W. Schrage does not object to the center of the NT
in Jesus Christ. To the contrary, he argues that those
who stop by saying that Jesus Christ is the center of
the NT have stopped too early.[95] In a similar vein M.
Hengel affirms a "christological center," but suggests
that there are a variety of formulae such as " 'solus
Christus', 'sola gratia', 'iustificatio impii' with which it
can be described."[96] At least two of these formulae have
had strong supporters. Before we turn to these it seems
advisable to mention several other suggestions in which
the "christological center" is more broadly defined.

33; Lohse, "Die Einheit des NT als theologisches Problem," pp. 152-
154; Haacker, "Einheit und Vielfalt in der Theologie des NT," pp.
40f.; Kümmel, The Theology of the NT, p. 332; and others.

[91]A. L. Moore, The Parousia in the New Testament (Leiden, 1966),
pp. 89f.

[92]P. 172.

[93]Ladd, "Eschatology and the Unity of NT Theology," p. 273.

[94]Ladd, A Theology of the NT, p. 33.

[95]Schrage, "Die Frage nach der Mitte und dem Kanon im Kanon
des NT," p. 438.

[96]M. Hengel, "Historische Methoden und theologische Auslegung
des Neuen Testaments," Kerygma und Dogma 19 (1973), 85-90,
esp. 90.

H. Riesenfeld of the University of Uppsala raises the question of how it could have happened that the "disparate elements of belief [in the NT], the only common denominator of which was that they in some way referred to a man named Jesus, who was supposed to have arisen from the dead, had been collected, integrated and considered homogenous in such an amazingly short space of time?"[97] A "mere Kerygma proclaiming a faith in the resurrection of a person named Jesus, and now considered to be heavenly Lord, will not be sufficient to explain why there was a diversity of christological titles and theological formulas, but only one Christian Church. . . ."[98] Ultimately the self-consciousness of Jesus alone can answer the question. "In the last resort the sense and the structural consistency of the kerygma proclaimed by the early Church depend upon the fact that Jesus during the time of his public ministry attributed to his person, his works and acts — and not least to his suffering and death — decisive importance for the coming and realization of the reign of God."[99] This is made clear in Jesus' usage of the title Son of Man which is typical of the pattern of thought of NT Christology.[100] Riesenfeld seems to argue that the Jesus kerygma contained an "explicit" and not merely an "implicit" Christology.

W. Beilner suggests that it is the task of NT theology to show how the historical Jesus became the proclaimed exalted Christ.[101] He believes that "NT theology is to be understood as a unity only from two basic aspects, namely from the proclaimed Jesus as the Christ and the "locus" of that proclamation, the existence of the church. These two elements form the bracket of all different NT theologies or layers of expression."[102] This

[97]Riesenfeld, "Reflections on the Unity of the NT," p. 41.
[98]P. 49.
[99]Ibid.
[100]Pp. 50f.
[101]W. Beilner, "Neutestamentliche Theologie. Methodische Besinnung," *Dienst und Lehre* (Wien, 1965), pp. 145-165, esp. 159.
[102]P. 158.

means for Beilner and his fellow Catholic Schelkle "that the unity of the NT has its ground in the one church."[103] The unity of the NT is conceived of differently by F. Mussner whose thesis it is that " 'the center of the gospel' is according to the NT the gospel of the dawn of the eschatological saving time in Jesus Christ."[104] This message "forms in a certain sense the unifying bracket in the NT canon and does not allow a canon within the canon." He warns, however, that one must not raise "a particular single kerygma . . . to a central place of the gospel or even make it into a unique gospel," because it "functions too easily as an explosive charge within the NT canon as is evident from history."[105]

Theologians such as W. Beilner, K. H. Schelkle, and F. Mussner are representative Catholic examples arguing for the unity of the NT[106] without necessarily making the proposed centers into an organizing principle on the basis of which a NT theology should be constructed. On the Protestant side we may mention particularly W. G. Kümmel and E. Lohse, both of whom have provided NT theologies. W. G. Kümmel notes that "the concern about a theology of the New Testament found itself from the outset confronted with the problem of diversity and unity in the New Testament."[107] With great perception he suggests "that the presentation and arrangement of a 'theology of the New Testament' can come about only as a *result* of work with the diverse forms of the New Testament proclamation."[108] In other words, no predetermined center can ever function as an organizing principle (*pace* Bultmann, Braun, Cullmann, etc.) for the presentation of a NT theology. In the "Conclusion" of his NT theology Kümmel returns

[103]Schelkle, *Theologie des NT*, III, 16; Beilner, Neutestamentliche Theologie," p. 160.

[104]Mussner, "Die Mitte des Evangeliums in ntl. Sicht," pp. 271, 290.

[105]F. Mussner, *Praesentia Salutis* (Munich, 1967), pp. 174ff.

[106]Other Catholic voices are reviewed by A. Kümmel, "Mitte des Neuen Testaments," pp. 79f.

[107]W. G. Kümmel, *The Theology of the New Testament According to its Major Witnesses: Jesus-Paul-John* (Nashville, 1973), p. 15.

[108]P. 17.

to the question of the "center of the New Testament."[109] His assumption is that the center of the NT found expression "in its purest version" in "(1) the message and figure of Jesus as these became perceptible to us in the earliest tradition of the synoptic gospels; then (2) the proclamation of the primitive community . . . ; and (3) the first theological reflection on this proclamation by Paul."[110] On the basis of these three blocks Kümmel suggests that the following twofold aspect about Jesus Christ constitutes the center of the NT: ". . . God has caused his salvation promised for the end of the world to begin in Jesus Christ, and that in this Christ event God has encountered us and intends to encounter us as the Father who seeks to rescue us from imprisonment in the world and to make us free for active love."[111] Inasmuch as Kümmel believes that this "common message . . . can be labeled as foundational and by which the message of the rest of the New Testament can be measured,"[112] we must react by raising a question. What objective criteria can Kümmel cite for his choice of the earliest synoptic traditions about Jesus, the kerygma of the primitive community, and the proclamation of Paul as the NT blocks of materials that yield the center of the NT with which the remainder of the NT is to be measured? As a Lutheran theologian Kümmel is committed to the material principle of a "canon within the canon,"[113] but in spite of this he has failed to justify the selection of the criteria chosen. E. Lohse is likewise committed to the principle of a "canon within the canon," which functions both as a principle of selection and a principle of judgment within the NT. He is not setting up his *own* criteria for a center of the NT in the form of certain blocks of writings at the exclusion

[109]Unfortunately the German term *Mitte* is translated with "heart" instead of the customary "center" in Kümmel's *Theology of the NT,* pp. 322-333.

[110]P. 324.

[111]P. 332.

[112]P. 324.

[113]W. G. Kümmel, "Notwendigkeit und Grenze des neutestamentlichen Kanons," *ZThK* 47 (1950), 277-313.

of others. He follows Luther's principle "what manifests Christ" (*"was Christum treibet"*)[114] and affirms that "the theology of the witnesses of the NT can only be unlocked from Christology."[115] This includes the fact that anthropology can only be defined through Christology. Lohse insists, correctly in our estimation, that the manifoldness of theological conceptions of the NT cannot be brought together through a single unifying concept such as salvation history (*pace* Cullmann) or anthropology (*pace* Braun).[116] The center and unity of the manifoldness of the NT expressions are found in the once-for-all Christ event on the cross in which God's love for the world was manifested.[117] Is not the center of the NT Jesus Christ?[118]

In harmony with the emphasis of the major Reformers, some NT scholars posit the Pauline idea of the "justification of the godless" (*iustificatio impii*) as the center of the NT. E. Käsemann not only wishes to see the message of justification of the godless as the center of Pauline theology,[119] but supporting the principle of "a canon within the canon,"[120] he suggests that it is the center of the whole NT.[121] Here Käsemann separates himself from his teacher Bultmann whose kerygmatic anthropology served as the center.[122] Käsemann maintains that "the New Testament actually

[114]Lohse, "Die Einheit des NT als theologisches Problem," p. 153.

[115]Lohse, *Grundriss der neutestamentlichen Theologie,* p. 14.

[116]Pp. 162f.

[117]P. 164.

[118]See also E. Schweizer, *Jesus Christus im vielfältigen Zeugnis des Neuen Testaments* (Stuttgart, 1968). P. Stuhlmacher, *Schriftauslegung auf dem Wege zur biblischen Theologie* (Göttingen, 1975), p. 178, speaks of "the message of reconciliation as the decisive center of Holy Scripture."

[119]E. Käsemann, "Gottes Gerechtigkeit bei Paulus," *Exegetische Versuche und Besinnungen,* II, 181-193.

[120]E. Käsemann, "Kritische Analyse," *Das Neue Testament als Kanon,* ed. E. Käsemann (Göttingen, 1970), p. 369.

[121]See for a detailed exposition of Käsemann's unity concept within his theology, Stock, *Einheit des NT,* pp. 13-24.

[122]A summary of the objections of Käsemann against Bultmann is provided by Stock, *Einheit des NT,* pp. 62-65.

wants to be understood as a whole as witness to Christ."[123] The different NT Christologies are "adequate, in order to emphasize clearly what manifests Christ. Because this is the way it is, the justification of the godless is the center of all Christian proclamation and therefore also of Scripture, . . ."[124] He explains emphatically that "for me the message of justification and *sola scriptura* are identical, the theological formula of the justification of the godless encompasses in my understanding all Scripture, including the Old Testament insofar as it has to do truly with Jesus Christ."[125] Although this "theological formula" is to be seen in "correlation with Christology," it is prior to Christology because any real Christology "is to be oriented . . . on justification of the godless,"[126] which "as canon within the canon . . . is the criterion for the testing of the spirits even with reference to Christian preaching in past and present."[127] W. Joest agrees: "The Pauline-reformation proclamation of justification [serves] indeed as the central interpretation of the Word of God. . . ."[128] Käsemann's student W. Schrage also puts the accent where Käsemann has it. For Schrage "*iustificatio impii* (Rom. 4:5) is the center and key theme of Pauline proclamation and theology."[129] He finds its echo also in other parts of the NT such as in the so-called Deuteropauline letters, 1 Peter, 1 John, and in Revelation.[130]

An indirect reaction to the "theological formula" of justification of the godless as the center of the NT, even

[123]Käsemann, *Das NT als Kanon,* p. 404.
[124]P. 405.
[125]P. 370.
[126]P. 405.
[127]Ibid.
[128]W. Joest, "Die Frage des Kanons in der heutigen evangelischen Theologie," *Was heisst Auslegung der Heiligen Schrift?* eds. W. Joest, F. Mussner, *et al.* (Regensburg, 1966), p. 198; idem, "Erwägungen zur kanonischen Bedeutung des Neuen Testaments," *Das Neue Testaments als Kanon,* pp. 258-281, esp. 276.
[129]Schrage, "Die Frange nach der Mitte und dem Kanon im Kanon des NT," p. 440.
[130]P. 441.

the whole Bible, comes from U. Luz. He argues for the "theology of the cross *(theologia crucis)* as the center of the New Testament."[131] Luz believes that the NT theologians of the "theology of the cross" *par excellence* are Mark and Paul[132] but that such other documents as the Fourth Gospel, Revelation, Hebrews,[133] 1 Peter,[134] and possibly others contain it. The following summarizes the proposal of Luz:

> The theology of the cross (1) understands the cross as the ground of salvation in an exclusive sense to which all other events of salvation (i.e. resurrection, parousia) are related and understood . . . (2) considers the cross of Christ as starting-point for *theology* in the sense that there is no doctrine of God which is independent of a theology of the cross . . . and (3) the cross is to be understood as the *point of orientation for theology* from which theological points of departure for anthropology, philosophy of history, ecclesiology, ethics, etc. are provided.[135]

Luz begins his quest for the center of the NT with Paul but arrives at a christological aspect different from Käsemann and his followers.

The NT is christocentric. This christocentricity has a variety of interrelated aspects. The exclusive emphasis on one or another aspect runs the risk of minimizing or maximizing one at the expense of another. The various aspects need to be carefully investigated, expounded, and seen in relation to each other. F. Mussner notes that "the Pauline doctrine of justification reveals immediately that the *iustificatio impii* by grace alone is based on the substitutionary atoning death of Jesus on the cross in which the saving righteousness of God 'is revealed' in the 'now.' The justification of man is in the

---

[131]U. Luz, "Theologia crucis als Mitte der Theologie des Neuen Testaments," *EvTh* 34 (1974), 116-141.
[132]Pp. 121-131 on Paul and pp. 131-139 on Mark.
[133]P. 118.
[134]P. 128.
[135]P. 116.

apostle's view grounded in a *factum historicum.*"[136] As a Lutheran theologian E. Lohse is not less interested in the concept of justification than Käsemann and his followers. He calls upon Luther himself to support his conclusion that "the teaching about justification has to be grounded alone in Christology."[137] H. Diem objects on other grounds. Justification is but a *partial* aspect of the Bible through which other aspects are unjustly criticized.[138]

No consensus has emerged regarding the question of the center of the New Testament. The reasons for this are manifold as the discussion of the debate has indicated. We must pause for some basic considerations. It has been noted repeatedly that one of the purposes of the quest for a center of the NT is to provide a basis for its unity on the one hand and for the systematic presentation or structure of a NT theology on the other. It appears that NT scholarship is at this point in the grip of a philosophical and theological speculative presupposition which claims that the multiform and multiplex NT materials in all their rich manifoldness will fit into and can be systematically ordered and arranged by means of a center. Here one of the most basic hermeneutical questions for the task of NT theology emerges. Can any center of the NT be sufficiently broad and thus adequate to bring about a systematization of the NT materials into a conceived structural unity? The fact of the proliferation of proposed centers for the NT indicates that this does not seem to be possible. It has become evident that even the most carefully worked out center whether in the form of a scheme, formula, concept, motif, or idea proves itself finally as one-sided, inadequate, and insufficient and thus inevitably leads to misconceptions as regards the variety, manifoldness, and richness of the NT. The phenomenon of constantly increasing numbers of new suggestions at what consti-

[136]Mussner, "Die Mitte des Evangeliums in ntl. Sicht," p. 282.

[137]Lohse, *Grundriss der neutestamentlichen Theologie*, p. 14.

[138]H. Diem, "Die Einheit der Schrift," *EvTh* 13 (1953), 391f., 397, 400.

tutes the center of the NT and how they contribute to
the writing of a NT theology is in itself a telling witness
to the evident inefficiency of the respective schemes,
formulas, concepts, motifs, or ideas for the task at hand.
On the basis of these undeniable limitations of the
various centers some have presented centers which are
longer in definition and/or larger in scope. It can be
said that even "salvation history" is stretched beyond
its proper limits as regards its capability of serving
as an umbrella under which the richness of the whole
NT can be brought.

We are not denying the legitimacy of the quest for
a center of the NT (and the OT). But as we are denying that any *external* structure based on categories of
thought alien to the NT (or the Bible) can be allowed to
be superimposed upon Biblical thought, viz., the God-
Man-Salvation (Theology-Anthropology-Soteriology)
scheme borrowed from dogmatics, so we are convinced
that any center of the NT (or the Bible) is not broad,
deep, and wide enough to do justice to the whole
canonical NT as regards its capability to serve as an
organizing principle. The quest for the center of the NT
(and the OT) as based on the inner Biblical witnesses
themselves is fully justified. It seems undeniable that
the NT is from beginning to end christocentric. Jesus
Christ is the dynamic, unifying center of the NT. God's
gracious saving activity comes to expression in the life
and activity, the suffering, death, and resurrection, as
well as in the exaltation and heavenly ministry of Jesus
Christ. Jesus Christ is the beginning, center, and end
of the NT. The NT's christocentricity must not be transformed into a structure on the basis of which a NT
theology is to be written.

C. The Center of the NT and the Canon Within the Canon

The current debate concerning the center of the NT
is closely related to the problem of canon criticism.

The previous discussion has revealed that the question of the center of the NT is interwoven with the question of "the canon within the canon." It is not our purpose here to review the rich literature on the subject.[139] We have noted time and again that the center of the NT is frequently used as a measuring rod whereby one can discern what the true gospel is and what it is not. The problem is in no way new, because Luther's principle *"was Christum treibet"* ("what manifests Christ") implies the criterion of "a canon within the canon"[140] and is a key among the roots of the "canon crisis in modern Protestantism."[141]

It is amazing to observe that modern scholars of one (Lutheran) confession, all of whom are equally strongly committed in their usage of the historical-critical meth-

[139]In addition to the various essays already referred to in n. 1 of this chapter the following studies since 1965 are particularly relevant: R. M. Grant, *The Formation of the New Testament* (New York, 1965); R. L. Morgan, "Let's Be Honest about the Canon: A Plea to Reconsider a Question the Reformers Failed to Answer," *Christian Century* 84 (1967), 717-719; A. C. Sundberg, "Toward a Revised History of the New Testament Canon," *Studia Evangelica* 4 (1968), 452-461; idem, "Canon of the NT," *IDB Sup.* (1976), 136-140; C. S. C. Williams, "The History of the Text and Canon of the New Testament to Jerome," *Cambridge History of the Bible*, ed. G. W. H. Lampe (New York, 1969), II, 27-53; E. Käsemann, ed., *Das Neue Testament als Kanon* (Göttingen, 1970); K.-H. Ohlig, *Woher nimmt die Bibel ihre Autorität? Zum Verhältnis von Schriftkanon, Kirche und Jesus* (Düsseldorf, 1970); I. Frank, *Der Sinn der Kanonbildung* (Freiburg, 1971); E. Kalin, "The Inspired Community: A Glance at Canon History," *Concordia Theological Monthly* 42 (1971), 541-549; H. F. von Campenhausen, *Die Entstehung der christlichen Bibel* (Tübingen, 1968); Eng. trans. *The Formation of the Christian Bible* (Philadelphia, 1972); H. Burkhardt, "Grenzen des Kanons — Motive und Masstäbe," *Theologische Beiträge* 1 (1970), 153-160; G. Maier, "Kanon im Kanon — oder die ganze Schrift?" *Theologische Beiträge* 3 (1972), 21-31; D. E. Groh, "H. von Campenhausen on Canon. Positions and Problems," *Interpretation* 28 (1974), 331-343; J. Barr, *The Bible in The Modern World* (New York, 1973); D. L. Dungan, "The New Testament Canon in Recent Study," *Interpretation* 29 (1975), 339-351.

[140]See K. Barth, "Das Schriftprinzip der reformierten Kirche," *Zeichen der Zeit* 3 (1925), 223; H. Strathmann, "Die Krise des Kanons der Kirche," *Das NT als Kanon*, p. 41, claims that Luther discovered in Rom. 1:17 "a canon within the canon." Cullmann, *Salvation in History*, pp. 297f.

[141]Lönning, *"Kanon im Kanon,"* pp. 39-49.

od and all of whom are committed to the principle of
"a canon within the canon," are unable to agree on what
this center of the NT is which is to function as "a canon
within the canon." We have seen that some of them,
for example, argue for the "justification of the godless"
(Käsemann, Joest, Schrage),[142] or for the "theology of
the cross" (Luz),[143] and others extract their critical
criteria from the message of the historical Jesus (Jeremias), or a combination of the message of Jesus and
the oldest kerygma (Kümmel, Marxsen),[144] or from
particular blocks of writings (H. Braun).[145] This evident
fact leads to only one conclusion: "Any selection of a
criterion [of unity] is bound to be subjective and arbitrary."[146] It is of course admitted that the quest for
a center and a criterion for unity is not to be confused
with an absolutizing of single aspects or with pet theological ideas.[147] But it will have to be admitted also
that the subjectivity with which a selection is made
from the whole and on the basis of which the whole
is subjected to content criticism calls into question the
objectivity of the method itself and the whole procedure.
I. Lönning's comprehensive study of the whole issue of
"a canon within the canon" from the time of the
Reformation to the present, which comes at major points
to conclusions similar to his teacher Käsemann, adds the
striking admonition that "we cannot make the 'canon
within the canon' into the canon."[148]

The well-known Catholic systematician H. Küng,

---

[142]See above, nn. 123, 128f.

[143]See above, n. 131.

[144]W. G. Kümmel, "Notwendigkeit und Grenze des neutestamentlichen Kanons," Das NT als Kanon, pp. 62-97, esp. 94; and above, nn.
107-112; W. Marxsen, "Das Problem des neutestamentlichen Kanons
aus der Sicht des Exegeten," Das NT als Kanon, pp. 233-246, esp. 246.

[145]H. Braun, "Hebt die heutige neutestamentlich-exegetische Forschung den Kanon auf?" Das NT als Kanon, pp. 228f.; cf. above, nn.
28f.

[146]Cullmann, Salvation in History, p. 298.

[147]So correctly Schrage, "Die Frage nach der Mitte und dem Kanon
im Kanon des NT," p. 418.

[148]Lönning, "Kanon im Kanon," p. 271.

whose theological position is in many ways akin to that of Käsemann, objects to the program of "a canon within the canon," because it "asks for nothing else but to be more biblical than the Bible, more NT-like than the NT, more gospel-like than the Gospel and even more Pauline than Paul."[149] He objects to a given preunderstanding on the basis of which one is to test the spirits. Paul never applied the principle of the testing of the spirits to the OT canon. Thus we have no right to use this principle for the NT canon.[150] He notes that such a pre-understanding is not grounded in the NT but rather in the Lutheran tradition. He asks therefore, "Is this not a position for which one cannot provide any reasons which would prevent another scholar to make another choice on the basis of *another* traditional preunderstanding for *another* center and thus to find exegetical support for *another* gospel?"[151] Ultimately any formula, principle, idea, etc., that is made into the center of the NT on the basis of which one engages in canon criticism with the selective principle of "a canon within the canon" is "subjective arbitrariness,"[152] because "a given preunderstanding about the nature of Christian faith is projected back into the NT as a critical canon within the canon."[153]

Another stricture made with regard to a center that serves as "a canon within the canon" which is employed for the purpose of content criticism or canon criticism is its inevitable reductionism.[154] The NT considered as a whole contains "truth in its fullness."[155] The principle of "a canon within the canon" cannot do justice to the totality of the NT. Any center designed for that pur-

[149]H. Küng, "Der Frühkatholizismus im NT als kontroverstheologisches Problem," *Das NT als Kanon,* pp. 175-204, esp. 192.

[150]P. 190.

[151]P. 191 (italics his).

[152]Ibid.; also H. Diem, *Theologie als kirchliche Wissenschaft* (2nd ed.; Munich, 1957), p. 206.

[153]Stock, *Einheit des NT,* p. 70.

[154]H. Küng, *Die Kirche* (Freiburg, 1967), p. 151.

[155]K. H. Schelkle, *Die Petrusbriefe. Der Judasbrief* (2nd ed.; Freiburg, 1964), p. 245.

pose tends toward a concentration on a single aspect. "What does this concentration consist of? It consists of reductionism."[156] This is the case because it is derived on the basis of a process of selection. Küng argues that selection from the totality of the NT canon leads to a multiplicity of denominations and to heresy. Only when one takes the canon of the NT seriously in its totality can one expect one church.[157] The Catholic scholar H. Schlier, a former student of Bultmann, also has reservations concerning the reduction of the full NT gospel by means of "a canon within the canon." "If one wishes to save the position of the faith of Luther . . . then one is forced to do away with the canon of Scripture. Scripture is Scripture. Any major or abstract Paulinism . . . finally declares almost all contents of Scripture as not binding."[158]

Various Protestant theologians have also raised serious questions concerning the principle of selection as it comes to expression in the concept of "a canon within the canon." E. Schweizer notes that Scripture is always "Scripture in function." Therefore, he rejects "a canon within the canon."[159] The views of the Lutheran systematician H. Diem and his categorical "No" to "a canon within the canon"[160] has exercised several NT scholars.[161] Likewise G. Ebeling refuses to affirm "a canon within the canon." For him such a principle runs the danger of being arbitrary. He speaks of a "legal view of the canon . . . which regards the unity of Scripture

[156]H. Küng, *Strukturen der Kirche* (Freiburg, 1962), p. 151; idem, *Die Kirche,* p. 27.

[157]Küng, "Der Frühkatholizismus im NT als kontroverstheologisches Problem," pp. 188f.

[158]H. Schlier, *Die Zeit der Kirche* (2nd ed.; Freiburg, 1958), p. 311.

[159]E. Schweizer, "Kanon?" *EvTh* 31 (1971), 339-357, esp. 354f.

[160]See particularly his "Die Einheit der Schrift," pp. 385-405, and his essay "Das Problem des Schriftkanons," *Das NT als Kanon,* pp. 159-174.

[161]See for example the reactions of Käsemann, *Das NT als Kanon,* pp. 359-371; and Schrage, "Die Frage nach der Mitte und dem Kanon im Kanon des NT," pp. 421-424. A good summary of Diem's position is provided by Stock, *Einheit des NT,* pp. 36-38, 100-112, including reactions from Protestants and Catholics.

as the unity of a dogmatic doctrinal system. Such a view can only be carried through to its logical conclusion either by doing what the Catholic Church does, namely, falling back on the hermeneutical function of tradition, or, in an apparently arbitrary fashion, establishing a canon within the canon in the form of a specific body of writings or a specific doctrine as a standard of criticism."[162] Ebeling suggests that because of the diversity and variety of the NT no single tradition "can be marked out as the *traditum tradendum* [tradition to be passed on]; but it is this that points to the decisive fact that the content of the *traditum tradendum* is . . . the very Person of Jesus himself as the incarnate Word of God, giving its authority to the Gospel. . . ."[163]

G. Maier is among the severest critics of the principle of "a canon within the canon." His point is the failure of the quest for "a canon within the canon." It has gone on for two hundred years but failed, because it is based on uncontrolled subjectivity. No scholar has been able to convince all others what such "a canon within the canon" should be.[164]

The variety of problems to which scholars have pointed in their discussions of the center of the NT, one that functions as "a canon within the canon" and serves as material principle of canon criticism, are apparently insurmountable. An approach to NT theology that seeks to be adequate to the totality of the NT cannot afford the arbitrariness (Küng, Ebeling, Diem), subjectivity (Cullmann, Maier), and reductionism (Küng) inherent in the choice of a selective principle in the form of a center either from without Scripture (tradition) or from within Scripture on the basis of

[162]G. Ebeling, *The Word of God and Tradition* (Philadelphia, 1968), p. 144.

[163]P. 146. The question is to be raised, however, whether the content of the NT remains open on account of the emphasis on the "Person Jesus." See also Stock, *Einheit des NT,* pp. 24-28, 82-88.

[164]G. Maier, "Kanon im Kanon—oder die ganze Schrift?" pp. 21-31; idem, *Das Ende der historisch-kritischen Methode* (2nd ed.; Wuppertal, 1975), pp. 10f., 44; Eng. trans. *The End of the Historical-Critical Method* (St. Louis, 1977), pp. 12ff.

which value judgments are made with regard to the content of Scripture as a whole or in its parts. Can the self-authenticating nature of the NT and the Bible as a whole[165] give way to an external or selective principle as its norm?

[165]See F. Mildenberger, "The Unity, Truth, and Validity of the Bible," *Interpretation* 29 (1975), 391-405, esp. 399.

IV. NT Theology and the OT

NT theology was separated from OT theology since the year 1800 when the first of four volumes of Georg Lorenz Bauer's *Biblische Theologie des Neuen Testaments* was published. Even though few books have been published in recent years that treat both the OT and NT with the title "Biblical theology,"[1] there is no lack of interest in the subject of the relationship between the Testaments.[2] We are reminded anew by G.

[1]See M. Burrows, *An Outline of Biblical Theology* (Philadelphia, 1946); G. Vos, *Biblical Theology* (Grand Rapids, Mich., 1948); J. Blenkinsopp, *A Sketchbook of Biblical Theology* (London, 1968).

[2]See the following studies in addition to those in nn. 70 and 80 below: A. A. van Ruler, *The Christian Church and the OT,* trans. G. W. Bromiley (Grand Rapids, 1971); S. Amsler, *L'AT dans l'église* (Neuchâtel, 1960); J. D. Smart, *The Interpretation of Scripture* (Philadelphia, 1961); P. Grelot, *Sens chrétien de l'AT* (Tournai, 1962); B. W. Anderson, ed., *The OT and Christian Faith* (New York, 1963; hereafter cited as *OTCF*); C. Westermann, *The OT and Jesus Christ* (Minneapolis, 1970); R. E. Murphy, "The Relationship Between the Testaments," *CBQ* 26 (1964), 349-359; "Christian Understanding of the OT," *Theology Digest* 18 (1970), 321f.; F. Hesse, *Das AT als Buch der Kirche* (Gütersloh, 1966); K. Schwarzwäller, *Das AT in Christus* (Zürich, 1966); "Das Verhältnis AT-NT im Lichte der gegenwärtigen Bestimmungen," *EvTh* 29 (1969), 281-307; P. Benoit and R. E. Murphy, eds., *How Does the Christian Confront the OT?* (New York, 1967); A. H. J. Gunneweg, "Über die Prädikabilität alttestamentlicher Texte," *ZThK* 65(1968), 389-413; N. Lohfink, *The Christian Meaning of the OT* (Milwaukee, 1968); H. D. Preuss, "Das AT in der Verkündigung der Kirche," *Deutsches Pfarrerblatt* 63 (1968), 73-79; Kraus, *Die Biblische Theologie,* pp. 193-305; E. O'Doherty, "The Unity of the Bible," *The Bible Today* 1 (1962), 53-57; C. Larcher, *L'Actualité chrétienne de l'Ancien Tes-*

Ebeling that one has to study the interconnection between the Testaments and "has to give an account of his understanding of the Bible as a whole, i.e. above all of the theological problems that come of inquiring into the inner unity of the manifold testimony of the Bible."[3] The fundamental theological reflections of the Tübingen NT scholar P. Stuhlmacher lead him to affirm that a Biblical theology of the NT "can and must be open toward the Old Testament as the decisive foundation of the formation of the tradition of the New Testament."[4] These remarks raise the questions of continuity and discontinuity, or whether one reads uniquely from the OT and NT or from the NT back into the OT, or reciprocally from the OT to the NT and the NT to the OT. Basic to the whole question is not merely an articulation of the theological problem of the interrelatedness between both Testaments but also an inquiry into the nature of this unity and disunity, whether it is one language, thought-form, or content. In order to facilitate our attempt to survey the issues involved, we may limit ourselves to discuss what are considered significant recent attempts to come to grips with the issues in-

---

tament d'après le Nouveau Testament (Paris, 1962); W. Neil, "The Unity of the Bible," The New Testament in Historical and Contemporary Perspective. Essays in Memory of G. H. C. Macgregor, eds. H. Anderson and W. Barclay (Oxford, 1965), pp. 237-259; Stock, Einheit des NT, pp. 160-170; P. A. Verhoef, "The Relationship Between the Old and New Testament," New Perspectives on the Old Testament, ed. J. B. Payne (Waco/London, 1970), pp. 280-303; F. Hahn, "Das Problem 'Schrift und Tradition' im Urchristentum," EvTh 30 (1970), 449-468; F. Lang, "Christuszeugnis und Biblische Theologie," EvTh 29 (1969), 523-534; H. Gese, "Erwägungen zur Einheit der biblischen Theologie," Vom Sinai zum Zion (Munich, 1974), pp. 11-30; H. Gross and F. Mussner, "Die Einheit von Altem und Neuem Testament," Internationale Katholische Zeitschrift 3 (1974), 544-555; F. C. Fensham, "The Covenant as Giving Expression to the Relationship between Old and New Testament," Tyndale Bulletin 22 (1971), 82-94; J. Sanders, Torah and Canon (2nd ed.; Philadelphia, 1974); idem, "Torah and Christ," Interpretation 29 (1975), 372-390.

[3] G. Ebeling, Word and Faith (Philadelphia, 1963), p. 96.

[4] P. Stuhlmacher, Schriftauslegung auf dem Wege zur biblischen Theologie (Göttingen, 1975), p. 127.

volved and which mirror the major positions in this century.

A. Patterns of Disunity and Discontinuity

The second century produced Marcion,[5] who under the impact of Gnosticism[6] stressed the total disunity between the OT and the NT, between Israel and the Church, and between the god of the OT and the Father of Jesus. The god of the OT was the Demiurge-Creator, an inferior, vindictive god of the law who has nothing to do whatever with the NT god who is the Father of Jesus, a god of love, grace, and mercy. Thus Marcion rejected the Hebrew Scriptures (OT) outrightly and also anything in the NT which came close to the Hebrew Scriptures or their thoughts as understood by him. This compelled Christianity to deal with the question of what is Christian truth and to decide upon the question of the canon.

1. *Overemphasis of NT — Underemphasis of OT*. A Marcionite strain with the superiority of the whole or key parts of the NT has existed in Christianity for a long time and is reflected in A. von Harnack (1851-1930) whose famous theme is summarized in this widely quoted sentence: "To have cast aside the Old Testament in the second century was an error which the Church rightly rejected; to have retained it in the sixteenth century was the fact which the Reformation was not yet able to avoid; but still to keep it after the nineteenth century as a canonical document within Protestantism results from a religious and ecclesiastical paralysis."[7] The same Marcionite strain is evident in Friedrich Delitzsch (1850-1922) who was a key figure in the Babel-

[5]A. von Harnack, *Marcion, Das Evangelium vom fremden* Gott (2nd ed.; Leipzig, 1924); J. Knox, *Marcion and the New Testament* (Chicago, 1942); E. C. Blackman, *Marcion and His Influence* (London, 1948).

[6]R. M. Grant, *A Short History of the Interpretation of the Bible* (2nd ed.; New York, 1966), pp. 60-65.

[7]Von Harnack, *Marcion,* pp. 221f.

Bible controversy at the beginning of this century.[8] "Seldom has the Old Testament been subjected to more vicious abuse than in this book [The Great Deception]."[9] The leading NT scholar Emanuel Hirsch published a study on *The OT and the Preaching of the NT* in 1936 in which he emphasizes a foundational distinction between the OT and NT in which both Testaments are seen in a permanent "antithetical tension."[10] Although Hirsch does not dismiss the OT from the Christian canon, his stress falls distinctly upon a radical discontinuity. H.-J. Kraus remarks that "one has to note with surprise that Rudolf Bultmann in his essays on the Old Testament seeks a solution of the biblical problem along the same lines."[11]

It is not so important whether or not R. Bultmann's negative stance with regard to the OT is due to the claim of a Marcionite strain[12] within him. What is important is that he seeks the connection between the Testaments in the factual course of history.[13] But Bultmann determines this connection in such a way that OT history is a history of failure. The application of the Lutheran law/gospel distinction and a modern type of Christomonism[14] leads him to view the OT as a "miscarriage *[Scheitern]* of history" which only through

[8]F. Delitzsch, *Die Grosse Täuschung*, 2 vols. (Stuttgart, 1920-21).

[9]J. Bright, *The Authority of the Old Testament* (Nashville, 1967), p. 65.

[10]E. Hirsch, *Das Alte Testament und die Predigt des Evangeliums* (Tübingen, 1936), pp. 27, 59, 83.

[11]H.-J. Kraus, *Geschichte der historisch-kritischen Erforschung des Alten Testaments* (2nd ed.; Neukirchen-Vluyn, 1969), pp. 431f.

[12]So Bright, *The Authority of the OT*, pp. 69-72; E. Voegelin, "History and Gnosis," *OTCF*, pp. 64-89, who calls Bultmann a gnostic thinker. C. Michalson, "Is the Old Testament the Propaedeutic to Christian Faith?" *OTCF*, pp. 64-89, warmly defends Bultmann against such a charge.

[13]Bultmann, "Prophecy and Fulfillment," *Essays on OT Hermeneutics*, ed. Claus Westermann (Richmond, Va., 1963), p. 73 (hereafter cited as *EOTH*). Cf. J. Barr, "The Old Testament and the New Crisis of Biblical Authority," *Interpretation* 25 (1971), 30-32.

[14]Bultmann in *EOTH*, pp. 50-75; and *OTCF*, pp. 8-35. See G. E. Wright's critique in *The OT and Theology* (New York, 1969), pp. 30-38.

this failure turns into a kind of promise.[15] "To the Christian faith the Old Testament is no longer revelation as it has been, and still is, for the Jews." To the Christian "the history of Israel is not history of revelation."[16] "Thus the Old Testament is the presupposition of the New"[17] and nothing more nor anything less. Bultmann argues for the complete theological discontinuity between the OT and NT. The relationship between both Testaments "is not theologically relevant at all."[18] Nonetheless this history has according to him a promissory character precisely because in the failure of the hopes centered in the covenant concept, in the failure of the rule of God and his people, it becomes clear that "the situation of the justified man arises only on the basis of this miscarriage [Scheitern]."[19] In answer to this position, Walther Zimmerli has rightly asked whether for the NT "the hopes and history of Israel are really only shattered." "Is there not fulfillment here, even in the midst of the shattering?" He recognizes clearly that the concept of failure or shattering becomes the means by which Bultmann is able "to elevate the Christ-message purely out of history in existential interpretation. . . ." Zimmerli suggests not without reason that the concept of a pure brokenness of Israel's history must of necessity lead to an unhistorical conception of the Christ-event, namely a "new Christ-myth."[20] He points out that an aspect of shattering is present even in the OT, where the prophets themselves bear witness to the freedom of Yahweh to "legitimately interpret his promise through his fulfillment, and the interpretation [by Yahweh] can be full of surprises even for the prophet

[15]Bultmann, EOTH, p. 73: ". . . the miscarriage of history actually amounts to a promise." See on this Barr, Old and New in Interpretation, pp. 162f.

[16]Bultmann, EOTH, p. 31.

[17]OTCF, p. 14.

[18]P. 13. Cf. Westermann's critique in EOTH, pp. 124-128.

[19]Bultmann, EOTH, p. 75.

[20]"Promise and Fulfillment," EOTH, pp. 118-120.

himself."[21] W. Pannenberg notes that the reason Bultmann finds no continuity between the Testaments "is certainly connected with the fact that he does not begin with the promises and their structure which for Israel were the foundation of history, . . . promises which thus endure precisely in change."[22]

The conviction of Friedrich Baumgärtel shares with Bultmann the emphasis on the discontinuity between the Testaments.[23] But Baumgärtel is not able to follow Bultmann's thesis of a total failure. He assumes an enduring "basic-promise [Grundverheissung]."[24] All the OT promises (promissiones) "really have no relevance for us"[25] except the timeless basic-promise (promissum) "I am the Lord your God."[26] He completely abandons the proof from prophecy as unacceptable to our historical consciousness. Beyond this Baumgärtel sees the meaning of the OT only in that its frustrated "salvation-disaster history" exemplifies the way of man under law. As such the OT contains a "witness of a religion outside the Gospel."[27] "Viewed historically it has another place than the Christian religion."[28] Here Baumgärtel comes close to the position of Bultmann in relating the Testaments to each other in terms of the Lutheran law/gospel dichotomy.[29] Baumgärtel, therefore, maintains that the historicity of Jesus Christ is not grounded in the OT but solely in the Incarnation.[30] One comes to recognize how in such an approach "the historicity of Jesus Christ falls when the history of Israel falls."[31] C.

[21]P. 107.

[22]Pannenberg, "Redemptive Event and History," EOTH, pp. 325f.

[23]F. Baumgärtel, Verheissung. Zur Frage des evangelischen Verständnisses des Alten Testaments (Gütersloh, 1952), p. 92.

[24]F. Baumgärtel, "The Hermeneutical Problem of the OT," EOTH, p. 151.

[25]P. 132.

[26]P. 151.

[27]P. 156.

[28]P. 135; cf. ThLZ, 86 (1961), 806.

[29]EOTH, p. 145.

[30]P. 156.

[31]Pannenberg, EOTH, p. 326.

Westermann points out that Baumgärtel ultimately admits "that the church could also live without the Old Testament."[32] Von Rad attacks the unhistorical concept of "basic promise" by characterizing the separation of such a single promise from particular historically realized promises and prophecies as a "presumptuous encroachment."[33] L. Schmidt has recently taken pains to unravel the issues in the relationship between OT and NT in the lengthy debate between von Rad and Baumgärtel[34] and concludes that Baumgärtel's concept of "basic-promise" is inadequate.[35]

Baumgärtel's former student Franz Hesse makes the same basic reduction of the manifold promises to the single basic-promise.[36] In the OT the promises failed. This is due to the chastening hand of God that made Israel harden their hearts. By turning God's word into its opposite, it is a warning and a dialectical witness to God's activity in Israel which culminates in Christ's cross.[37] Hesse pronounces the sharpest theological strictures on the OT on the ground that certain historical data supposedly do not fit the facts.[38] Therefore the OT can have meaning for the Christian only in pointing him toward the salvation which is found in the NT.[39] The criticisms against Baumgärtel apply also to Hesse. It will not do, as happened again and again in the case of F. D. E. Schleiermacher[40] and still happens with

[32]"Remarks on the Theses of Bultmann and Baumgärtel," *EOTH,* p. 133.

[33]"Verheissung," *EvTh,* 13 (1953), 410. See also the incisive criticism by Gunneweg, *ZThK* 65 (1968), 398-400.

[34]L. Schmidt, "Die Einheit zwischen Alten und Neuen Testament im Streit zwischen Friedrich Baumgärtel und Gerhard von Rad," *EvTh* 35 (1975), 119-138.

[35]Esp. pp. 135f.

[36]*Das AT als Buch der Kirche,* p. 82.

[37]"The Evaluation and Authority of the OT Texts," *EOTH,* pp. 308-313.

[38]Pp. 293-299.

[39]P. 313.

[40]*The Christian Faith* (2 vols.; New York, 1963).

Baumgärtel[41] and Hesse,[42] to discuss the NT arguments of fulfillment of prophecy as nothing but an anti-Jewish apologetic, relevant only to the NT period.[43] It is a mistake to believe, as Bultmann does, that the meaning of the "proof from Scripture" has as its purpose to "prove" what can only be grasped by faith, or to approach and criticize the NT's method of quotation from the point of view of modern literary criticism.[44] Over against this limited position one must maintain that the NT quotations presuppose the unity of tradition and indicate keywords and major motifs and concepts in order to recall a larger context within the OT.

2. *Underemphasis of NT — Overemphasis of OT.* At the opposite end of the spectrum are attempts that posit a disunity or discontinuity between the Testaments by overemphasizing the OT at the expense of the NT. Some scholars make the OT all-important theologically and historically. The late Dutch dogmatician A. A. van Ruler attempted to put the OT on a superior level to the NT as regards Christian thought and teaching. Van Ruler's thesis is summed up in these sentences: "The Old Testament is and remains the true Bible."[45] The NT is but "its explanatory glossary *[Wörterverzeichnis]*."[46] In strict dialectic "the New Testament interprets the Old Testament as well as the Old the New."[47] The central concern in the whole Bible is not reconciliation and redemption but the kingdom of God. For this the OT is of special importance; it brings legitimization, foundation, interpretation, illustration, historicization, and eschatologization.[48] Van Ruler thereby reduces the relationship between the Testaments to the single spiritual

[41]*Verheissung,* pp. 75ff.
[42]*Das AT als Buch der Kirche,* pp. 82ff.
[43]Pannenberg, *EOTH,* p. 324.
[44]Bultmann, *EOTH,* pp. 50-55, 72-75.
[45]Van Ruler, *The Christian Church and the OT,* p. 72.
[46]P. 74 n. 45.
[47]P. 82.
[48]Pp. 75-98.

denominator of the kingdom of God,[49] reading the NT
very one-sidedly without recognizing the distinction between theocracy and eschatology.[50]

In view of the superiority given to the OT by van
Ruler, it is in place to consider a chief point in van
Ruler's argument. In the second chapter the following
question is treated: Does the OT itself already see
Christ? In dealing with this question van Ruler is essentially critical in nature. Prominence is given to that
which emphasizes discontinuity between the Testaments. One of the main points is that in the OT the
Messiah is a man, in the NT, God Himself; hence the
deity of Christ cannot be derived from the former.[51]
One of the key notions of the whole book is summed
up in the following statement: "If I may put it briefly
and sharply, Jesus Christ is an emergency measure that
God postponed as long as possible (cf. Mt. 21:33-46).
Hence we must not try to find him fully in the Old
Testament, even though as Christian theologians we
investigate the Old Testament in orientation to God."[52]
J. J. Stamm has pointed out that van Ruler relates the
OT facts inaccurately and inappropriately for the sake
of contrast.[53] It is correct that van Ruler takes account
only of the nature of the Israelite king and not at the
same time of the authoritative position connected with
his office. If one also takes the authoritative nature of the
office into consideration, "then one can certainly only
say that in the OT and NT the Messiah is divine, there,
per adoptionem, here, *ex origine*."[54] Van Ruler has not
found any followers in calling Jesus merely "an emergency measure of God."

Another Dutch systematic theologian who has the

[49]Pp. 95-98.
[50]See Th. C. Vriezen, "Theocracy and Soteriology," *EOTH*, pp.
221-223.
[51]Van Ruler, *The Christian Church and the OT*, pp. 51f.
[52]P. 69.
[53]J. J. Stamm, "Jesus Christ in the Old Testament," *EOTH*, pp.
200-210.
[54]P. 208.

tendency to make the OT all-important is K. H. Miskotte.[55] Although he contrasts the OT with the NT by
such schemata as Law/Gospel, shadow/reality, and
promise/fulfillment, he maintains that the OT contains
a "surplus" over against the NT. The "surplus" of the
OT comes to expression in four points on which the NT
is practically silent: skepticism, revolt, erotics, and
politics. Although OT piety and ethics contain elements
of joy of living, of appreciation of earthly goods, which
seem most attractive to modern man, Christian ethics
that would simply set up the various aspects of theocracy or marriage customs of the OT as the standard
to which the modern world or the church would have
to conform without first confronting them with the cross
of Christ would fail signally in its duty. We can agree
with the statement by Th. C. Vriezen that "the Cross
is not merely an element of the Biblical message, but
a source of light in the centre which casts its grace
over all the other elements. . . ."[56]

The Reformed biblical scholar W. Vischer stands out
among biblical theologians for his adoption of a thoroughgoing Christological approach to the OT.[57] He
claims that the Bible, including the OT, must be interpreted in the light of its true intention, its true theme.
That true theme is Christ: "The Bible is the Holy Scripture only insofar as it speaks of Christ Jesus."[58] Vischer,
therefore, reads the OT for its witness to Christ. He
finds that it testifies everywhere of Christ — not in the
sense, to be sure, that He is directly to be found in the
OT, but in the sense that the OT in all its parts points
to Him and His crucifixion. He explains that the OT
tells us *what* Christ is and the NT *who* He is.[59] If we
do not understand what the Christ of the OT is, we

[55]K. H. Miskotte, *When the Gods are Silent* (New York, 1967).
[56]Th. C. Vriezen, *An Outline of Old Testament Theology* (2nd ed.;
Newton, Mass., 1970), p. 98.
[57]W. Vischer, *The Witness of the OT to Christ,* 2 vols. (Philadelphia, 1949).
[58]Vol. I, p. 14.
[59]P. 7.

shall never recognize and confess Jesus as the Christ.[60]

On the basis of these principles Vischer provides interpretations of the OT that are fully Christological. He claims that the OT as a whole not only points to Christ and testifies of Christ, but in each smallest detail the Christian eye may recognize Christ. "We do not understand a single word in the whole Bible if we do not find Jesus Christ in this word."[61] The words "Let there be light" (Gen. 1:3) refer to the "glory of God in the face of Christ."[62] The sign of Cain in Genesis 4:15 is the cross.[63] The patriarch Enoch and his ascension point to Jesus' ascension and prior resurrection.[64] The prophecy that Japheth would "dwell in the tents of Shem" is fulfilled in the church of both Gentiles and Jews.[65] Speaking of the midnight Presence with whom Jacob wrestled at the Jabbok (Gen. 32), Vischer asks who this person was and answers that it was Jesus Christ.[66]

Vischer has been the target of a great deal of criticism, even unjust and scornful criticism. He feels that a purely historical exegesis of the OT is not enough, for that would leave the OT a document of an ancient religion of little apparent relevance for the Christian. Vischer is known as an extremely competent scholar who insists upon a historical and philological approach to the Bible.[67] There is much in Vischer's approach that is of great value and should not be rejected too easily. As the same time Vischer gives the impression that he has overstepped some limitations of his approach. He writes, "The life-story of all these men [of the OT] are part of His [Jesus'] life-story. Therefore, they are written with

[60]Pp. 12, 26.

[61]Vischer as cited by W. Hertzberg, *ThLZ* 4 (1949), 221.

[62]Vischer, *The Witness of the OT to Christ,* I, 44.

[63]Pp. 75f.

[64]Pp. 87f.

[65]Pp. 104f.

[66]P. 153.

[67]Vischer's exegetical methodology is recently set forth very clearly in his "La methode de l'exegese biblique," *Revue de theologie et de philosophie* 10 (1960), 109-123.

so little biographical interest for the individual persons. What is written about them is actually written as a part of the biography of the One through whom and toward whom they live."[68] It seems that Vischer would feel in a position to reconstruct a biography of Jesus from the OT. If this were possible, it would be difficult to perceive why the OT speaks in the first place about Abraham, Moses, etc. Why does it not speak right away about Jesus? Would it speak of Him only in such mysterious form? Vischer read the OT consistently from the side of the NT. Does he deprive thereby the OT's own distinctive witness? Is there not also a current of life flowing from the OT to the NT? Nevertheless, we can agree with John Bright that "Vischer certainly deserves thanks for being among the first to remind us that we cannot rest content with a purely historical understanding of the OT but must press on to see it in its Christian significance."[69]

The tendency toward Marcionism with its emphasis on discontinuity and disunity between the Testaments is present in full-fledged form in A. Harnack who called for this dismissal of the OT, and in Friedrich Delitzsch for whom the OT was an unchristian book. An attenuated Marcionist strain is manifested by E. Hirsch for whom the Testaments stand in "antithetical tension" to each other, and to a lesser extent by Bultmann, Baumgärtel, and Hesse.[70] The opposite extreme makes the OT all-important historically and theologically for the Christian. It appears in a variety of forms in van Ruler, Miskotte, and Vischer. In other words, on one side of

[68]W. Vischer, *Die Bedeutung des AT für das christliche Leben* (Zurich, 1947), p. 5.

[69]Bright, *The Authority of the OT*, p. 88.

[70]The following studies criticize this position from rather different perspectives: U. Mauser, *Gottesbild und Menschwerdung. Eine Untersuchung zur Einheit des Alten und Neuen Testaments* (Tübingen, 1971); G. Siegwalt, *Le Loi, chemin du Salut. Étude sur la signification de la loi de l'AT* (Neuchâtel, 1971); W. Zimmerli, *Die Weltlichkeit des AT* (Göttingen, 1971); J. D. Smart, *The Strange Silence of the Bible in the Church* (London, 1970); J. Bright, *The Authority of the OT* (Nashville, 1967), pp. 58-79.

the spectrum are those who stress diversity between the Testaments to such a degree that there is total disunity and complete discontinuity between OT and NT, while on the other side are those that overemphasize the OT and relegate the NT to a less important position. The Christological-theocratic emphases of van Ruler and Vischer, for example, pose special difficulties because they telescope and virtually eliminate the varieties of the Biblical testimonies. They suffer from a reductionism of the multiplicity of OT thought, which merely becomes a pale reflection of the Messiah to come. Here the somewhat shrill cry of "Christomonism"[71] has a point. G. E. Wright, J. Barr, and R. E. Murphy[72] emphasize a Trinitarian approach that meets the needs of delineating the relationship between the Testaments better. This approach preserves the *sensus litteralis* of the OT testimony and avoids the development of a hermeneutical method based merely on the NT usage of OT texts. Once the true meaning of Christ is grasped within the context of the Trinity, then one can say that Christ is the destination and at the same time the guide to the true understanding of the OT. W. Vischer once posed the question that remains crucial: "Is the interpretation which reads the whole OT as a witness for the Messiah Jesus correct or does it violate the OT writings?"[73] L. Goppelt has put his finger on the crucial

[71]Wright, *The OT and Theology*, pp. 13-38. He protests against resolving the tension between the OT and NT in terms of a "new kind of monotheism based on Christ" ("Historical Knowledge and Revelation," *Understanding and Translating the OT*, p. 302).

[72]Wright, *Understanding and Translating the OT*, pp. 301-303; Barr, *Old and New in Interpretation*, pp. 151-154; Murphy, *Theology Digest* (1970), p. 327.

[73]*Christuszeugnis*, p. 32. Of course, Vischer gives an affirmative answer to the question. He designates Jesus as the "hidden meaning of the OT writings" (p. 33). In his book *Die Bedeutung des AT für das christliche Leben* (Zürich, 1947), p. 5, he writes: "All movements of life of which the OT reports move from him [Jesus] and towards him. The life-stories of all these men are part of his life-story. Therefore they are written with so little biographical interest for the individual persons. What is written about them is actually written as a part of the biography of the One through whom and towards

spot in pointing out that "the theme of Christ and the Old Testament . . . is a key question for theology as a whole."[74] No Christian theologian can avoid that question.

B. Patterns of Unity and Continuity

At the beginning of our discussion we raised the question of whether we ought to read uniquely from the OT to the NT or from the NT back to the OT, or reciprocally from the OT to the NT and from the NT to the OT. A number of well-known theologians have addressed themselves to this question. As examples we may refer to H. H. Rowley who reminds us that "the Old Testament continually looks forward to something beyond itself; the New Testament continually looks back to the Old."[75] Two of the most famous Old Testament theologians of this century have maintained that both Testaments shed light upon each other in their mutual relations. W. Eichrodt declares, "In addition to this historical movement from the Old Testament to the New there is a current of life flowing in reverse direction from the New Testament to the Old. This reverse relationship also elucidates the full significance of the realm of Old Testament thought."[76] In similar vein G. von Rad emphasizes that the larger context of the OT is the NT and vice versa.[77] H. W. Wolff sug-

---

whom they live." This would mean that we can reconstruct a biography of Jesus from the OT. If Vischer's position were correct, it is difficult to perceive why the OT speaks in the first place about Abraham and Moses. Why does it not speak right away about Jesus, and why does it speak of him only in such "hidden" form?

[74]L. Goppelt, *Theologie des NT* (Göttingen, 1976), II, 388.

[75]H. H. Rowley, *The Unity of the Bible,* p. 95.

[76]W. Eichrodt, *Theology of the Old Testament* (Philadelphia, 1961), I, 26.

[77]G. von Rad, *Old Testament Theology* (Edinburgh, 1965), II, 369 (hereafter cited as OTT): "The larger context into which we have to set the Old Testament phenomena if they are to be meaningfully appreciated is not, however, a general system of religious and ideal values, but the compass of a specific history, which was

gests that "the total meaning of the Old Testament" is "revealed in the New Testament."[78] These scholars point to a reciprocal relationship between the Testaments. H. H. Rowley reminds us that "there is a fundamental unity so that with all their diversity they [the Testaments] belong so intimately together that the New Testament cannot be understood without the Old and *neither can the Old Testament be fully understood without the New*."[79] It is clear that the emphasis of these theologians is placed upon the internal keys which unlock both Testaments. The OT gives a torso-like appearance without the NT and the NT has no foundation without the OT.[80]

It is not our purpose to provide a comprehensive sketch of the various lines of connection to which Bib-

---

set in motion by God's words and deeds and which, as the New Testament sees it, finds its goal in the coming of Christ. Only in this event is there any point in looking for what is analogous and comparable. And it is only in this way of looking at the OT and the New Testaments that the correspondences and analogies between the two appear in their proper light."

[78]H. W. Wolff, "The Hermeneutics of the Old Testament," *EOTH*, p. 181.

[79]Rowley, *The Unity of the Bible*, p. 94 (italics his).

[80]Among the studies relating to the subject of the unity of the Testaments the following make a special contribution in addition to the ones cited in footnotes 2 and 70 of this chapter: A. J. B. Higgins, *The Christian Significance of the OT* (London, 1949); P. Auvray et al., *L'AT et les chrétiens* (Paris, 1951); F. V. Filson, "The Unity of the OT and the NT: A Bibliographical Survey," *Interpretation* 5 (1951), 134-152; H. H. Rowley, *The Unity of the Bible* (London, 1953); D. E. Nineham, ed., *The Church's Use of the Bible* (London, 1963); H. Seebass, "Der Beitrag des AT zum Entwurf einer biblischen Theologie," *Wort und Dienst* 8 (1965), 20-49; H. Cazelles, "The Unity of the Bible and the People of God," *Scripture* 18 (1966), 1-10; F. N. Jasper, "The Relation of the OT to the New," *Expository Times* 78 (1967/68), 228-232, 267-270; F. Lang, "Christuszeugnis und Biblische Theologie," *EvTh* 29 (1969), 523-534; A. H. van Zyl, "The Relation between OT and NT," *Hermeneutica* (1970), 9-22; M. Kuske, *Das AT als Buch von Christus* (Göttingen, 1971); S. Sidel, "Das Alte und das NT, Ihre Verschiedenheit und Einheit," *Tübinger Praktische Quartalschrift*, 119 (1971), 314-324; J. Wenham, *Christ and the Bible* (Chicago, 1972); F. F. Bruce, *The NT Development of OT Themes* (Grand Rapids, Mich., 1973); Harrington, *The Path of Biblical Theology* (Dublin, 1974), pp. 260-336.

lical scholars have pointed in recent discussions. We will limit ourselves to patterns of unity within diversity which in our opinion are the most outstanding and most promising in recent scholarly discussions. All of these reflect an essential reciprocity between the Testaments.

1. *Historical Connection.* As they attempt to come to grips with the question of the unity between both Testaments, scholars customarily emphasize the historical nature of the essential story of the Bible. The common mark of both the OT and the NT is the continuous history of God's people. The OT is viewed as the historical preparation of the NT. History is prominent in the Bible. The primary interest in the Bible is God's action on behalf of the redemption of His people and the nations. Thus the unity between the OT and the NT results from the fact that the Bible is concerned "throughout with God and with His dealings with mankind"[81] by one and the same triune God who is present and active in the history of ancient Israel, in Jesus Christ, and in the Spirit-led life and witness of the NT church.

For ancient Israel this history is the encounter with her God. "The very idea that history is a process with beginning, middle, and end is original with Israel."[82] It is the purpose and will of God that unifies the historical process. The historical career of Israel is directed by the will of God to fulfill His designs. These designs are ever more clearly unfolded during OT and NT times. Spiritual Israel stands in a direct line of continuity with literal Israel in that the former is connected with the latter and shares in the same aims and goals.

2. *Scriptural Dependence.* One of the theological connections between the OT and the NT is the quotations in the NT from OT passages. Various theologians refer

81F. V. Filson, "The Unity Between the Testaments," *The Interpreter's One-Volume Commentary on the Bible* (Nashville, 1971), p. 992.

82J. L. McKenzie, "Aspects of Old Testament Thought," *The Jerome Biblical Commentary*, eds. R. E. Brown, J. A. Fitzmyer, and R. E. Murphy (Englewood Cliffs, N.J., 1968), p. 755.

to this connection as "Scriptural proof."[83] It has been recently emphasized that "the idea of proof is of importance because the quotations are placed in the context of an argument and referred to as part of the promulgation of the Gospel."[84] The fact and number of these quotations can easily be assessed by turning to the pages of Nestle-Aland's Greek NT which marks 257 passages as being explicit citations.[85]

From the modern historical-critical point of view some of these quotations are not in accordance with a seemingly recovered meaning of the OT texts. This has been raised as a serious objection against seeing a legitimate line of connection between the Testaments in their references to each other. Certainly the NT quotations of the OT call for thorough investigation. It is difficult to accept the idea of an arbitrary Scriptural reference just for the sake of obtaining material for illustrations.[86] We cannot agree with Bultmann that the use of the OT can be best explained as a projection of the convictions of the NT writers.[87] The solution according to which the NT's use of the OT can be explained in terms of the accommodation to the technique and method of contemporary, rabbinical methods of exegesis is helpful only to a limited degree.[88] This point of view does not distinguish between the aim and scope of the rabbinical

[83]On the whole, see R. T. France, *Jesus and the Old Testament* (London, 1971).

[84]Verhoef, "The Relationship Between the Old and the New Testaments," p. 282.

[85]R. Nicole, "New Testament Views of the Old Testament," *Revelation and the Bible*, ed. C. F. H. Henry (1958), p. 137, counts at least 295 separate references of which 224 are direct citations introduced by a certain definite formula. K. Grobel, "Quotations," *IDB* (Nashville, 1962), III, 977, writes that the OT "is explicitly quoted some 150 times and tacitly quoted some 1,100 additional times."

[86]Hesse, *Das Alte Testament als Buch der Kirche*, p. 38.

[87]R. Bultmann, "Prophecy and Fulfillment," *EOTH*, pp. 50-75, which has been criticized by C. Westermann, *EOTH*, pp. 124-128.

[88]E. E. Ellis, *Paul's Use of the Old Testament* (Grand Rapids, Mich., 1957), p. 143; see the detailed study of R. Longenecker, *Biblical Exegesis in the Apostolic Period* (Grand Rapids, Mich., 1975).

and Qumran exegesis on the one hand,[89] and the unique perspective of the NT usage of the OT on the other hand. P. A. Verhoef has pointed out that "over and against critical views we maintain that the New Testament in citing the Old Testament nowhere presupposes a fundamental breach between the Testaments."[90] This is in full correspondence with the acceptance of the canon of both Testaments in the Christian church. It is true that the references to the OT were not made in a systematic manner, but this does not diminish the significance of an extensive procedure of quotation.

3. *Vocabulary.* Another line of connection between the Testaments is found in the relation of the vocabulary or words of the Bible.[91] Jesus and the apostles used familiar terms. To put it differently, the theological language that Jesus and the apostles used was the language known to them and to their listeners. This theologically impregnated language was the product of a long tradition. "Without a background of the OT and Israelite faith, the message of Jesus would have been unintelligible." It is widely recognized that "almost every key theological word of the New Testament is derived from some Hebrew word that had a long history of use and development in the Old Testament."[92]

Scholarship has given much attention to the investigation of the background of the words of the NT and their roots in the OT.[93] There are various ways in which

[89]F. F. Bruce, *Biblical Exegesis in the Qumran Texts* (Grand Rapids, Mich., 1959), pp. 66-77; R. H. Gundry, *The Use of the Old Testament in St. Matthew's Gospel* (Leiden, 1967); J. A. Fitzmyer, "The Use of Explicit Old Testament Quotations in Qumran and in the New Testament," *NTS* 7 (1960-61), 297-333.

[90]Verhoef, "The Relationship Between the Old and New Testament," p. 284.

[91]This is particularly stressed by J. L. McKenzie, "Aspects of OT Thought," *The Jerome Biblical Commentary*, eds. R. E. Brown, *et al.* (Englewood Cliffs, N.J., 1968), p. 767.

[92]Ibid.

[93]G. R. Kittel and G. Friedrich, eds., *Theological Dictionary of the New Testament* (1962-1975), 8 vols.; L. Coenen *et al.*, eds., *Theologisches Begriffslexikon zum Neuen Testament* (3rd ed.; Wuppertal, 1972), 3 vols.; X. Leon-Dufour, *Dictionary of Biblical Theology* (New

words appear. Ultimately each individual context determines the meaning in this context. Nevertheless the variety of usages of single words sheds much light upon the semantic ranges of meaning. There is scarcely any key word of the OT that has not been enriched in the NT. While we are aware that different meanings are expressed by the same word, there is not one word for each distinct idea or theme. We will have to apprehend the connecting line between the "Greek words and their Hebrew meanings,"[94] i.e., between the OT and the NT.

4. *Themes.* J. Bright has assessed the unity of basic theological themes of the OT and the NT in the following way: "Each of the major themes of the Old has its correspondent in the New, and is in some way resumed and answered there."[95] By virtue of this fact a hermeneutical bridge is built between the Testaments which gives us access to each of the OT's texts and defines for us the procedure that we must follow in attempting to interpret them in their Christian significance.

It is impossible to provide a list of the many themes that connect the two Testaments.[96] One thinks immediately of creation, promise, faith, election, righteousness, love, sin, forgiveness, judgment, salvation, eschatology, messianism, people of God, remnant, and many others. One of the themes that has recently been stressed as giving expression to the relationship between the Testaments is the covenant.[97] But even the covenant theme as a single theme cannot hold the golden key which

---

York, 1968); C. Brown, ed., *The New International Dictionary of New Testament Theology* (1975-78), 3 vols.

[94]D. Hill, *Greek Words and Hebrew Meanings: Studies in the Semantics of Soteriological Terms* (London, 1967); J. Barr, *The Semantics of Biblical Language* (London, 1961); idem, *Biblical Words for Time* (London, 1962).

[95]Bright, *The Authority of the OT*, p. 211.

[96]J. Guillet, *Themes of the Bible* (South Bend, Ind., 1960); F. F. Bruce, *New Testament Development of Old Testament Themes* (Grand Rapids, Mich., 1969).

[97]Fensham, "The Covenant as Giving Expression to the Relationship between Old and New Testament," pp. 86-94.

unlocks all the mysteries of the relation between the Testaments.

5. *Typology*. A prominent way of relating the two Testaments to each other is to study persons, institutions, or events in the OT in their typological relationship to the NT.[98] In such a perspective the types described in the OT are regarded as models or prefigurations of persons, institutions, or events in the NT. Typology develops along horizontal and vertical lines.[99]

The discussion on typology received new inpetus by W. Eichrodt[100] and G. von Rad.[101] Eichrodt uses typology "as the designation for a peculiar way of looking at history." The types "are persons, institutions, and events of the Old Testament which are regarded as divinely established models or prerepresentations of corresponding realities in the New Testament salvation history."[102] His exposition appears to agree with the traditional views of earlier Christianity. But he differs from the views of von Rad, whose basic premise is that "the

[98]Among the key literature on the subject of typology are the following: L. Goppelt, *Typos: Die typologische Deutung des Alten Testaments* (2nd ed.; Darmstadt, 1966); idem, "Typos," *Theological Dictionary of the New Testament* 8 (1972), 246-259; A. Schulz, *Nachfolgen und Nachahmen* (Munich, 1962), pp. 309-331; Ellis, *Paul's Use of the OT*, pp. 126-139; Larcher, *L'actualité chret. de l'AT*, pp. 489-513; G. W. H. Lampe and J. J. Woolcombe, *Essays on Typology* (London, 1957); P. Fairbairn, *The Typology of Scripture* (Grand Rapids, Mich., n.d.); W. Eichrodt, "Is Typological Exegesis an Appropriate Method?" *EOTH*, pp. 224-245; G. von Rad "Typological Interpretation of the Old Testament," *EOTH*, pp. 17-39; idem, *Old Testament Theology*, II, 364-374; P. A. Verhoef, "Some Notes on Typological Exegesis," *New Light on Some OT Problems* (Praetoria, 1962), pp. 58-63; H. D. Hummel, "The OT Basis of Typological Interpretation," *Biblical Research* 9 (1964), 38-50; J. H. Stek, "Biblical Typology Yesterday and Today," *Calvin Theological Journal* 5 (1970), 133-162; N. H. Ridderbos, "Typologie," *Vox Theologica* 31 (1960/61), 149-159.

[99]Hummel, "The OT Basis of Typological Interpretation," pp. 40-50.

[100]"Is Typological Exegesis an Appropriate Method?" *EOTH*, pp. 224-245.

[101]"Typological Interpretation of the NT," *EOTH*, pp. 17-39; *OTT*, II, 364-374.

[102]*EOTH*, p. 225.

Old Testament is a history book."[103] It is the history of God's people, and the institutions and prophecies within it, that provide prototypes to the antitypes of the NT within the whole realm of history and eschatology.[104] Von Rad is very broadly based, as can be gathered from his relating Joseph to Christ as type to antitype.[105]

Some scholars reject the typological approach completely.[106] However, the importance of the typological approach is not to be denied, if it is not developed into a hermeneutic method which is applied to all texts like a divining-rod. Typological correspondence must be rigidly controlled on the basis of direct relationship between various OT elements and their NT counterparts in order that arbitrary and fortuitous personal views may not creep into exegesis.[107] One should be cautious enough not to be trapped into applying typology as *the* single definite theological ground-plan whereby the unity of the Testaments is established. The advocacy of typological unity between the Testaments is not primarily concerned to find a unity of historical facts between the OT prefiguration and its NT counterpart,[108] though this is not to be denied altogether; it is more

[103]*EOTH,* p. 25; cf. *OTT,* II, 357.

[104]*OTT,* II, 365.

[105]*OTT,* II, 372.

[106]F. Baumgärtel, *ThLZ* 86 (1961), 809-897, 901-906. R. Lucas, "Considerations of Method in OT Hermeneutics," *The Dunwoodie Review* 6 (1966), 35: "Typology lacks that criterion which would establish both its limitation and validity. . . . It is a theology of biblical texts. It leaves the Old Testament behind, in the last analysis, and discovers its significance outside and beyond its historical testimony." Murphy, *Theology Digest* 18 (1970), 324, believes that typology is not creative enough for the possibilities of theology and in comparison to the early Church "it is simply less appealing to the modern temper." See also Barr, *Old and New in Interpretation,* pp. 103-148, who is not willing to separate typology from allegory.

[107]See also, with regard to a proper use of typology, the remarks by H. W. Wolff, "The Hermeneutics of the OT," *EOTH,* pp. 181-186; and Vriezen, *An Outline of OT Theology,* pp. 97, 136f.

[108]Von Rad, *EOTH,* pp. 17-19, advocates that the typological approach seeks to "regain reference to the facts attested in the New Testament," i.e., to discover the connection in the historical process.

concerned to recognize the connection in terms of a structural similarity between type and antitype. It is undeniable that the typological analogy begins with a relationship which takes place in history. For example, the typological analogy between Moses and Christ in 2 Corinthians 3:7ff. and Hebrews 3:1-6 begins with a relationship that takes place in history; but the concern is not with all the details of the life and service of Moses, but primarily with his "ministry" and "glory" in the former passage and with his "faithfulness" as leader and mediator in the divine dispensation in the second passage. It is equally true that the NT antitype goes beyond the OT type.[109] Even if it is correct, at least to some degree, that the course of history which unites type and antitype emphasizes the distinction between them, while the connection is primarily discovered in its structural analogy and correspondence, this should not be used as an argument against typology unless typology is seen only in terms of a historical process.[110] The conceptual means of the typological correspondence has its distinct place in its expression of the qualification of the Christ-event, but it is in itself not able to express fully the Christ-event in terms of OT history. Therefore additional approaches will need to complement the typological one. The Bible is too rich in relations between

[109]Eichrodt, *EOTH*, pp. 225f.

[110]This is where Pannenberg, *EOTH*, p. 327, goes astray. For him the only analogy that has any value is the historical one. Pannenberg adopts the "promise and fulfillment" schema without realizing that this "structure" (p. 325), as he repeatedly calls it, functions in his own presentation as another instance of a timeless principle being employed to replace history. Pannenberg emphasizes that freeness, creativeness, and unpredictability are central in history, but he finds this central aspect of history preserved only in that the fulfillment often involves the "breaking down" of the prophecy as a "legitimate interpretation," a "transformation of the content of prophecy," which is "fulfilled otherwise" than the original recipients of the prophetic word expected (p. 326). Here Pannenberg has unconsciously conceded the incompatibility between history and its structure. Thus even in Pannenberg's position, structure and construction tend to replace history and render his use of the promise-fulfillment structure unhistorical.

God and man for it to be confined to one special connection. Whereas we must hesitate to accept typological references in definite cases, every attempt to view the whole from a single point of view must beware of wishing to explain every detail in terms of this one aspect and to impose an overall picture upon the variety of possible relations. While the OT context must be preserved in its prefiguration so that NT meanings are not read into the OT texts, it seems that a clear NT indication is necessary so that subjective imaginative fancies and arbitrary typological analogies can be avoided. That is to say that the question of the *a posteriori* character of the typological approach should not be suppressed.

6. *Promise-Fulfillment*. An extremely significant pattern of continuity between the Testaments is the promise-fulfillment schema. This schema has received special attention by C. Westermann, W. Zimmerli, G. von Rad, and others.[111] In this way the fulfillment has an open end, looking on to the future.[112] This eschatological aspect is present in both Testaments. Westermann remarks: "Promise and fulfillment constitute an integral event which is reported in both the Old and New Testaments of the Bible." In view of the multiplex character of the relationship between the Testaments, Westermann admits that under the single idea of promise-fulfillment "it is not possible to sum up everything in the relation of the Old Testament to Christ."[113] On a more comprehensive scale, we must admit that the promise-fulfillment schema does not sum up everything

[111] C. Westermann, "The Way of Promise through the OT," *OTCF*, pp. 200-224; *The OT and Jesus Christ* (Minneapolis, 1970); W. Zimmerli, "Promise and Fulfillment," *EOTH*, pp. 89-122; G. von Rad, "Verheissung," *EvTh* 13 (1953), 406-413; R. E. Murphy, "The Relationship Between the Testaments," *CBQ* 26 (1964), 349-359; idem, "Christian Understanding of the OT," *Theology Digest* 18 (1970), 321-332.

[112] This tension between promise and fulfillment is a dynamic characteristic of the OT. Since this is a basic kind of interpreted history which the OT and NT themselves present to us, J. M. Robinson's attempt (*OTCF*, p. 129) to dismiss the category of promise-fulfillment as a structure imposed on Biblical history from without is abortive.

[113] *The OT and Jesus Christ*, p. 78.

in the relation between the Testaments. As fundamental and fruitful as the promise-fulfillment approach is, it is not by itself able to describe the multiplex nature of the relationship between the Testaments.

If we raise the question how the OT can be related adequately and properly to the NT, we have admittedly decided on an *a priori* basis that both are related to each other in some way. We must be conscious of this decision, which always has a bearing on our questioning of the OT materials. This prior decision does not come easy. This is true especially when the OT is viewed in the way in which von Rad looks at it, namely that "the Old Testament can only be read as a book of ever increasing anticipation."[114] This claim presupposes a particular understanding of the OT history of tradition, that is, one which is from the beginning focusing upon the transition to the NT. Von Rad's view finds its justification only in terms of a direct line of connection that moves from the testimony of the initial action of God toward judgment and on to the expectation of God's renewed action in which God yet proves his divine character. It is amazing to see how Israel never allowed a promise to come to nothing, how she thus swelled Yahweh's promise to an infinity, and how, placing absolutely no limit on God's power yet to fulfill, she transmitted the promises still unfulfilled to generations to come. Thus we must ask with von Rad, "does not the way in which comparative religion takes hold of the Old Testament in abstraction, as an object which can be adequately interpreted without reference to the New Testament, turn out to be fictitious from the Christian point of view?"[115] On the other hand, there is nothing mysterious about coming to grips with the question of the relationship between the Testaments. Initially, therefore, we do not begin from the NT and its manifold references to the OT. This method has often been

[114]*OTT*, II, 319.
[115]*OTT*, II, 321.

adopted, most recently again by B. S. Childs as we have noted above. It has also led all too often to contrasting the Testaments with a sharpness that does not do justice to the great hermeneutical flexibility of the relationship between them. A proper method will then initially be an attempt to show characteristic ways in which the OT leads forward to the NT. The NT can then on the basis of this initial approach also enlighten the content of the OT.

7. *Salvation History*. Several of the unifying patterns between the Testaments cannot be separated from the pattern of salvation history[116] of which we have spoken frequently in previous chapters. We have had occasion to indicate that even salvation history is not *the* one golden key which unlocks all the mysteries in the relationship of the Testaments. Salvation history is not to be dismissed out of hand,[117] because "the NT affirmation that Jesus is the Messiah implies the unity of history under a single divine plan of salvation."[118] Salvation history points to a unity of perspective.[119]

8. *Unity of Perspective*. Many eminent scholars agree that there is a perspective pointing to the future that unites the OT and NT. Th. C. Vriezen puts it this way: "The true heart of both Old Testament and New Testament is, therefore, the eschatological perspective."[120] H. H. Rowley writes as follows: "The full consummation of the hopes of the Old Testament lie still in the distant future, . . . nor does the New Testament fail to perceive this. . . . It still places the final glory in the future."[121] Just as did the OT believer, so the believer in

[116]See the NT theologies referred to under the heading "Salvation History Approaches" in Chapter 2, pp. 106-125.

[117]So D. Braun, "Heil als Geschichte," *EvTh* 27 (1967), 57-76. For an appreciative evaluation of salvation history, see Kraus, *Biblische Theologie,* pp. 185-187.

[118]McKenzie, "Aspects of OT Thought," p. 766.

[119]See esp. Verhoef, "Relationship Between Old and New Testament," pp. 292f.

[120]Vriezen, *An Outline of Old Testament Theology,* p. 123.

[121]Rowley, *The Unity of the Bible,* pp. 109f.

Christ "comes to stand in a new way under an arc of tension between promise and fulfillment. . . ."[122] All supplication for fulfillment in the congregation of the New Covenant merges in the single plea, "Come, Lord Jesus!" (Rev. 22:20; 1 Cor. 16:22). Thus within the arc of promise and fulfillment God's redemptive purpose, His salvation history, unfolds itself from the OT to the NT and beyond to the end of time.

The OT does relate a history of salvation. But in many respects it is an unusual history of salvation, because it is a truncated history of salvation. The expected Messiah did not come in OT times. In this sense the OT is a book that is incomplete, pointing beyond itself, ending in a posture of waiting. Down to its very last page it speaks of a fulfillment of the promise in the future tense. The God who acted in creation, in the Exodus, and Conquest, guiding His people, will act again one day. The completion of this incomplete history of salvation is a primary concern of the NT. The turning point of all history has taken place in Jesus Christ. The God who acted in Israel's history has acted decisively in human history through Jesus Christ. This is the center of the NT's message. The NT completes the OT's incompleteness and yet moves beyond to the final *eschaton*. From the OT to the NT and beyond there is one continuous movement in the direction of the *eschaton*, the coming of the Day of the Lord. Indeed the entire history of revelation is one pilgrimage, looking forward to the City whose builder and maker is God (Heb. 11:10). On this pilgrimage there are many stops, many initial fulfillments, but each one of them becomes a point of departure again until all promises will finally be fulfilled at the end of time. It has been pointed out rightly that the NT contains also a futuristic eschatology. The predictions concerning the last days

[122]Zimmerli, *EOTH,* p. 114.

in the synoptic Gospels and the other writings of the
NT continue the expectation of the OT.[123]

The unity between the OT and NT is then also a
unity of its common perspective, plan, and purpose for
men and of God's ongoing action to realize these.[124] The
OT tells of the history of Israel in terms of salvation
history and prepares for and leads up to the coming of
Jesus as the Christ of Israel and the Saviour of all men.
It is certainly to be admitted that not everything in the
OT can be subsumed under the rubric of salvation history,[125] because it was a history that led on to Christ
and equally to the rejection of Christ. For the sake of
clarification it needs to be pointed out that we have in
the Bible not only the revelation of God, but also the
reaction of men. We must recognize that the reaction
of men is not normative and does not figure in the
whole scheme of the relationship between the Testaments. The "history" of the reaction of Israel and Judaism which led to the rejection of Christ could not have
been a part of the history of salvation.[126] Despite the
repeated frustrations of God's plan and purpose for men,
God still saw to it that the outstanding promises would
yet be realized through Him in the future. The whole
Bible then drives forward to the consummation of all
things in heaven and on earth. "This is the pervasive
theme of both Old and New Testaments."[127] The work
of Christ is continued in the work of the Holy Spirit and
will be completed in the consummation of all things.

In view of these considerations, it would seem that
the only adequate way to come to grips with the multiplex nature of the relationship between the Testaments
is to opt for a multiplex approach. Such a multiplex
approach leaves room for indicating the variety of connections between the Testaments and avoids, at the

[123]Verhoef, "Relationship Between Old and New Testament," p.
293.
[124]Filson, *The Interpreter's One-Volume Commentary*, p. 992.
[125]Bright, *The Authority of the OT*, p. 196.
[126]M. Meinertz, *Theologie des Neuen Testaments* (1950), I, 54.
[127]Verhoef, "Relationship Between Old and New Testament," p. 293.

same time, the temptation to explain the manifold testimonies in every detail by one single point of view or approach and so to impose a single structure upon testimonies that witness to something else. A multiplex approach will lead to a recognition of similarity and dissimilarity, old and new, continuity and discontinuity, etc., without in the least distorting the original historical witness and literal sense nor falling short in the larger kerygmatic intention and context to which the OT itself testifies and which the NT assumes.

It is not surprising that in the recent debate about the complex nature of the relationship between the Testaments the question of the proper context has become crucial. Von Rad himself speaks of "the larger context to which a specific Old Testament phenomenon belongs. . . ."[128] He reflects the concern of H. W. Wolff, who maintains that "in the New Testament is found the context of the Old, which, as its historical goal, reveals the total meaning of the Old Testament. . . ."[129] The systematic theologian Hermann Diem expresses himself to the extent that "for the modern interpretation of Scripture it can be no question needing judgment whether the interpretation will follow the apostolic witness and read the OT with their eyes or whether it will read presuppositionless, which would mean to read it as a phenomenon of general history of religion. . . ."[130] In a similar vein Kurt Frör maintains that "the canon forms the given and compulsory context for all single texts and single books of both Testaments."[131] The idea of "context" should not be limited to the nearest relationship of a pericope, not even to the connection within a book or historical work. With regard to the larger connections the canon as a given fact receives hermeneutic relevance. "The first step on the path of the continuation of the

[128]*OTT*, II, 369.

[129]*EOTH*, p. 181.

[130]H. Diem, *Theologie als kirchliche Wissenschaft* (Gütersloh, 1951), I, 75; cf. his *Was heisst schriftgemäss?* (Gütersloh, 1958), pp. 38f.

[131]*Biblische Hermeneutik* (3rd ed.; München, 1967), p. 65.

self-interpretation of the text is to give ear to the remaining Scriptural witnesses."[132] Hans-Joachim Kraus has sensed what Eichrodt meant when the latter emphasized that "only where this two-way relationship between the Old and New Testaments is understood do we find a correct definition of the problems of OT theology and of the method by which it is possible to solve it."[133] As regards Kraus his assessment of the matter of the context shows that "the question of the *context* is decisive for the connection of texts and themes. This means for the OT undertaking of Biblical-theological exegesis: How do the Old and New Testaments refer to certain kerygmatic intentions apparent in a text?"[134]

In this connection it is of great importance to explicate what it means that NT theology—and also OT theology—is bound to the given connections of the texts in the canon. Alfred Jepsen writes that "the interpretation of the Old Testament, being the interpretation of the church's canon, is determined by its connection with the New Testament and by the questions that follow from this."[135] We need to emphasize strongly that Biblical events and meanings must not be looked for behind, beneath, or above the texts,[136] but *in* the texts, because the divine deeds and words have received form and found expression in them. Biblical-theological interpretation attempts to study a passage within its own original historical context, the *Sitz im Leben* into which a word was spoken or an action took place, and also the life settings and contextual relations and connections in the later materials as well as the *Sitz im Leben* in the given context of the book in which it is preserved and the larger kerygmatic intention. In all of this the given

132Diem, *Was heisst schriftgemäss?* p. 38.
133Eichrodt, *Theology of the OT,* I, 26.
134Kraus, *Die Biblische Theologie,* p. 381 (italics his).
135"The Scientific Study of the OT," *EOTH,* p. 265.
136This is the way in which Hesse, *Kerygma und Dogma,* IV (1958), 13, seeks to secure a reality that he feels is not there. F. Mildenberger, *Gottes Tat im Wort* (Gütersloh, 1964), pp. 93ff., argues for unity of the canon as a rule of understanding but revives a new kind of pneumatic exegesis.

context of both Testaments has a bearing on interpretation.[137] Thus the matter of the given context in the nearest and more removed relationships within both Testaments will always have a decisive bearing for Biblical-theological interpretation and for the Biblical theologian's task of doing NT theology.[138]

One of the great turning-points in today's interest in NT theology is the reflection on the interrelationship between the Testaments. Fruitful beginnings may be seen in various attempts that point in forceful ways to the fact that the Testaments witness to multiple interrelationships. W. Eichrodt has pointed out that there is a reciprocal relationship between the Testaments, namely "in addition to this historical movement from the Old Testament to the New there is a current of life flowing in reverse direction from the New Testament to the Old. This reverse relationship also elucidates the full significance of the realm of OT thought." Then follows the striking claim that "only where this two-fold relationship between the Old and New Testaments is understood do we find a correct definition of the problem of OT theology and of the method by which it is possible to

[137]Childs, *Biblical Theology in Crisis*, pp. 99ff., has developed the relevance of the "larger canonical context" as the appropriate horizon for Biblical theology and applied it to his own methodological approach.

[138]Despite von Rad's emphasis on a charismatic-kerygmatic interpretation, his approach goes along the lines of *Heilsgeschichte*. Von Rad's emphasis on typology (*OTT*, II, 323ff.) presupposes a wider salvation-historical framework and connects two points on this background, as is true of the current revival of typological interpretation. On the relationship between typology and salvation history, see Cullmann, *Salvation in History*, pp. 132-135. G. Fohrer's negative reaction against the notion of salvation history ("Prophetie und Geschichte," *ThLZ* 89 [1964], 481ff.) comes on the basis that both salvation and doom are part of salvation history. To a great extent the history of salvation is a history of disaster. Yet even here the continuity is preserved in that later the proclamation of salvation is taken up without the preaching of the message of judgment disappearing. Fohrer's thesis, that the aim of God's action is the rule of God over the world and nature, is not opposed to salvation history but a characteristic part of it.

solve it."[139] G. von Rad's emphasis on the larger Biblical context of the OT[140] is seconded by H. W. Wolff,[141] H.-J. Kraus,[142] B. S. Childs,[143] and others who strive toward a Biblical theology.[144]

The complex nature of the interrelationship between the Testaments requires a multiplex approach. No single category, concept, or scheme can be expected to exhaust the varieties of interrelationships.[145] Among the patterns of historical and theological relationships between the Testaments are the following: (1) A common mark of both Testaments is the continuous history of God's people and the picture of God's dealings with mankind.[146] (2) New emphasis has been put upon the connection between the Testaments on the basis of Scriptural quotations.[147] (3) Among the interrelationships between the Testaments appears the common use of theological key

[139]Eichrodt, *Theology of the OT,* I, 26.

[140]Von Rad, *OTT,* II, 320-325.

[141]Wolff, *EOTH,* p. 181: "In the New Testament is found the context of the Old, which, as its historical goal, reveals the total meaning of the Old Testament."

[142]Kraus, *Die biblische Theologie,* pp. 33-36, 279-281, 344-347, 380-387.

[143]Childs, *Biblical Theology in Crises,* pp. 99-107.

[144]In both Protestant and Catholic scholarship there is a marked increase in the number of voices asking for a Biblical theology: F. V. Filson, "Biblische Theologie in Amerika," *ThLZ* 75 (1950), 71-80; M. Burrows, *An Outline of Biblical Theology* (Philadelphia, 1946); G. Vos, *Biblical Theology* (Grand Rapids, Mich., 1948); C. Spicq, "L'avènement de la Théologie Biblique," *Revue biblique* 35 (1951), 561-574; F. M. Braun, "La Theologie Biblique," *Revue Thomiste* 61 (1953), 221-253; R. de Vaux, "A propos de la Theologie Biblique," *ZAW* 68 (1956), 225-227; P. Robertson, "The Outlook for Biblical Theology," pp. 65-91; Harrington, *The Path of Biblical Theology,* pp. 260-335, 371-377.

[145]In this respect we agree with W. H. Schmidt, " 'Theologie des Alten Testaments' vor und nach Gerhard von Rad," *Verkündigung und Forschung* (Beiheft zur *EvTh* 17; Munich, 1972), p. 24.

[146] F. V. Filson, "The Unity Between the Testaments," *The Interpreter's One-Volume Commentary on the Bible,* p. 992.

[147]Childs, *Biblical Theology in Crisis,* pp. 114-118; Verhoef, "The Relationship Between the Old and New Testaments," p. 282; R. H. Gundry, *The Use of the OT in St. Matthew's Gospel* (Leiden, 1967); R. T. France, *Jesus and the OT* (London, 1971).

terms.[148] "Almost every key theological word of the New Testament is derived from some Hebrew word that had a long history of use and development in the Old Testament."[149] As among the other connecting links, unity does not mean uniformity, even when one speaks of "Greek words and their Hebrew meanings."[150] (4) The interrelationship between the Testaments comes also to expression through the essential unity of major themes. "Each of the major themes of the Old [Testament] has its correspondent in the New, and is in some way resumed and answered there."[151] Such themes as rulership of God, people of God, exodus experience, election and covenant, judgment and salvation, bondage and redemption, life and death, creation and new creation, etc., present themselves for immediate consideration. (5) A guarded and circumspect use of typology is indispensable for an adequate methodology that attempts to come to grips with the historical context of the OT and its relationship to the NT.[152] Typology must be sharply separated from allegory,[153] because it is essentially a historical and theological category between OT and NT events. Allegory has little concern with the historical character of the OT. (6) The category of promise/prediction and fulfillment elucidates another aspect of the interrelatedness of the Testaments. This interrelationship is fundamental and decisive not only for inner OT unity and the understanding of the relationship of the OT to Jesus Christ but also for the interrelationship

[148]So H. Haag in *Mysterium Salutis. Grundriss heilsgeschichtlicher Dogmatik*, eds. J. Feiner and M. Lohr (1965), I, 440-457.

[149]J. L. McKenzie, "Aspects of OT Thought," *The Jerome Biblical Commentary*, p. 767.

[150]D. Hill, *Greek Words and Hebrew Meanings: Studies in the Semantics of Soteriological Terms;* cf. J. Barr, *The Semantics of Biblical Language.*

[151]J. Bright, *The Authority of the OT,* p. 211. Cf. F. F. Bruce, *The NT Development of OT Themes.*

[152]See above, footnote 98.

[153]This basic separation has been attacked by Barr, *Old and New in Interpretation*, pp. 103-111, but rightly defended by Eichrodt, *EOTH*, pp. 227f.; Lampe, *Essays on Typology*, pp. 30-35; and France, *Jesus and the OT*, pp. 40f.

between the Testaments. As important as this category is, it is not exhaustive of the total relationship of OT to NT. (7) The concept of salvation history links both Testaments together. Secular history and salvation history are not to be conceived as two separate realities. Particular historical events have a deeper significance, perceived through divine revelation; such events are divine acts in human history. (8) Finally we have the unity of perspective, that future orientation inherent in both Testaments. The NT fulfills the OT's incompleteness and yet moves beyond to the final *eschaton*.

If properly conceived, these multiple interrelationships between the Testaments may be considered to be key elements in the elucidation of the unity of the Testaments without forcing uniformity upon the diverse Biblical witnesses. Neither Testament is in itself monochromatic nor is the relationship between both to be viewed in a monochromatic way. Any attempt toward a NT theology is expected to reflect the polychromatic nature of the NT; a true theology of the NT will also reveal a polychromatic relationship to the OT. The full spectrum of colors is expected to reveal a compatible blend and not a painful clash.

V. Basic Proposals Toward
A NT Theology:
A Multiplex Approach

Our attempt to focus on major unresolved issues which are at the center of the current problems in NT theology has revealed that there is a basic crisis[1] in current methodologies and approaches. The inevitable question that has arisen is, Where do we go from here? Our criticism of the paths already taken has indicated that a more adequate approach must be worked out. A productive way to proceed from here appears to have to rest upon the following basic proposals towards a NT theology.

1. Biblical theology must be understood to be a theological-historical discipline. This is to say that the Biblical theologian engaged in either Old or New Testament theology must claim as his task both to discover and describe what the text *meant* and also to explicate what it *means* for today. The Biblical theologian attempts to "get back there,"[2] i.e., he wants to do away with the temporal gap by bridging the time span between his day and that of the Biblical witnesses through the his-

[1]J. M. Robinson, "Kerygma and History in the New Testament," *The Bible in Modern Scholarship*, ed. J. P. Hyatt (Nashville, 1965), pp. 114-150, esp. 117, speaks of a *Grundlagenkrise.*

[2]This phrase comes from G. E. Wright, "The Theological Study of the Bible," *The Interpreter's One-Volume Commentary on the Bible* (Nashville, 1971), p. 983.

torical study of the Biblical documents. The nature of the Biblical documents, however, inasmuch as they are themselves witnesses of the eternal purpose of God as manifested through divine acts and words of judgment and salvation in history, requires a movement from the level of the historical investigation of the Bible to the theological one.[3] The Biblical witnesses are themselves not only historical witnesses in the sense that they originated at particular times and particular places; they are at the same time theological witnesses in the sense that they testify as the word of God to the divine reality and activity as it impinges on the history of man. Thus the task of the Biblical theologian is to interpret the Scriptures meaningfully, with the careful use of proper tools of historical and philological research, attempting to understand and describe in "getting back there" what the Biblical testimony meant; and to explicate what the Biblical testimony means for modern man in his own particular historical situation.[4]

The New Testament theologian is to draw his categories, themes, motifs, and concepts from the Biblical texts themselves. In the past he has drawn too often on the "concepts-of-doctrine" (*Lehrbegriffe*)[5] or the scheme of God-Man-Salvation (Theology-Anthropology-Soteriology) in dependence on dogmatics, or both. The recent situation of NT theology has revealed that the

[3]H. G. Wood, "The Present Position of New Testament Theology: Retrospect and Prospect," *New Testament Studies* 4 (1957/58), 169: "New Testament theology must be the subject of an objective historical inquiry, but if we are Christians, our interest in the subject is neither exclusively nor predominantly historical."

[4]F. Beisser, "Irrwege und Wege der historisch-kritischen Bibelwissenschaft. Auch ein Vorschlag zur Reform des Theologiestudiums," *Neue Zeitschrift für systematische Theologie und Religionsphilosophie* 15 (1973), 192-214, reminds us of the following: "It is known to everyone that the Biblical writings do not merely wish to be historical reports, but in the first instance witnesses of faith. . . . With this presupposition [of faith] exegesis can never be satisfied with the aim of describing how it was in the past. In every exegetical investigation the question therefore moves to the foreground: What does that which was found mean for faith?" (p. 214).

[5]See Chapter I, pp. 35-36.

introduction of contemporary philosophy in one form or another into this discipline has replaced the older problem. The apparent substitution of modern philosophical a prioris for the older dogmatic a prioris for the sake of interpretation does not seem to have solved the problem. A. Dulles points to one of the modern perils of Biblical theology. "Any number of supposedly biblical theologies in our day are so heavily infected with contemporary personalist, existential, or historical thinking as to render their biblical basis highly suspect."[6] In our investigation of the various NT theologies of leading writers we have seen the results to which this has led. In the discipline of NT theology the NT authors are frequently cross-examined "on the basis of a modern philosophy or a modern dogmatics. In many cases it is possible to get answers from the interrogated authors, but it is not clear if they really have ever thought of the subjects which we want them to talk about."[7] J. Munck goes on to suggest quite correctly that "it would be a healthy change if we tried to find and express the thoughts of the NT authors without the help of a modern dogmatics or a popular philosophy."[8] NT theology must not be dominated by external norms whether they come from dogmatics or a given philosophy. In this way NT theology is able to say something to both and raise its own questions. NT theology is to use NT categories, motifs, themes, and concepts. Often these Biblical categories, motifs, etc. are most suggestive and dynamic for expressing the rich revelation of the deep mysteries of God in the NT.

The proper method for NT (and OT) theology must be both theological *and* historical from the starting-point. This is the necessary correlate of conceiving NT (and

[6]A. Dulles, "Response to Krister Stendahl's 'Method in the Study of Biblical Theology,'" *The Bible in Modern Scholarship*, pp. 210-216, esp. 214.

[7]J. Munck, "Pauline Research Since Schweitzer," *The Bible in Modern Scholarship*, pp. 166-177, esp. 175.

[8]P. 176.

OT) theology as a theological-historical discipline. A theology of the NT presupposes careful exegetical work based upon sound principles and procedures. Exegesis in turn is in need of NT theology. Neither one can exist without the other. Without NT theology the work of exegetical interpretation may easily become endangered by isolating individual texts or units from the whole. The various NT writings are larger wholes made up of a series of units. These units in turn are made up of a series of sentences or clauses which consist of words joined to each other to express a particular thought, or parts of a larger thought, or a whole chain of thoughts. Each of these parts contributes to an understanding of the total end product—the NT as preserved for us. At the same time an understanding of the end product contributes to the understanding of the single parts. Careful, clear-sighted, and sound exegesis will always be able critically to check NT theology and NT theology will always be able to inform the exegetical procedures. It is a truism that NT theology remains the crown of NT studies.

At this point we must pause to note H.-J. Kraus' reminder that "one of the most difficult questions confronting Biblical theology today is that of the starting-point, the meaning and function of historical-critical research."[9] The recent debate on the nature and function of the historical-critical method,[10] which had re-

---

[9]Kraus, *Die Biblische Theologie,* p. 363; cf. p. 377. On this point Childs (*Biblical Theology in Crisis,* pp. 141f.) writes: "The historico-critical method is an inadequate method for studying the Bible as the Scriptures of the church because it does not work from the needed context. . . . When seen from the context of the canon both the question of what the text meant and what it means are inseparably linked and both belong to the task of interpretation of the Bible as Scripture. To the extent that the use of the critical method sets up an iron curtain between the past and present, it is an inadequate method for studying the Bible as the church's Scripture." For the inadequacy of the historical-critical method with regard to the new quest of the historical Jesus, see G. E. Ladd, "The Search for Perspective," *Interpretation* 26 (1971), 41-62.

[10]The pertinent literature is cited in Chapter I, footnotes 32-35.

ceived its classical formulation by E. Troeltsch[11] at the turn of the century, reveals that there is much discontent regarding its adequacy. The method is so differently practiced that it is difficult even to speak of *the* historical-critical method.[12]

A leading OT theologian, G. von Rad, keenly sensed one of the problems and suggested that the OT theologian, and we may add the NT theologian, cannot move on the pathway of a "critically assured minimum," if he actually attempts to grasp "the layers of depth of historical experience, which historical-critical research is unable to fathom."[13] The reason for the inability of the historical-critical method to grasp all layers of depth of historical experience, i.e., the inner unity of happening and meaning based upon the inbreaking of transcendence into history as *the* final reality to which the Biblical text testifies, rests upon its limitation to study history on the basis of its own presuppositions. The NT scholar W. Wink has recently spoken on the bankruptcy of the historical-critical method.[14] G. Maier's recent book announces the end of the historical-critical method.[15] Broadsides against the historical-critical method come from various quarters but are the severest from scholars schooled in the method.[16] Some point to the inadequacy of the principle of analogy,[17] one of the three pillars of

[11]E. Troeltsch, "Über historische und dogmatische Methode in der Theologie" (1898), reprinted in *Theologie als Wissenschaft,* ed. G. Sauter (Munich, 1971), pp. 105-127.

[12]Beisser, "Irrwege und Wege der historisch-kritischen Bibelwissenschaft," p. 192.

[13]G. von Rad, *Old Testament Theology,* I, 108.

[14]W. Wink, *The Bible in Human Transformation: Toward a New Paradigm for Biblical Study* (Philadelphia, 1973), pp. 1-18. He suggests a dialectical paradigm with strong emphasis on sociology and psychoanalysis.

[15]G. Maier, *The End of the Historical-Critical Method* (St. Louis, 1977). He speaks of a "historical-biblical method" that is to replace the "historical-critical method."

[16]E. Krentz, *The Historical-Critical Method* (Philadelphia, 1975), p. 81.

[17]T. Peters, "The Use of Analogy in Historical Method," *CBQ* 35 (1973), 473-482.

the method, while others have attacked its anthropocentricity,[18] its lack of a future dimension,[19] and other inherent problems.[20] It is pointed out that the historical-critical method is limited by its own concept of understanding and that it is therefore bound by its own limitations of argumentation.[21] "Historical criticism brings a concept of truth to the Bible that is not able to give full access to reality in history."[22] The reason for these limitations and for its inability to grasp all layers of depth of historical experience and reality in its totality rests in the method's self-imposed understanding of history.

The historical-critical method comes out of the Enlightenment.[23] It has a particular view of historical understanding[24] illustrated in Troeltsch's principle of correlation. History is viewed as a closed continuum, an unbroken series of causes and effects in which there is no room for transcendence.[25] This means "(1) that no critical historian could make use of supernatural intervention as a principle of historical explanation because this shattered the continuity of the causal nexus, and

[18]See esp. Pannenberg, *Basic Questions in Theology* (1970), I, 39-50.

[19]F. Hahn, "Probleme historischer Kritik," *ZNW* 63 (1972), 1-17, esp. 15-17.

[20]See P. Stuhlmacher, "Kritischer müssten mir die Historisch-Kritischen Sein," *Theologische Quartalschrift* 153 (1973), 244-251; *Schriftauslegung*, pp. 23f., 33, 98, 120-126. J. H. Leith, "The Bible and Theology," *Interpretation* 30 (1976), 227-241, writes: "The influence of the presuppositions of the critic and the precariousness of the methods have resulted in a history of conflicting conclusions and results" (p. 238).

[21]Stuhlmacher, *Schriftauslegung*, p. 19.

[22]Krentz, *The Historical-Critical Method*, p. 86.

[23]Ebeling, *Word and Faith*, pp. 42f. Krentz, *The Historical-Critical Method*, p. 85, calls the historical-critical method or historical criticism "the child of the Enlightenment and historicism; it is still dominated by Troeltsch's principles (systematic criticism, analogy, and universal correlation)."

[24]Stuhlmacher, *Schriftauslegung*, pp. 14f., 18.

[25]Von Rad, *Old Testament Theology*, II, 418: "For Israel, history consisted only of Jahweh's self-revelation by word and action. And on this point conflict with the modern view of history was sooner or later inevitable, for the latter finds it perfectly possible to construct a picture of history without God. It finds it very hard to assume that there is divine action in history. God has no natural place in its schema."

(2) that no event could be regarded as a final revelation of the absolute since every manifestation of truth and value was relative and historically conditioned."[26] If "the historian cannot presuppose supernatural intervention in the causal nexus as the basis for his work,"[27] can he ever deal adequately with the Biblical text which communicates just such intervention? A negative answer is forthcoming, because the historical-critical method is unable to deal with full reality in history. P. Stuhlmacher, for example, states that the historical-critical method will either lead to "a conflict between theological intention and the tendentiousness of the method or introduce historical criticism into theological thought as a disturbing or destructive element."[28] This is due to the presuppositions and philosophical premises about the nature of history. This problem is incisively referred to by C. E. Braaten: "The historian often begins by claiming that he conducts his research purely objectively, without presuppositions, and ends by surreptitiously introducing a set of presuppositions whose roots lie deeply embedded in an anti-Christian *Weltanschauung*."[29] A NT theology which rests upon a view of history that is based on an unbroken continuum of causes and effects cannot do justice to the Biblical view of history and revelation nor to the Scripture's claim to truth.[30] Von Rad has come to recognize that "a consistently applied historico-critical method could [not] really do justice

[26]Van A. Harvey, *The Historian and the Believer* (2nd ed.; New York, 1969), pp. 31f.

[27]R. W. Funk, "The Hermeneutical Problem and Historical Criticism," *The New Hermeneutic*, ed. J. M. Robinson and J. B. Cobb, Jr. (New York, 1964), p. 185. Cf. R. Bultmann, *Existence and Faith* (Cleveland, 1960), p. 291.

[28]P. Stuhlmacher, "Zur Methoden- und Sachproblematik einer interkonfessionellen Auslegung des Neuen Testaments," *Evangelisch-Katholischer Kommentar zum NT. Vorarbeiten* Heft 4 (Neukirchen-Vluyn, 1973), pp. 11-55, esp. p. 46.

[29]C. E. Braaten, "Revelation, History, and Faith in Martin Kähler," in M. Kähler, *The So-Called Historical Jesus and the Historic Biblical Christ* (Philadelphia, 1964), p. 22.

[30]D. Wallace, "Biblical Theology: Past and Future," *Theologische Zeitschrift* 19 (1963), 90; cf. Barr, "Revelation through History," pp. 201f.

to the Old Testament scripture's claim to truth."[31] What von Rad has stated of the OT applies likewise to the NT. What needs to be emphatically stressed is that there is a transcendent or divine dimension in Biblical history which the historical-critical method is unable to deal with. "If all historical events must by definition be explained by sufficient historical causes, then there is no room for the acts of God in history, for God is not a historical character."[32] If one's view of history is such that one cannot acknowledge divine intervention in history through deed and word, then one is unable to deal adequately and properly with the testimony of Scripture. We are, therefore, led to conclude that the crisis respecting history in OT and NT theology does not result from the scientific study of the evidences, but stems from the historical-critical method's own crisis[33] and its inadequacy to deal with the role of transcendence in history due to philosophical premises about the nature of history. If the reality of the Biblical text testifies to a suprahistorical dimension which transcends the self-imposed limitations of the historical-critical method, then one must employ a method that can account for this dimension and can probe into all the layers of depth of historical experience and deal adequately and properly with the Scripture's claim to truth.[34]

We have stated that the proper method for Biblical theology is to be both theological *and* historical from the beginning. Too often it is assumed that exegesis has the historical-critical function to work out the meaning of *single* texts, and NT (or OT) theology the task to

---

[31]Von Rad, *Old Testament Theology*, II, 417.

[32]Ladd, "The Search for Perspective," p. 50.

[33]Krentz, *The Historical-Critical Method*, p. 84, speaks of historical criticism as being in a "methodological crisis."

[34]Von Rad, *Old Testament Theology*, I, 108. E. Osswald, "Geschehene und geglaubte Geschichte," *Wissenschaftliche Zeitschrift der Universität Jena* 14 (1965), 711: "With the aid of critical science one can certainly make no statement about God, because there is no path that leads from the objectifying science of history to a real theological expression. The rational process of knowing history remains limited to the spatial-temporal dimension. . . ."

join reconstruction to interpretation into a theological *whole,* namely a sequential procedure. H.-J. Kraus has rightly called for a "Biblical-theological process of interpretation" in which exegesis is from its starting point Biblical-theological in orientation.[35] If we add to this aspect that a proper and adequate method of research dealing with the Biblical text needs to take into account the reality of God and his inbreaking into history,[36] because the Biblical text testifies to the transcendent dimension in historical reality,[37] then we have a basis upon which historical *and* theological interpretation can go hand in hand from the start without needing to be artificially separated into sequential processes.[38] On this basis one is able to "get back there" into the world of the Biblical writer by bridging the temporal and cultural gap, and can attempt to understand historically and theologically what the text meant. It is then possible to

[35]*Die Biblische Theologie,* p. 377.

[36]This point is also made by Floyd V. Filson, "How I Interpret the Bible," *Interpretation* 4 (1950), 186: "I work with the conviction that the only really objective method of study takes the reality of God and his working into account, and that any other point of view is loaded with presuppositions which actually, even if subtly, contain an implicit denial of the full Christian faith."

[37]Troeltsch writes, "The means by which criticism becomes in the first possible is the application of analogy. . . . This omnipotence of analogy implies the identity in principle of all historical happening" ("Über historische und dogmatische Methode in der Theologie," p. 108). Von Rad offers here an incisive observation with regard to the course of history as presented by the historical-critical method, in *Theologie des Alten Testaments* (Munich, 1960), II, 9: "It is interpreted history on the basis of historical-philosophical presuppositions, which do not allow any possible recognition of God's action in history, because only man is notoriously considered to be the creator of history." Mildenberger, *Gottes Tat im Wort,* p. 31 n. 37, agrees with von Rad and adds that historical criticism "presupposes a closed relation of reality which cannot grant 'supernatural' causes."

[38]On this point von Rad, *Theologie des AT,* II, 12, has made the following observation: "The theological interpretation of OT texts does not actually begin when the exegete, trained in literary criticism and history (either this or that!), has done his job, as if we had two exegetical processes, first a historical-critical one and then a 'theological one.' A theological interpretation that seeks to grasp a statement about God in the text is active from the very beginning of the process of understanding."

express more adequately and comprehensively what the text means for man in the modern world and historical situation.

This methodological procedure does not seek to skip history in favor of theology. The Biblical theologian working with the method that is both historical and theological recognizes fully the relativity of human objectivity.[39] Accordingly he is aware that he must never let his faith cause him to modernize his materials on the basis of the tradition and community of faith in which he stands. He must ask questions of the Biblical text on its own terms; he makes room that his tradition and the content of his faith may be challenged, guided, enlivened, and enriched by his finds. He recognizes also that a purely philological, linguistic, and historical approach is never enough to disclose the full and complete meaning of a historical text. One can apply all the exegetical instruments available from historical, linguistic, and philological research and never reach the heart of the matter unless one yields to the basic experience out of which the Biblical writers speak, namely faith. Without so yielding, one will hardly come to a recognition of the full reality that finds expression in the Biblical testimony. We do not wish to turn faith into a method, nor do we intend to disregard the demand of the Biblical books, as documents from the past, to translate them as objectively as possible by careful employment of the respective and proper methods of interpretation. But we mean that the interpretation of Scripture is to become part of our own real experience. The theological-historical interpretation is to be at the service of faith, if it is to fathom all layers of historical experience and to penetrate into the full meaning of the text and the reality expressed in it. We must, therefore, affirm that when interpretation seeks to grasp statements and testimonies witnessing to God's self-disclosure as the Lord of time and event, who has chosen to reveal himself in actual datable happenings of human history

[39]So also Stendahl, *IDB*, I, 422.

through acts and words of judgment and salvation, then the process of understanding such statements and testimonies must be from the start both historical *and* theological in nature in order to comprehend fully the complete reality that has come to expression.

2. The Biblical theologian engaged in NT theology has his subject indicated beforehand inasmuch as his endeavor is a theology of the *New Testament.* It is founded on materials taken from the NT. The NT comes to him through the Christian church as part of the inspired Scriptures. Introduction to the NT seeks to throw light on the pre-literary and literary stages and forms of the NT books by tracing their history and formation as well as the text-forms and the canonization of the NT. The history of early Christianity is studied in the context of the history of antiquity with special emphasis on the surrounding cultures from which we have many texts and where archaeology has been invaluable in providing the historical, cultural, and social setting for the Bible.

New Testament theology questions the various books or blocks of writings of the NT as to their theology.[40] For the NT is composed of writings whose origin, content, forms, intentions, and meaning are very diverse. The nature of these matters makes it imperative to look at the material at hand in light of the context which is primary to us, namely, the form in which we meet it first, as a verbal structure of an integral part of a literary whole.[41] Viewed in this way a NT theology will not be a

[40]This has been stressed for NT theology especially by Heinrich Schlier ("The Meaning and Function of a Theology of the NT," *Dogmatic vs. Biblical Theology,* ed. H. Vorgrimler [Baltimore, 1964], pp. 88-90); for OT theology by Kraus (*Die Biblische Theologie,* p. 364), by D. J. McCarthy ("The Theology of Leadership in Joshua 1-9," *Biblica* 52 [1971], 166), and with his own emphasis by Childs (*Biblical Theology in Crisis,* pp. 99-107).

[41]Contemporary (non-Biblical) literary critics place special emphasis upon the "new criticism," which the Germans call *Werkinterpretation.* Cf. W. Kayser, *Das sprachliche Kunstwerk* (10th ed.; Bern-München, 1964); Emil Staiger, *Die Kunst der Interpretation* (4th ed.; Zürich, 1963); Horst Enders, ed., *Die Werkinterpretation* (Darmstadt, 1967).

"history of religion"[42] or a "history of the transmission of
tradition"[43] or something else.[44] A theology of the NT
provides primarily a summary interpretation and explanation of each NT document or the NT blocks of
writing with a view to let their various concepts, themes,
and motifs emerge and to reveal their relatedness to each
other. The primary procedure of explicating the theology of the NT books or blocks of writings in the final
form as verbal structures of literary wholes has the
advantage of recognizing the similarities *and* differences
between the various books or blocks of writings. This
means, for example, that the theologies of the individual
gospels will be able to stand independently next to each
other. Each voice can be heard in its testimony to the

The primary concern according to the practitioners of the "new criticism" is to occupy oneself with the study of a finished piece of literature. The "new criticism" insists on the formal integrity of the literary
piece as a work of art, the *Kunstwerk*. Such a work must be appreciated in its totality; to look behind it in an attempt at discovering
its history of origin is irrelevant. The emphasis is on the finished literary product *qua* work of art. An increasing number of OT scholars
have taken up the emphasis of the "new criticism." Among them are:
Z. Adar, *The Biblical Narrative* (Jerusalem, 1959); S. Talmon, " 'Wis-
dom' in the Book of Esther," *Vetus Testamentum* 13 (1963), 419-
455; M. Weiss, "Wege der neueren Dichtungswissenschaft in ihrer
Anwendung auf die Psalmenforschung," *Biblica* 42 (1961), 225-302;
"Einiges über die Bauformen des Erzählens in der Bibel," *Vetus Testamentum* 13 (1963), 455-475; "Weiteres über die Bauformen des
Erzählens in der Bibel," *Biblica* 46 (1965), 181-206. NT scholars
have as yet not followed this procedure. Certain aspects of the structur-
alist approach seem to lead into the direction of greater emphasis upon
the final form of NT documents.

[42]One will recall the redirection and renaming of the discipline of
NT theology by William Wrede. See Chapter I, pp. 26-31.

[43]For OT theology the diachronic method adopted by G. von Rad is
a typical example; see Hasel, *OT Theology*, pp. 46-49. A history of
the transmission of tradition method is equally applied to OT and
NT by H. Gese, *Vom Sinai zum Zion* (Munich, 1974), pp. 11-30.

[44]Kraus, *Die Biblische Theologie*, p. 365: " 'Biblical theology' should
be *biblical* theology in that it accepts the canon in the given textual
connections as *the historical truth* which is in need of explanation,
whose final form is in need of being presented by interpretation and
summary. This should be the actual task of Biblical theology. Every
attempt at a different procedure would not be Biblical theology, but
'history of revelation,' 'history of religion,' or even 'history of tradition' " (italics his).

activity of God and the divine self-disclosure. Another advantage of this approach, one that is crucial for the whole enterprise of NT theology, is that no systematic scheme, pattern of thought, or extrapolated abstraction is superimposed upon the NT materials. Since no single theme, scheme, or motif is sufficiently comprehensive to include within it all varieties of NT viewpoints, one must refrain from using a particular concept, formula, basic idea, etc., as the center of the NT whereby a systematization of the manifold and variegated NT testimonies is achieved. On the other hand, we must affirm that as God is the center of the OT[45] so Jesus Christ is the center of the NT.[46] We seek to refrain from systematizing on the basis of a single theme, scheme, motif, etc., the reasons for which have been stated earlier.

3. A presentation of NT theology may begin best with the message of Jesus as it is available from the various NT documents. This assumes that it is possible to glean the message of Jesus from the respective gospels and the few sayings quoted in other NT documents and that there is a basic historical reliability in what has been preserved in the NT documents. This may be followed by the theologies of Matthew, Mark, and Luke-Acts. In such a consideration it will be recognized that the various Gospels have their own distinctive purpose both in the selection and presentation of the material preserved.

The Pauline theology may be gained by depicting the theology of the different Pauline letters and their common as well as differing themes and motifs. The key to Pauline theology is not easy to come by, as various recent attempts indicate.[47]

Some may choose to present Petrine theology perhaps

[45]G. F. Hasel, "The Problem of the Center in the OT Theology Debate," *ZAW* 86 (1974), 65-82.

[46]See Chapter III.

[47]See J. Jeremias, *Der Schlüssel zur Theologie des Apostels Paulus* (Gütersloh, 1971); G. Eichholz, *Die Theologie des Paulus im Umriss* (Göttingen, 1972); H. Ridderbos, *Paul. An Outline of His Theology* (Grand Rapids, Mich., 1975).

before that of Paul as well as the theology of other NT documents testifying to the preaching and teaching of early Christianity. Here the dating of the respective NT writings will become a factor in the sequence of the presentation of NT theology.

The Johannine theology as provided both in the Fourth Gospel and the Johannine epistles appears to come last with the exception of the theology of Revelation which gives the impression of standing in a category by itself among the theologies of the NT and may be presented last.

4. A NT theology not only seeks to know the theology of the various books or groups of writings; it also attempts to draw together and present the major themes of the NT. To live up to its name, NT theology must allow its themes, motifs, and concepts to be formed for it by the NT itself. The range of NT themes, motifs, and concepts will always impose itself on the theologian insofar as they silence his own, once the theological perspectives of the NT are really grasped. On principle, a theology of the NT must tend toward themes, motifs, and concepts and must be presented with all the variety and all the limitations imposed on them by the NT itself.

The presentation of these longitudinal perspectives of the NT testimonies can be achieved only on the basis of a multitrack treatment. The richness of the NT testimonies can be grasped by such a multiplex approach as is commensurate with the nature of the NT. This multiplex approach with the multitrack treatment of longitudinal themes frees the Biblical theologian from the notion of an artificial and forced unilinear approach determined by a single structuring concept, whether it is covenant, communion, kingdom of God, or something else, to which all NT testimonies, thoughts, and concepts are made to refer or are forced to fit.

5. As the NT is interrogated for its theology, it answers first of all by yielding various theologies, namely those of the individual books and groups of writings, and then by yielding the theologies of the various lon-

gitudinal themes. But the name of our discipline as *theology* of the NT is not only concerned to present and explicate the variety of theologies. The concept foreshadowed by the name of the discipline has *one* theology in view, namely *the* theology of the NT.

The final aim of NT theology is to demonstrate the unity that binds together the various theologies and longitudinal themes, concepts, and motifs. This is an extremely difficult undertaking which contains many dangers. If there is behind the experience of those who left us the NT Scriptures a unique divine reality, then it would seem that behind all variegation and diversity of theological reflection there is a unity within the NT writings. The ultimate object of a theology is then to draw the unity out of its concealment as much as possible and to make it transparent.

The task of achieving this objective must not be performed too hastily. The constant temptation to find unity in a single structuring theme or concept must be avoided. Here misgivings should arise not only because NT theology would be reduced to a cross-sectional or some other development of a single theme or concept, but the real task would be lost sight of, which is precisely not to overlook or pass by the variegated and diverse theologies while at the same time to present and articulate the unity which seemingly binds together in a concealed way the divergent and manifold NT testimonies. One can indeed speak of such a unity in which ultimately the divergent theological utterances and testimonies are intrinsically related to each other from the theological viewpoint on the basis of a presupposition that derives from the inspiration and canonicity of the NT as Scripture.

A seemingly successful way to come to grips with the question of unity is to take the various major longitudinal themes and concepts and explicate where and how the variegated theologies are intrinsically related to each other.[48] In this way the underlying bond of the one theology of the NT may be illuminated. In the quest to find and explicate the unity one must refrain from making the theology of one book or group of books the norm of what is NT theology. We have seen that this has happened too frequently. Some scholars have made the theology of Paul or a particular aspect of it into the norm or "canon within the canon" of early Christian faith on the basis of which other parts are criticized. The procedure proposed here seeks to avoid this method. It also allows the too often neglected theologies of certain NT writings such as Hebrews, James, Jude, and others to stand side by side with other theologies. They make their own special contributions to NT theology on equal basis with those more recognized ones, because they too are expressions of NT realities. The question of unity implies tension, but tension does not of necessity mean contradiction. It would appear that where conceptual unity seems impossible the creative tension thereby produced will turn out to be a most fruitful one for NT theology.

6. The Biblical theologian understands NT theology as being part of a larger whole. The name "theology of the New Testament" implies the larger context of the Bible made up of both Testaments. An integral NT theology stands in a basic relationship to the OT and to OT theology. For the Christian theologian the NT has the character of Scripture and he will constantly reflect on what this means particularly in relation to the other Testament.

These proposals indicate a multiplex and multiform approach to NT theology. This approach seeks to do justice to the various NT writings and attempts to avoid an explication of the manifold witnesses through a single structure, unilinear points of view, or even a compound approach of a limited nature. The approach

[48]A. Deissmann, "Zur Methode der Biblischen Theologie des NT," PTNT, pp. 78-80, had already called for a presentation of the total early Christian theology as a main task of NT theology.

briefly outlined has the advantage of remaining faithful to the rich variety of NT thought, to both similarity
and dissimilarity as well as old and new, without in the
least distorting the original historical witness of the text
in its literal sense and in the larger Scriptural context
to which the NT belongs. It allows unity to emerge
within all diversity and manifoldness without forcing
it into the mold of uniformity. It will not be an easy
task to present a NT theology along the lines outlined
here, but it is hoped that this challenge is of the kind
that will gain victory over any temptation that seeks
an easier path.

Selected Bibliography

(Note: The following list includes primarily a selection of works written in the last 100 years. Preference has been given, where possible, to works which represent various points of view and/or have in some fashion or another contributed in the current debate.)

Adeney, W. F. *The Theology of the New Testament*. London, 1894.

Albertz, M. *Die Botschaft des Neuen Testaments*. Bd. I, 1, Berlin, 1946; Bd. I, 2, Zollikon-Zurich, 1952; Bd. II, 1, Zollikon-Zurich, 1954; Bd. II, 2, Zollikon-Zurich, 1957.

———. "Die Krisis der sogenannten neutestamentlichen Theologie," *Zeichen der Zeit* 8 (1954), 370-376.

———. "Kerygma und Theologie im Neuen Testament," *ZNW* 46 (1955), 267 f. and *ThLZ* 81 (1956), 341-344.

Albright, W. F. "Return to Biblical Theology," *Christian Century* 75 (1958), 1328-1331.

Alexander, N. "The United Character of the New Testament Witness of the Christ-Event," *The New Testament in Historical and Contemporary Perspective. Essays in Memory of G. H. C. Macgregor,* ed. Hugh Anderson (Oxford, 1965), 1-33.

Allen, E. L. "The Limits of Biblical Theology," *JBR* 25 (1956), 13-18.

Althaus, P. *Faith and Fact in the Kerygma Today*. Philadelphia, 1959.

Aulén, G. *Jesus in Contemporary Historical Research*. Nashville, 1976.

Bachmann, Ph. "Zur Methode der biblischen Theologie des Neuen Testaments," *Festgabe, der philos. Fakultät der Friedrich-Alexander-Universität Erlangen* (Erlangen, 1925), 7-26.

Balthasar, H. U. v. "Die Vielheit der biblischen Theologien und der Geist der Einheit im Neuen Testament," *Schweizer Rundschau* 67 (1968), 159-169.

———. "Einigung in Christus," *Freiburger Zeitschrift für Philosophie und Theologie* 15 (1968), 171-189.

Barr, James. *Old and New in Interpretation: A Study of the Two Testaments.* New York, 1968.

———. *The Bible in the Modern World.* New York, 1973.

———. "Story and History in Biblical Theology," *Journal of Religion* 56 (1976), 1-17.

———. "Biblical Theology," *IDB Sup.* (Nashville, 1976), 104-111.

———. "Trends and Prospects in Biblical Theology," *JTS* 25 (1974), 265-282.

Barth, Karl. *Der Römerbrief.* Bern, 1918.

———. "Rudolf Bultmann—An Attempt to Understand Him," *Kerygma and Myth II,* ed. H. W. Bartsch (London, 1962).

Barth, M. "Die Methode von Bultmanns 'Theologie des Neuen Testaments'," *Theologische Zeitschrift* 11 (1955), 1-27.

———. "Whither Biblical Theology," *Interpretation* 25 (1971), 350-354.

Batey, R. *New Testament Issues.* New York, 1970.

Bauer, G. L. *Biblische Theologie des Neuen Testaments.* 4 vols. Leipzig, 1800-1802.

Baumgärtel, F. *Verheissung. Zur Frage des evangelischen Verständnisses des Alten Testaments.* Gütersloh, 1952.

Baur, F. C. *Vorlesungen über neutestamentliche Theologie,* ed. F. F. Baur. Leipzig, 1864.

Beilner, W. "Neutestamentliche Theologie," *Dienst an der Lehre. Studien zur heutigen Philosophie und Theologie* (Wiener Beitrage zur Theologie X; Wien, 1965), 145-165.

Beisser, F. "Irrwege und Wege der historisch-kritischen Bibelwissenschaft: Auch ein Vorschlag zur Reform des Theologiestudiums," *Neue Zeitschrift für system. Theologie und Religionsphilosophie* 15 (1973), 192-214.

Beker, J. C. "Reflections on Biblical Theology," *Interpretation* 24 (1970), 303-320.

Benoit, P. "Exégèse et theólogie Biblique," *Exégèse et théologie III* (Paris, 1968), 1-13.

Bertram, G. "Neutestamentliche Religionsgeschichte und Theologie," *Deutsche evangelische Erziehung* 46 (1935), 355-362.

Betti, E. *Die Hermeneutik als allgemeine Methodik der Geisteswissenschaften.* Tübingen, 1967.

Betz, O. "History of Biblical Theology," *IBD,* I, 432-437.

Blenkinsopp, J. "Biblical and Dogmatic Theology: The Present Situation," *CBQ* 26 (1964), 70-85.

———. *A Sketchbook of Biblical Theology.* New York, 1968.

Bonsirven, J. *Théologie du Nouveau Testament.* Paris, 1951.

Trans. *Theology of the New Testament*. Westminster, Md., 1963.

Bourke, J. "A Survey of Biblical Theology," *Life of the Spirit* 18 (1963), 51-68.

Bousset, W. *Kyrios Christos. Geschichte des Christusglaubens von den Anfängen des Christentums bis Irenaeus*. Göttingen, 1913; 6th ed. Darmstadt, 1967. Trans. *Kyrios Christos*. Nashville, 1970.

Bouttier, M. "Théologie et Philosophie du NT," *Etudes Theologiques et Religieuses* 45 (1970), 188-194.

Bowman, J. W. "From Schweitzer to Bultmann," *Theology Today* 11 (1954), 160-178.

———. *Prophetic Realism and the Gospel. A Preface to Biblical Theology*. Philadelphia, 1955.

Brandon, S. G. F. "Is there a New Testament Theology?" *Modern Churchman* 3 (1960), 124-130.

Branton, J. "Our Present Situation in Biblical Theology," *Religion in Life* 26 (1956/57), 5-18.

Braun, D. "Heil als Geschichte. Zu Oscar Cullmanns neuem Buch," *EvTh* 27 (1967), 57-76.

Braun, F.-M. "La théologie biblique," *Revue Thomiste* 53 (1953), 221-253.

Braun, H. "The Problem of a New Testament Theology," *Journal for Theology and Church* 1 (1965), 169-185.

———. *Jesus. Der Mann aus Nazareth und seine Zeit*. Stuttgart/Berlin, 1969.

Briggs, R. C. *Interpreting the New Testament Today*. Nashville, 1973.

Bright, J. *The Authority of the OT*. Nashville, 1967.

Brown, C. "Bultmann Revisited," *Churchman* 88 (1974), 167-187.

Brown, S. *Apostasy and Perseverance in the Theology of Luke*. Rome, 1969.

Bruce, F. F. *New Testament Development of Old Testament Themes*. 3rd ed. Grand Rapids, Mich., 1973.

Brückner, M. "Die neuen Darstellungen der neutestamentlichen Theologie," *Theologische Rundschau* 16 (1913), 363-386, 415-436.

Büchsel, F. *Theologie des Neuen Testaments. Geschichte des Wortes Gottes im Neuen Testament*. Gütersloh, 1935.

Bultmann, R. "Heilsgeschichte und Geschichte. Zu O. Cullmann, Christus und die Zeit," *ThLZ* 73 (1948), 659-666.

———. *Theologie des Neuen Testaments*. Tübingen, 1948-1953. Trans. *Theology of the NT*. 2 vols. London, 1965.

———. "Das Problem des Verhältnisses von Theologie und Verkündigung im Neuen Testament," *Aux sources de la tradition chrétienne. Festschrift für M. Goguel* (Neuchatel/Paris, 1950), 32-42.

———. *Das Urchristentum im Rahmen der antiken Religionen.* Zurich, 1959. Trans. *Primitive Christianity in Its Contemporary Setting.* Edinburgh, 1956.

———. *Jesus.* Berlin, 1926. Trans. *Jesus and the Word.* 2nd ed. London, 1958.

———. *Die Geschichte der synoptischen Tradition.* Göttingen, 1921. 2nd. ed., 1931. Trans. *The History of the Synoptic Tradition.* New York, 1963.

Burkhardt, H. "Grenzen des Kanons—Motive und Masstäbe," *Theologische Beiträge* 1 (1970), 153-160.

Burrows, M. *An Outline of Biblical Theology.* Philadelphia, 1946.

———. "The Task of Biblical Theology," *JBR* 14 (1946), 13-15.

Campenhausen, H. von. *The Formation of the Christian Bible.* Trans. by J. A. Baker. Philadelphia, 1972.

Carlston, C. E. *The Parables of the Triple Tradition.* Philadelphia, 1975.

———. "Review of J. Jeremias, *New Testament Theology. The Proclamation of Jesus,*" *JBL* 91 (1972), 260-262.

Cazelles, H. "The Unity of the Bible and the People of God," *Scripture,* 18 (1966), 1-10.

Charlot, John. *New Testament Disunity.* New York, 1970.

Childs, B. S. *Biblical Theology in Crisis.* Philadelphia, 1970.

Clavier, H. "Remarques sur la méthode en theologie biblique," *Novum Testamentum* 14 (1972), 161-190.

Clemons, J. T. "Critics and Criticisms of Salvation History," *Religion in Life* 41 (1972), 89-100.

Coenen, L., *et al.,* eds. *Theologisches Begriffslexikon zum Neuen Testament.* 3 vols. 3rd ed. Wuppertal, 1972.

Conzelmann, H. "Die Frage der Einheit der Neutestamentlichen Schriften," *Moderne Exegese und historische Wissenschaft. Dokumentation der Tagung des Deutschen Instituts für Bildung und in Niederaltaich vom 6. bis 11. Okt. 1969,* eds. J. M. Hollenbach und H. Staudinger (Trier, 1972), 67-76.

———. "Fragen an Gerhard von Rad," *Evangelische Theologie* 24 (1964), 113-125.

———. *Grundriss der Theologie des Neuen Testaments.* München, 1967. Trans. *An Outline of the Theology of the New Testament.* New York, 1969.

———. *Die Mitte der Zeit.* Tübingen, 1953. Trans. *The Theology of St. Luke.* London, 1961.

Cordero, M. García. *Teología de la Biblia II and III: Nuevo Testamento.* Madrid, 1972.

Courth, Franz. "Der historische Jesus als Auslegungsnorm des

Glaubens?" *Münchener Theologische Zeitschrift* 25 (1974), 301-316.

Cox, Claude E. "R. Bultmann: Theology of the New Testament," *Restoration Quarterly* 17 (1974), 144-161.

Craig, C. T. "Biblical Theology and the Rise of Historicism," *JBL* 62 (1943), 281-294.

Cullmann, O. *Christus und die Zeit. Die urchristliche Zeit- und Geschichtsauffassung.* Zollikon-Zürich, 1946. Trans. *Christ and Time.* London, 1962.

———. *The Christology of the NT.* rev. ed. New York, 1964.

———. *The Early Church.* Philadelphia, 1956.

———. *Heil als Geschichte. Heilsgeschichtliche Existenz im Neuen Testament.* Tübingen, 1965. Trans. *Salvation in History.* New York, 1967.

———. "La Nécessité et la fonction de l'exégèsis philogique et historique de la Bible," *Verbum Caro* 3 (1949), 2-13.

Dahl, N. A. "Die Theologie des Neuen Testaments," *Theologische Rundschau* 22 (1954), 21-49.

Davies, W. D. "Scene in New Testament Theology," *JBR* 20 (1952), 231-238.

Deissmann, A. "Zur Methode der biblischen Theologie des Neuen Testamentes," *ZThK* 3 (1893), 126-139.

Demke, Ch. "Die Frage nach der Möglichkeit einer Theologie des Neuen Testaments," *Theologische Versuche 2,* eds. J. Rogge und G. Schille (Berlin, 1970), 129-139.

Dentan, R. C. *Preface to OT Theology.* 2nd ed. New York, 1963.

Dequeker, L. "Old and New in the Bible. Guidelines for a Better Understanding of the Relationship between the Old and New Testaments," *Louvain Studies* 3 (1971), 189-205.

Descamps, A. "Reflexions sur la methode en théologie biblique," *Sacra Pagina 1,* Miscellanea Biblica Congressus Internationalis Catholici de Re biblica (Gembloux, 1959), 132-157.

De Vaux, R. "A propos de la théologie biblique," *Zeitschrift für die alttestamentliche Wissenschaft* 68 (1956), 225-227.

Dibelius, M. "Aus der Werkstatt der neutestamentlichen Theologie," *Christliche Welt* 27 (1913), 938-941, 964-967.

———. "Biblische Theologie und biblische Religionsgeschichte II des NT," *Religion in Geschichte und Gegenwart* (2nd ed., Tübingen, 1927), I, 1091-1094.

Diem, H. "Die Einheit der Schrift," *EvTh* 13 (1953), 385-405.

———. *Theologie als kirchliche Wissenschaft.* 2nd ed. Munich, 1957.

———. *Was heisst schriftgemäss?* Gütersloh, 1958.

Dodd, C. H. *The Apostolic Preaching and its Developments.* London, 1936.

———. *According to the Scriptures. The Substructure of New Testament Theology.* London, 1952.

———. *The Authority of the Bible.* New York, 1929.

———. "The Foundation of Christian Theology," *Theology Today* 7 (1950-51), 308-320.

———. "A Problem of Interpretation," *Studiorum Novi Testamenti Societas,* Bull. II (1951), 1-18.

Doty, W. G. *Contemporary New Testament Interpretation.* Englewood Cliffs, N.J., 1972.

Dulles, A. "Response to Krister Stendahl's 'A Method in the Study of Biblical Theology'," *The Bible in Modern Scholarship,* ed. J. Ph. Hyatt (Nashville, 1965), 210-216.

Ebeling, G. *The Word and Faith.* London, 1963.

———. *Theology and Proclamation: Dialogue with Bultmann.* Philadelphia, 1966.

———. *The Word of God and Tradition.* Philadelphia, 1968.

———. "The Meaning of 'Biblical Theology'," *Word and Faith* (London, 1963), 81-86.

Egg, G. *Adolf Schlatters kritische Position, gezeigt an seiner Matthäusinterpretation.* Stuttgart, 1968.

Eichholz, G. *Die Theologie des Paulus im Umriss.* Göttingen, 1972.

Ellis, E. E. *Paul's Use of the Old Testament.* Grand Rapids, Mich., 1959.

———. *Paul and His Recent Interpreters.* Grand Rapids, Mich., 1961.

Estes, D. F. *An Outline of New Testament Theology.* New York, 1900.

Evans, C. F. *Is 'Holy Scripture' Christian?* London, 1971.

Fallon, J. E. "Towards a Biblical Theology," *Dominicana* 49 (1964), 221-228.

Fascher, E. "Eine Neuordnung der neutestamentlichen Fachdisziplin? Bemerkungen zum Werk von M. Albertz: Die Botschaft des Neuen Testaments," *ThLZ* 83 (1958), 609-618.

———. "Christologie oder Theologie? Bemerkungen zu O. Cullmanns Christologie des Neuen Testamentes," *ThLZ* 87 (1962), 881-910.

Feine, Paul. *Theologie des Neuen Testaments.* Leipzig, 1910.

Feiner, J. and Lohr, M., eds. *Mysterium Salutis. Grundriss heilsgeschichtlicher Dogmatik.* Freiburg, 1965.

Fensham, F. C. "Covenant, Promise and Expectation in the Bible," *Theologische Zeitschrift* 23 (1967), 305-322.

———. "The Covenant as Giving Expression to the Relationship between Old and New Testament," *Tyndale Bulletin* 22 (1971), 82-94.

Ferrero-Blanco, J. J. *Iniciación a la teología bíblica*. Barcelona, 1967.

Festorazzi, F. "Il problema del metodo nella teologia biblica," *Scuola Cattolica* 91 (1963), 253-276.

Filson, F. V. "Biblische Theologie in Amerika," *ThLZ* 75 (1950), 71-80.

———. "A New Testament Student's Approach to Biblical Theology," *JBR* 14 (1946), 22-28.

———. "New Testament Theology in the Last Decade," *JBR* 19 (1951), 191-196.

———. "The Unity Between the Testaments," *The Interpreter's One-Volume Commentary on the Bible* (Nashville, 1971), 989-993.

———. "The Unity of the OT and the NT: A Bibliographical Survey," *Interpretation* 5 (1951), 134-152.

Fitzmyer, J. A. "Pauline Theology," *The Jerome Biblical Commentary*, eds. R. E. Brown, J. A. Fitzmyer, R. E. Murphy (Englewood Cliffs, N. J., 1968), 800-827.

Flender, H. *St. Luke, Theologian of Redemptive History*. London, 1967.

Fohrer, G. "Der Mittelpunkt einer Theologie des Alten Testaments," *Theologische Zeitschrift* 24 (1968), 161-172.

Fontaine, J. *Formation progressive de la théologie neo-testamentaire*. Arras, 1905.

———. *Théologie du Nouveau Testament*. Arras, 1905.

———. *Théologie du Nouveau Testament et l'évolution des dogmes*. Paris, 1907.

———. *La Théologie néo-testamentaire sa structure interne: les faits, les dogmes et la foi*. Arras, 1905.

France, R. T. *Jesus and the Old Testament*. London, 1971.

Frank, I. *Der Sinn der Kanonbildung*. Freiburg, 1971.

Franklin, E. *Christ the Lord: A Study in the Purpose and Theology of Luke-Acts*. London, 1975.

Friedrich, J., ed. *Rechtfertigung. Festschrift für E. Käsemann zum 70. Geburtstag*, eds. J. Friedrich, W. Pohlmann, and P. Stuhlmacher. Tübingen, 1976.

Fröhlich, K. "Die Mitte des Neuen Testaments: Oscar Cullmanns Beitrag zur Theologie der Gegenwart," *Oikonomia. Heilsgeschichte als Thema der Theologie* (Hamburg-Bergstedt, 1967), 203-219.

Frye, R. M. "On the Historical-Critical Method in New Testament Studies: A Reply to Professor Achtemeier," *Perspective* 14 (1973), 28-33.

Fuchs, E. *Zur Frage nach dem historischen Jesus*. Tübingen, 1960. Trans. *Studies on the Historical Jesus*. SBT 42; London, 1964.

———. "Probleme der neutestamentlichen Theologie. Rez. von

E. Stauffer, Die Theologie des Neuen Testaments," *Verkündigung und Forschung* (1942/46), 168-182.

———. "Die Theologie des Neuen Testaments und der historische Jesus," *Zur Frage nach dem historischen Jesus* (Tübingen, 1960), 377-404.

———. *Zum hermeneutischen Problem in der Theologie.* Tübingen, 1959.

———. *Hermeneutik,* 2nd ed. Cannstadt, 1958.

Funk, R. W. "The Hermeneutical Problem and Historical Criticism," *The New Hermeneutic,* eds. J. M. Robinson and J. B. Cobb, Jr. (New York, 1964), 164-197.

———. *Language, Hermeneutic, and Word of God.* New York, 1966.

Furnish, V. "New Directions in New Testament Theology," *Perkins School of Theology Journal* 19 (1965/66), 5-11.

Gamble, Connolly, Jr. "The Nature of Biblical Theology," *Interpretation* 5 (1951), 462-467.

Gast, F. A. "Biblical Theology," *The Reformed Church Review* 2 (1898), 236-251.

Geiger, W. *Spekulation und Kritik. Die Geschichtstheologie F. C. Baurs.* Munich, 1964.

Gese, H. "Erwägungen zur Einheit der biblischen Theologie," *Vom Sinai zum Zion* (Munich, 1974), 11-30.

Geyer, Hans-Georg. "Geschichte als theologisches Problem," *EvTh* 22 (1962), 92-104.

Giblet, J. "Unité et diversité dans les écrits du Nouveau Testament," *Istina* 20 (1975), 23-34.

Gilbert, G. H. "Biblical Theology; its History and its Mission," *Biblical World* 6 (1895), 6-14, 358-366.

Gogarten, F. *Demythologizing and History.* London, 1955.

Goppelt, L. *Die apostolische und nachapostolische Zeit.* 2nd ed. Göttingen, 1966. Trans. *The Apostolic and Post-Apostolic Times.* Philadelphia, 1962.

———. "Paulus und die Heilsgeschichte," *Christologie und Ethik* (Göttingen, 1968), 220-233.

———. "Die Pluralität der Theologien im Neuen Testament und die Einheit des Evangeliums als ökumenisches Problem," *Evangelium und Einheit. Bilanz und Perspektiven der ökumenischen Bemühungen,* ed. V. Vajta (Göttingen, 1971), 103-125.

———. "Der Ertrag einer Epoche. Vier Darstellungen der Theologie des Neuen Testaments," *Lutherische Monatshafte* 11 (1972), 96-98.

———. *Theologie des Neuen Testaments.* 2 vols. Göttingen, 1975-76.

———. *Typos. Die typologische Deutung des Alten Testaments im Neuen.* Darmstadt, 1966.

———. "Review of Herbert Braun, Jesus. Der Mann aus Nazareth und seine Zeit," *ThLZ* 95 (1970), 744-748.

Gould, E. P. *The Biblical Theology of the New Testament.* New York, 1900.

Grant, F. C. *An Introduction to New Testament Thought.* Nashville, 1950.

Grant, R. M. *The Formation of the New Testament.* New York, 1965.

———. *A Short History of the Interpretation of the Bible,* 2nd ed. New York, 1966.

Grässer, E. *Wort Gottes in der Krise?* Gütersloh, 1969.

———. "Review of W. G. Kümmel, *Die Theologie des NT,*" *Deutsches Pfarrerblatt* 70 (1970), 254-255.

Grech, P. "Background Studies in New Testament Theology," *Dublin Review* 240 (1966), 247-260.

———. "Contemporary Methodological Problems in New Testament Theology," *BTB* 2 (1972), 262-280.

Grelot, P. *Sens chrétien de l'AT.* Tournai, 1962.

Gross, H. and F. Mussner. "Die Einheit von Altem und Neuem Testament," *Internationale Katholische Zeitschrift* 3 (1974), 544-555.

Guillet, J. "Die Mitte der Botschaft: Jesu Tod und Auferstehung," *Internationale Katholische Zeitschrift* 2 (1973), 225-238.

———. *Themes of the Bible.* South Bend, Ind., 1960.

Gundry, R. H. *The Use of the Old Testament in St. Matthew's Gospel.* Leiden, 1967.

Güttgemanns, E. "Literatur zur Neutestamentlichen Theologie. Randglossen zu ausgewählten Neuerscheinungen," *Verkündigung und Forschung* 12 (1967), 38-87.

———. "Literatur zur Neutestamentlichen Theologie. Überblick über Fortgang und Ziele der Forschung," *Verkündigung und Forschung* 15 (1970), 41-75.

———. "Linguistisch-literaturwissenschaftliche Grundlegung einer neutestamentlichen Theologie," *Linguistica Biblica* 13/14 (1972), 2-18.

———. *Offene Fragen zur Formgeschichte des Evangeliums.* Munich, 1970.

Haacker, K. "Einheit und Vielfalt in der Theologie des Neuen Testaments. Ein methodenkritischer Beitrag," *Beiträge zur hermeneutischen Diskussion,* ed. W. Böld (Wuppertal, 1968), 78-102.

Haenchen, E. "Das alte 'Neue Testament' und das neue 'Alte Testament'," *Die Bibel und wir. Gesammelte Aufsätze,* II (Tübingen, 1968), 13-27.

Hahn, F. "Das Problem 'Schrift und Tradition' im Urchristentum," *EvTh* 30 (1970), 449-468.

———. "Probleme historischer Kritik," *ZNW* 63 (1972), 1-17.

Haroutunian, J. "The Bible and the Word of God. The Importance of Biblical Theology," *Interpretation* 1 (1947), 291-308.

Harrington, W. J. "New Testament Theology, Two Recent Approaches," *BTB* 1 (1971), 171-189.

———. "The Method and Scope of Biblical Theology," *Doctrine and Life* 22 (1972), 71-90.

———. *The Path of Biblical Theology*. Dublin, 1973.

Harvey, J. "Symbolique et théologie biblique," *Sciences Ecclesiastiques* 9 (1957), 147-157.

Harvey, Van A. *The Historian and the Believer*. New York, 1966.

Hasel, G. F. "The Problem of History in OT Theology," *AUSS* 8 (1970), 32-46.

———. "Review of H. Conzelmann, *Grundriss der Theologie des NT*," *AUSS* 8 (1970), 86-89.

———. "Capito, Schwenckfeld and Crautwald on Sabbatarian Anabaptist Theology," *Mennonite Quarterly Review* 46 (1972), 41-57.

———. "The Problem of the Center in the OT Theology Debate," *ZAW* 86 (1974), 65-82.

———. *Old Testament Theology: Basic Issues in the Current Debate*. 2nd ed. Grand Rapids, Mich., 1975.

Hasenhüttl, G. "Dialogue between the Dogmatic Theologian and the Exegete," *Concilium* 10 (1971), 39-46.

Haufe, G. "Auf dem Wege zu einer theologischen Hermeneutik des Neuen Testaments," *Bericht von der Theologie. Resultate. Probleme. Konzepte,* ed. G. Kulicke, *et al.* (Berlin, 1971), 56-79.

———. "Review of K. H. Schelkle, *Theol. d. NT, Bd. I*," *ThLZ* 94 (1969), 909-910.

———. "Review of W. G. Kümmel, *Die Theologie des Neuen Testaments*," *ThLZ* 96 (1971), 108-111.

Hefner, P. "Theology's Task in a Time of Change: The Limitations of Biblical Theology," *Una Sancta* 24 (1967), 39-51.

Hengel, M. "Theorie und Praxis im Neuen Testament?" *Evangelische Kommentare* 3 (1970), 744-745.

———. "Historische Methoden und theologische Auslegung des Neuen Testaments," *Kerygma und Dogma* 19 (1973), 85-90.

Hesse, F. *Das AT als Buch der Kirche*. Gütersloh, 1966.

———. *Abschied von der Heilsgeschichte*. Zurich, 1971.

Hessen, J. *Griechische oder biblische Theologie? Das Problem der Hellenisierung des Christentums in neuer Beleuchtung*. Leipzig, 1956. 2nd ed. München/Basel, 1962.

Hicks, R. L. "Present-Day Trends in Biblical Theology," *Anglican Theological Review* 32 (1950), 137-153.

Higgins, A. J. B. *The Christian Significance of the OT*. London, 1949.

———. "The Growth of New Testament Theology," *Scottish Journal of Theology* 6 (1953), 275-286.

Hill, D. "What is 'Biblical Theology'?" *Biblical Theology* 15 (1965), 17-23.

Hillman, W. "Wege zur neutestamentlichen Theologie," *Wissenschaft und Weisheit* 14 (1951), 56-67, 82, 200-211; 15 (1952), 15-32, 122-136.

———. "Grundzüge der urchristlichen Glaubensverkündigung," *Wissenschaft und Weisheit* 20 (1957), 163-180.

Hirsch, E. *Das Alte Testament und die Predigt des Evangeliums.* Tübingen, 1936.

Hodgson, L. *Biblical Theology and the Sovereignty of God.* Cambridge, 1947.

Hodgson, P. C. *The Formation of Historical Theology. A Study of Ferdinand Christian Baur.* New York, 1966.

Hofmann, J. C. K. *Biblische Theologie des neuen Testaments,* ed. W. Volk (Die heilige Schrift neuen Testaments zusammenhängend untersucht, 11. Theil). Nördlingen, 1886.

Holtzmann, H. J. *Lehrbuch der neutestamentlichen Theologie.* 2 vols. Freiburg/Leipzig, 1897.

Hornig, G. *Die Anfänge der historisch-kritischen Theologie.* Göttingen, 1961.

Hübner, J. *Die Theologie Johannes Keplers zwischen Orthodoxie und Naturwissenschaft.* Tübingen, 1975.

Hughes, H. D. "Salvation-History as Hermeneutic," *Evangelical Quarterly* 48 (1976), 79-89.

Hummel, H. D. "The OT Basis of Typological Interpretation," *Biblical Research* 9 (1964), 38-50.

Hunter, A. M. *The Unity of the New Testament.* London, 1943.

———. *The Message of the New Testament.* Philadelphia, 1944.

———. *Interpreting the New Testament 1900-1950.* London, 1951.

———. "Contemporary Religious Trends: New Testament Theology — Where and Whither?" *Expository Times* 66 (1954/55), 269-272.

———. *Introducing New Testament Theology.* London/Philadelphia, 1958.

———. "Modern Trends in New Testament Theology," *The New Testament in Historical and Contemporary Perspective. Essays in Memory of G. H. C. Macgregor* (Oxford, 1965), 133-148.

Jacob, E. "Possibilités et limites d'une Théologie biblique," *Revue d'Histoire et de Philosophie Religieuses* 46 (1966), 116-130.

Jansen, John F. "The Biblical Theology of Gerhardus Vos," *Princeton Seminary Bulletin* 66 (1974), 23-34.

Jasper, F. N. "The Relation of the Old Testament to the New," *Expository Times* 78 (1967/68), 228-232, 267-270.

Jaspers, K. *R. Bultmann. Die Frage der Entmythologisierung.* Munich, 1954.

———. *Philosophical Faith and Revelation.* New York, 1967.

———, and R. Bultmann. *Myth and Christianity.* New York, 1958.

Jeremias, J. *The Problem of the Historical Jesus.* Philadelphia, 1964.

———. *The Eucharistic Words of Jesus.* 2nd ed. London, 1966.

———. *Neutestamentliche Theologie. Erster Teil. Die Verkündigung Jesu.* Gütersloh, 1971. Trans. *New Testament Theology: The Proclamation of Jesus.* New York, 1971.

———. *Der Schlüssel zur Theologie des Apostels Paulus.* Gütersloh, 1971.

Jervell, J. *Luke and the People of God.* Minneapolis, 1972.

Kaftan, J. *Neutestamentliche Theologie, Im Abriss dargestellt.* Berlin, 1927.

Kähler, M. "Biblische Theologie," *Realencyklopädie für protestantische Theologie und Kirche,* 3. Aufl. (Leipzig, 1897), 192-200.

———. *The So-Called Historical Jesus and the Historical Biblical Christ.* Philadelphia, 1964.

Kaiser, W. C. "The Centre of Old Testament Theology: The Promise," *Themelios* 10 (1974), 1-10.

Kalin, E. "The Inspired Community: A Glance at Canon History," *Concordia Theological Monthly* 42 (1971), 541-549.

Käsemann, E. "The Canon of the NT and the Unity of the Church," *Essays on NT Themes* (London, 1964), 95-107.

———. *NT Questions of Today.* London, 1969.

———, ed. *Das Neuen Testament als Kanon.* Göttingen, 1970.

———. "The Problem of a New Testament Theology," *NTS* 19 (1973), 235-245.

———. *Perspectives on Paul.* Philadelphia, 1971.

Keck, L. E. "Problems of New Testament Theology. A Critique of Alan Richardson's *An Introduction to New Testament Theology,*" *Novum Testamentum* 7 (1964), 217-241.

Kelsey, D. H. *The Uses of Scripture in Recent Theology.* Philadelphia, 1975.

Kistemaker, S. J. "Current Problems and Projects in NT Research," *Journal of the Evangelical Theological Society* 18 (1975), 17-28.

Klein, G. *Rekonstruktion und Interpretation. Gesammelte Aufsätze zum Neuen Testament.* Göttingen, 1969.

———. " 'Reich Gottes' als biblischer Zentralbegriff," *EvTh* 30 (1970), 642-670.

———. "Bibel und Heilsgeschichte. Die Fragwürdigkeit einer Idee," *ZNW* 62 (1971), 1-47.

Knudsen, R. H. *Theology in the New Testament. A Basis for Christian Faith.* Los Angeles, 1964.

Koester, H. "The Historical Jesus: Some Comments and Thoughts on Norman Perrin's *Rediscovering the Teaching of Jesus," Christology and a Modern Pilgrimage*, ed. H. D. Betz (Philadelphia, 1971), 123-136.

Kraeling, E. G. "Toward a Biblical Theology," *The OT Since the Reformation* (New York, 1955), 210-225.

Kraus, H.-J. *Geschichte der historisch-kritischen Erforschung des AT.* 2nd ed. Neukirchen-Vluyn, 1969.

———. *Die Biblische Theologie. Ihre Geschichte und Problematik.* Neukirchen-Vluyn, 1970.

Krentz, E. *The Historical-Critical Method.* Philadelphia, 1975.

Krüger, Gustav. *Das Dogma vom Neuen Testament. Programm der Universität Giessen.* Giessen, 1896.

Kümmel, A. "Mitte des Neuen Testaments," *Mélanges offerts au Franz Leenhardt L'Évangile Hier et Aujourd'hui* (Geneva, 1968), 71-85.

Kümmel, W. G. *Die Theologie des Neuen Testaments nach seinen Hauptzeugen Jesus, Paulus, Johannes.* Göttingen, 1969. Trans. *The Theology of the New Testament According to Its Major Witnesses: Jesus-Paul-John.* Nashville, 1973.

———. *Das Neue Testament im 20. Jahrhundert.* Stuttgart, 1970.

———. *The New Testament: The History of the Investigation of its Problems.* Nashville, 1972.

———. "Heilsgeschichte im Neuen Testament?" *Neues Testament und Kirche: Für Rudolf Schnackenburg*, ed. J. Gnilka (Freiburg, 1974), 434-457.

———. "Current Theological Accusations Against Luke," *Andover Newton Quarterly* 16 (1975), 131-145.

Künneth, W. "Zur Frage nach der Mitte der Schrift," *Dank an Paul Althaus* (Gütersloh, 1958), 121-140.

———. *Ostergedanken.* Lahr, 1963.

Kuske, M. *Das AT als Buch von Christus.* Göttingen, 1971.

Kuss, O. *Theologie des Neuen Testaments.* 2nd ed. Regensburg, 1963.

———. "Exegese und Theologie des Neuen Testaments als Basis und Ärgernis jeder nachneutestamentlichen Theologie," *Münster Theologische Zeitschrift* 21 (1970), 181-215.

Ladd, G. E. "Biblical Theology, History, and Revelation," *Review and Expository* 54 (1957), 195-204.

———. "Eschatology und the Unity of New Testament Theology," *Expository Times* 68 (1956/57), 268-273.

———. "Unity and Variety in New Testament Faith," *Christianity Today* 10 (1965), 21-24, 197-200.

———. "The Search for Perspective," *Interpretation* 25 (1971), 41-62.

———. *The New Testament and Criticism*. Grand Rapids, Mich., 1967.

———. *Jesus and the Kingdom. The Eschatology of Biblical Realism*. 2nd ed. Waco, Texas, 1970.

———. *A Theology of the New Testament*. Grand Rapids, Mich., 1974.

Lampe, G. W. H. and J. J. Woolcombe. *Essays on Typology*. London, 1957.

Landes, G. M. "Biblical Exegesis in Crisis: What is the Exegetical Task in a Theological Context?" *Union Seminary Quarterly Review* 26 (1971), 273-298.

Lang, F. "Christuszeugnis und Biblische Theologie Alten und Neuen Testaments in der Sicht heutiger Exegese," *EvTh* 29 (1969), 523-534.

Larcher, C. *L'Actualite chretienne de l'Ancien Testament d'apres le Nouveau Testament*. Paris, 1962.

Leary, A. P. "Biblical Theology and History," *Church Quarterly Review* 157 (1956), 402-414.

Lehman, C. R. *Biblical Theology, Vol. 2: New Testament*. Scottsdale, Pa., 1974.

Leith, John H. "The Bible and Theology," *Interpretation* 30 (1976), 227-241.

Lemonnyer, R. P. *Théologie du Nouveau Testament*. Paris, 1928. Trans. *The Theology of the New Testament*. London, 1930.

Lindsey, J. "Biblical Theology," *International Standard Bible Encyclopedia* (1943), I, 469-472.

Lohfink. N. *The Christian Meaning of the OT*. Milwaukee, 1968.

Lohse, E. *Grundriss der neutestamentlichen Theologie*. Stuttgart, 1974.

———. "Die Einheit des Neuen Testaments als theologisches Problem. Überlegungen zur Aufgabe einer Theologie des Neuen Testaments," *EvTh* 35 (1975), 139-154.

Longenecker, R. N. "NT Theology," *Zondervan Pictorial Encyclopedia of the Bible IV* (Grand Rapids, Mich., 1975), 428-434.

Lönning, Inge. *"Kanon im Kanon."* Zum dogmatischen Grundlagenproblem des neutestamentlichen Kanons. Munich, 1972.

Lorenz, F. *Streit um Jesus*. Munich, 1969.

Luz, Ulrich. *"Theologia crucis* als Mitte der Theologie im Neuen Testament," *EvTh* 34 (1974), 116-141.

Lymann, M. E. "The Unity of the Bible," *JBR* 14 (1946), 5-12.

Lyonnet, S. "De notione et momento Theologiae Biblicae," *Verbum Domini* 34 (1956), 142-153.

MacKenzie, R. A. F. "The Concept of Biblical Theology," *Proceedings of the Catholic Theological Society of America* 10 (1955), 48-66.

McMorrow, L. "Encyclopedia of Biblical Theology," *Irish Theological Quarterly* 38 (1971), 168-174.

MacRae, G. "New Testament Theology. Some Problems and Principles," *Scripture* 16 (1964), 97-106.

Maier, G. "Kanon im Kanon—oder die ganze Schrift?" *Theologische Beiträge* 3 (1972), 21-31.

———. *Das Ende der historisch-kritischen Methode.* 2nd ed. Wuppertal, 1975. Trans. *The End of the Historical-Critical Method.* St. Louis, 1977.

Marrow, S. B. "Biblical Theology," *New Catholic Encounter* 2 (1967), 545-550.

Marsh, J. "The Theology of the New Testament," *Peake's Commentary of the Bible* (2nd ed., London, 1962).

Mathers, D. "Biblical and Systematic Theology," *Canadian Journal of Theology* 5 (1959), 15-24.

Mauser, U. *Gottesbild und Menschwerdung. Eine Untersuchung zur Einheit des Alten und Neuen Testaments.* Tübingen, 1971.

Meinertz, M. *Theologie des Neuen Testamentes.* 2 vols. Bonn, 1950.

———. "Randglossen zu meiner Theologie des Neuen Testamentes," *Theologische Quartalschrift* 132 (1952), 411-431.

———. "Sinn und Bedeutung der neutestamentlichen Theologie," *Münchener Theologische Zeitschrift* 5 (1954), 159-170.

Merk, O. *Biblische Theologie des Neuen Testament in ihrer Anfangszeit.* Marburg, 1972.

Mildenberger, F. "Die Gegenläufigkeit von historischer Methode und kirchlicher Anwendung als Problem der Bibelauslegung," *Theologische Beiträge* 3 (1972), 57-64.

———. "Unity, Truth, and Validity of the Bible," *Interpretation* 29 (1975), 391-405.

Minear, P. S. "Wanted: a Biblical Theology," *Theology Today* 1 (1944), 47-58.

Morgan, R. "Let's Be Honest about the Canon: A Plea to Reconsider a Question the Reformers Failed to Answer," *Christian Century* 84 (1967), 717-719.

———. *The Nature of New Testament Theology. The Contribution of William Wrede and Adolf Schlatter.* London, 1973.

Munck, J. "Pauline Research Since Schweitzer," *The Bible in Modern Scholarship,* pp. 166-177.

Murphy, R. E. "The Relationship Between the Testaments," *CBQ* 26 (1964), 349-359.

———. *How Does the Christian Confront the OT?* New York, 1967.

———. "Christian Understanding of the Old Testament," *Theology Digest* 18 (1970), 321-332.

Mussner, F. "Die Mitte des Evangeliums in neutestamentlicher

Sicht," *Catholica* 15 (1961), 271-292.

———. "'Evangelium' und 'Mitte des Evangeliums'. Ein Beitrag zur Kontroverstheologie," *Gott in Welt. Festschrift für K. Rahner* (Freiburg, 1964), I, 492-514.

———. "NT Theology: III Johannine Theology," *Sacramentum Mundi* 4 (1968), 227-231.

———. "Die Einheit von Altem und Neuem Testament," *Internationale Katholische Zeitschrift* 3 (1974), 544-555.

Neil, W. "The Unity of the Bible," *The New Testament in Historical and Contemporary Perspective. Essays in Memory of G. H. C. Macgregor* (Oxford, 1965), 237-259.

Neill, S. *The Interpretation of the New Testament 1861-1961.* London, 1964.

———. *Jesus Through Many Eyes. Introduction to the Theology of the New Testament.* Nashville, 1976.

Newport, J. "New Developments in New Testament Theology," *Review and Expositor* 49 (1952), 41-56.

Nicol, I. G. "Event and Interpretation. Oscar Cullmann's Conception of Salvation History," *Theology* 77 (1974), 14-21.

Nikolainen, A. T. "Om planläggningens problem i en titalframställning av Nya testaments teologi" [On the problem of Devising the Plan for a Total Presentation of the Theology of the New Testament], *Svensk Exeg Arsbok* 37-38 (1972-73), 310-319.

———. *Uuden testamentin tulkinta ja tutkimus.* Porvoo-Helsinki, 1971.

Nineham, D. E., ed. *The Church's Use of the Bible.* London, 1963.

Nuland, J. v. "Sémantique et théologie biblique Bijdragen," *Tijdschrift voor Filosofie en Theologie* 30 (1969), 140-153.

O'Doherty, E. "The Unity of the Bible," *The Bible Today* 1 (1962), 53-57.

Ohlig, K.-H. *Woher nimmt die Bibel ihre Autorität? Zum Verhältnis von Schriftkanon, Kirche und Jesus.* Düsseldorf, 1970.

Pannenberg, W. *Basic Questions in Theology.* 2 vols. Philadelphia, 1970-71.

———. "Biblische Theologie," *Theologie als Wissenschaft* (1973), 384-392.

Perrin, N. "The Challenge of New Testament Theology Today," *New Testament Issues,* ed. R. A. Batey (New York/London, 1970, 15-34.

———. *The New Testament: An Introduction.* New York, 1974.

———. *A Modern Pilgrimage in New Testament Christology.* New York, 1974.

———. *Jesus and the Language of the Kingdom.* New York, 1976.

———. "Jesus and the Theology of the New Testament," read

at the Catholic Biblical Association, Denver, Colo., Aug. 18-21, 1975.

Peters, James. "Salvation History as a Model for Theological Thought," *Scottish Journal of Theology* 23 (1970), 1-12.

Peters, T. "The Use of Analogy in Historical Method," *CBQ* 35 (1973), 473-482.

Phythian-Adams, W. J. T. "The Foundation of Biblical Theology," *Church Quarterly Review* 135 (1942/43), 1-24.

———. "Biblical Theology in the Life of the Church," *Church Quarterly Review* 135 (1942/43), 141-174; 136 (1943/44), 1-35.

Piper, O. A. "Biblical Theology and Systematic Theology," *Journal of Bible and Religion* 25 (1957), 106-111.

———. "Christology and History," *Theology Today* 19 (1962), 333.

Prat, F. *The Theology of St. Paul, I-II.* Westminster, Md., 1952.

Prenter, R. "Die systematische Theologie und das Problem der Bibelauslegung," *ThLZ* 81 (1956), 577-586.

Quesnell, Q. *This Good News. An Introduction to the Catholic Theology of the New Testament.* London, 1963.

Rad, G. v. "Antwort auf Conzelmanns Fragen," *EvTh* 24 (1964), 388-394.

———. "Offene Fragen im Umkreis einer Theologie des AT," *ThLZ* 88 (1963), 409.

Rahner, K. "Biblische Theologie und Dogmatik in ihrem wechselseitigen Verhältnis," *Lexikon für Theologie und Kirche* (Freiburg, 1958), II, 449-451.

———. "Theology in the NT," *Theological Investigations* V (1966), 23-41.

———. "Bible, Biblical Theology," *Sacramentum Mundi,* I (London, 1968), 171-176.

Ramlot, M.-L. "Une décade de théologie biblique," *Revue Thomiste* 64 (1964), 65-96.

Reicke, B. "Einheitlichkeit oder verschiedene 'Lehrbegriffe' in der neutestamentlichen Theologie," *Theologische Zeitschrift* 9 (1953), 401-415.

Richardson, A. "The Nature of Biblical Theology," *Theology* 39 (1939), 166-176.

———. "Historical Theology and Biblical Theology," *Canadian Journal of Theology* 1 (1955), 156-157.

———. *An Introduction to the Theology of the New Testament.* London, 1958.

———. "Second Thoughts: Present Issues in New Testament Theology," *Expository Times* 75 (1963/64), 109-113.

———. "What is New Testament Theology?" *Studia Evangelica* VI (1973), 455-465.

Ridderbos, N. H. *Paul and Jesus.* Grand Rapids, Mich., 1957.

———. "Typologie," *Vox Theologica* 31 (1960/61), 149-159.

———. *Paul: An Outline of His Theology*. Grand Rapids, Mich., 1975.

Riesenfeld, H. "Reflections on the Unity of the New Testament," *Religion* 3 (1973), 35-51.

Robertson, Palmer. "The Outlook for Biblical Theology," *Toward a Theology for the Future*, eds. D. F. Wells and C. H. Pinnock (Carol Stream, Ill., 1971), 65-91.

Robinson, J. M. *A New Quest of the Historical Jesus*. SBT 25; London, 1959.

———, and J. B. Cobb, Jr. *The Later Heidegger and Theology*. New York, 1963.

———, and J. B. Cobb, Jr. *Theology in History*. New York, 1967.

———. *World in Modern Theology and in New Testament Theology*, *Soli Deo Gloria* (*Festschrift für W. C. Robinson, Sr.*). Richmond, Va., 1968.

———, and H. Koester. *Trajectories Through Early Christianity*. New York, 1970.

———. "Die Zukunft der Neutestamentlichen Theologie," *Neues Testament und christliche Existenz: Festschrift für Herbert Braun zum 70. Geburtstag am 4. Mai 1973*, ed. Hans Dieter Betz and Luise Schottroff (Tübingen, 1973), 387-400. Trans. "The Future of New Testament Theology," *Religious Study Review* 2 (1976), 17-23.

Rowley, H. H. *The Unity of the Bible*. London, 1953.

Rust, Eric C. *Salvation History*. Richmond, 1962.

Ryrie, C. C. *Biblical Theology of the New Testament*. Chicago, 1959.

Sabourin, L. "Notion and Function of Biblical Theology," *Sin, Redemption, and Sacrifice* (Rome, 1970), xiii-xvi.

Sanders, J. N. *Torah and Canon*. 2nd ed. Philadelphia, 1974.

———. "Torah and Christ," *Interpretation* 29 (1975), 372-390.

Sauter, Gerhard. *Vor einem neuen Methodenstreit in der Theologie?* (Theologische Existenz heute 164). Munich, 1970.

———, ed. *Theologie als Wissenschaft*. Munich, 1971.

Scheffczyk, L. "Biblische und dogmatische Theologie," *Trierer Theologische Zeitschrift* 67 (1958), 193-209.

Schelkle, K. H. "Was bedeutet 'Theologie des Neuen Testaments?'," ed. J. B. Bauer, *Evangelienforschung. Ausgew. Aufsätze deutscher Exegeten* (Graz/Wien/Köln, 1968), 299-312.

———. "NT Theology: II. Pauline Theology," *Sacramentum Mundi* 4 (1968), 220-227.

———. *Theologie des Neuen Testaments*, 4 vols. Düsseldorf, 1968-74. Trans. *Theology of the New Testament*, 4 vols. Collegeville, Minn., 1971-77.

Schlatter, A. *Der Glaube im Neuen Testament. Eine Untersuchung zur neutestamentliche Theologie*. Darmstadt, 1885.

———. "Atheistische Methoden in der Theologie," *Zur Theologie des Neuen Testaments und zur Dogmatik* (Munich, 1969), 134-150.

———. *Die Theologie des Neuen Testaments und die Dogmatik* (Beiträge zur Förderung christlicher Theologie 13, 2). Gütersloh, 1909.

———. *Die Theologie des Neuen Testaments. Bd. 1: Das Wort Jesu, Bd. 2: Die Lehre der Apostel.* Calw-Stuttgart, 1909-1910.

Schlier, Heinrich. "The Meaning and Function of the New Testament," *Dogmatic vs. Biblical Theology*, ed. H. Vorgrimler (Baltimore, 1964), 26-90.

———. *Besinnung auf das Neue Testament.* Freiburg, 1964.

———. *Die Zeit der Kirche.* 2nd ed. Freiburg, 1958.

Schmid, H. H. "Schöpfung, Gerechtigkeit und Heil, 'Schöpfungstheologie' als Gesamthorizont biblischer Theologie," *ZThK* 70 (1973), 1-19.

Schmidt, L. "Die Einheit zwischen Altem und Neuem Testament im Streit zwischen Friedrich Baumgärtel und Gerhard von Rad," *EvTh* 35 (1975), 119-139.

Schnackenburg, R. *Neutestamentliche Theologie. Der Stand der Forschung.* Munich, 1963. 2nd ed. Munich, 1965. Trans. *New Testament Theology Today.* London, 1963.

———. "Der Stand der neutestamentlichen Theologie," *Diskussion über die Bibel*, ed. L. Klein (Mainz, 1963), 30-46. Trans. "The Position of the Theology of the New Testament," *The Bible in a New Age*, ed. L. Klein (London, 1965), 35-49.

Scholder, K. *Ursprünge und Probleme der Bibelkritik in 17. Jahrhundert. Ein Beitrag zur Entstehung der historisch-kritischen Theologie.* Munich, 1966.

Schrage, Wolfgang. "Die Frage nach der Mitte und dem Kanon im Kanon des Neuen Testaments in der neueren Diskussion," *Rechtfertigung. Festschrift für E. Käsemann zum 70. Geburtstag*, eds. J. Friedrich, W. Pöhlmann and P. Stuhlmacher (Tübingen, 1976), 415-442.

Schubert, K. "Geschichte und Heilsgeschichte," *Kairos* 15 (1973), 89-101.

Schulz, S. *Die Stunde der Botschaft: Einführung in die Theologie der vier Evangelisten.* Hamburg, 1967.

Schwarzwäller, K. *Das AT in Christus.* Zürich, 1966.

———. "Das Verhältnis Altes Testament — Neues Testament im Lichte der gegenwärtigen Bestimmungen," *EvTh* 29 (1969), 281-307.

Schweizer, E. *Jesus Christus im vielfältigen Zeugnis des Neuen Testaments.* Siebenstern/Taschenbuch, 1968.

———. "Kanon?" *EvTh* 31 (1971), 339-357.

Scott, E. F. "The Present Position of New Testament Theology," *Harvard Theological Review* 6 (1913), 60-75.

Seebass, H. "Der Beitrag des Alten Testaments zum Entwurf einer biblischen Theologie," *Word und Dienst* 8 (1965), 20-41.

———. *Biblische Hermeneutik.* Stuttgart, 1974.

Sevenster, J. N. *De boodschap van het Nieuwe Testament.* Assen, 1939.

Sidel, S. "Das Alte und das NT, Ihre Verschiedenheit und Einheit," *Tübinger Praktische Quartalschrift* 119 (1970), 314-324.

Smart, J. D. *The Interpretation of Scripture.* Philadelphia, 1961.

———. *The Strange Silence of the Bible in the Church.* London, 1970.

Smend, R. "Johann Philipp Gablers Begründung der biblischen Theologie," *EvTh* 22 (1962), 345-357.

———. *Die Mitte des Alten Testaments.* Zürich, 1970.

Sontag, F. "Philosophy and Biblical Theology: A Prologue," *Religion in Life* 33 (1964), 224-237.

Spicq, C. "L'avènement de la théologie biblique," *Revue de Sciences Philosophiques et Théologiques* 35 (1951), 561-574.

———. "Nouvelles réflexions sur la théologie biblique," *Revue des Sciences Philosophiques et Théologiques* 42 (1958), 209-219.

———. "Bulletin de théologie biblique du Nouveau Testament," *Freiburger Zeitschrift für Philosophie und Theologie* 6 (1959), 50-61.

———. "The Work of Biblical Theology," *Theology Digest* 7 (1959), 29-34.

Stachel, G. *Die neue Hermeneutik. Ein Überblick.* Munich, 1968.

Stagg, F. *New Testament Theology.* Nashville, 1962.

Stanley, D. M. "Towards a Biblical Theology of the New Testament. Modern Trends in Catholic Scriptural Scholarship," *Contemporary Developments in Theology* (West Hartford, 1959), 267-281.

———, and R. E. Brown. "Aspects of New Testament Thought," *The Jerome Biblical Commentary,* eds. R. E. Brown, J. A. Fitzmyer, R. E. Murphy (Englewood Cliffs, N.J., 1968), 768-799.

Stauffer, E. *Die Theologie des Neuen Testaments.* Stuttgart/Berlin, 1941. Trans. *New Testament Theology.* London, 1955.

———. "Prinzipienfragen der neutestamentlichen Theologie," *Evangelische-lutherische Kirchenzeitung* 4 (1950), 327-329.

Stek, J. H. "Biblical Typology Yesterday and Today," *Calvin Theological Journal* 5 (1970), 133-162.

Stendahl, K. "Biblical Theology, Contemporary," *IDB,* I, 418-432.

———. "Method in the Study of Biblical Theology," *The Bible in Modern Scholarship. Papers read at the 100th Meeting of the Society of Biblical Literature,* ed. J. P. Hyatt (Nashville,

1965), 196-209.

Stephenson, A. A. "Biblical Theology and Scholastic Theology," *Scripture and Ecumenism. Protestant, Catholic, Orthodox,* ed. L. Swindler (Pittsburgh, 1965), 151-186.

Stevens, G. B. *The Theology of the New Testament.* Edinburgh, 1901. 2nd ed. 1906.

Stewart, J. S. "On a Neglected Emphasis in New Testament Theology," *Scottish Journal of Theology* 4 (1951), 292-301.

Stock, A. *Einheit des Neuen Testaments. Eröterung hermeneutischer Grundpositionen der heutigen Theologie.* Zurich/Einsiedeln/Köln, 1969.

Strecker, G. "Das Problem der Theologie des Neuen Testaments," *PTNT,* 1-31.

———, ed. *Das Problem der Theologie des Neuen Testaments.* Darmstadt, 1975.

Stuhlmacher, Peter. *Schriftauslegung auf dem Wege zur biblischen Theologie.* Göttingen, 1975.

Talbert, C. H. *Literary Patterns, Theological Themes and the Genre of Luke-Acts.* Missoula, 1974.

———. "Shifting Sands: The Recent Study of the Gospel of Luke," *Interpretation* 30 (1976), 381-395.

Taylor, V. "Review of A. Richardson, *An Introduction to the Theology of the New Testament,*" *Expository Times* 70 (1958/59), 168.

Taylor, W. "Biblical Theology," *Zondervan Pictorial Encyclopedia of the Bible* (1975), 593-600.

Thornhill, J. "Towards an Integral Theology," *Theological Studies* 24 (1963), 264-277.

Trilling, W. *Vielfalt und Einheit im Neuen Testament. Zur Exegese und Verkündigung des Neuen Testaments.* Einsiedeln/Köln, 1968.

Troeltsch, E. "Über historische und dogmatische Methode," *Gesammelte Studien II* (Tübingen, 1913), reprinted in *Theologie als Wissenschaft,* ed. G. Sauter (Munich, 1971), 105-127.

Van Ruler, A. A. *The Christian Church and the OT,* trans G. W. Bromiley. Grand Rapids, Mich., 1971.

Vawter, B. "Johannine Theology," *The Jerome Biblical Commentary,* eds. R. E. Brown, J. A. Fitzmyer, R. E. Murphy (Englewood Cliffs, N.J., 1968), 825-839.

Verhoef, P. A. "Some Notes on Typological Exegesis," *New Light on Some OT Problems* (Praetoria, 1962), 58-63.

———. "Some Thoughts on the Present-Day Situation in Biblical Theology," *Westminster Theological Journal* 33 (1970), 1-19.

———. "The Relationship Between the Old and New Testaments," *New Perspectives on the Old Testament,* ed. J. B. Payne (Waco/London, 1970), 280-303.

Viard, A. "Bulletin de théologie biblique," *Revue des Sciences Philosophiques et Théologiques* 42 (1958), 324-348; 43 (1959), 301-324.

Vicary, D. R. "Liberalism, Biblical Criticism, and Biblical Theology," *Anglican Theological Review* 34 (1950), 114-121.

Vischer, W. *Das Christuszeugnis des AT*. Zurich, 1934. Trans. *The Witness of the OT to Christ*. London, 1949.

———. *Die Bedeutung des AT für das christliche Leben*. Zurich, 1947.

———. "La methode de l'exegese biblique," *Revue de theologie et de philosophie* 10 (1960), 109-123.

Vögtle, A. "New Testament Theology: I. Data and Methods," *Sacramentum Mundi,* ed. K. Rahner (London, 1969), IV, 216-220.

———. "Progress and Problems in New Testament Exegesis," *Dogmatic versus Biblical Theology* (London, 1964), 67-86.

———. "Kirche und Schriftprinzip nach dem Neuen Testament," *Bibel und Leben* 12 (1971), 153-162.

Von Harnack, A. *Marcion, Das Evangelium vom fremden Gott*. 2nd ed. Leipzig, 1924.

Vorgrimler, H., ed. *Dogmatic versus Biblical Theology*. London, 1964.

Vos, G. *Biblical Theology. Old and New Testament*. Grand Rapids, Mich., 1948.

Wallace, D. H. "Biblical Theology: Past and Future," *Theologische Zeitschrift* 19 (1963), 88-105.

———. "Historicism and Biblical Theology," *Studia Evangelica* 3 (1964), 223-227.

Walther, J. A. "The Significance of Methodology for Biblical Theology," *Perspective* 10 (1969), 217-233.

Warnach, V. "Gedanken zur neutestamentlichen Theologie," *Gloria Dei* 7 (1952/53), 65-75.

———. *Agape. Die Liebe als Grundmotif der neutestamentlichen Theologie*. Düsseldorf, 1951.

Watson, P. S. "The Nature and Function of Biblical Theology," *Expository Times* 73 (1961/62), 195-200.

Weidner, F. *Biblical Theology of the New Testament*. 2 vols. Chicago/London, 1891.

Weinel, H. *Biblische Theologie des Neuen Testaments*. Tübingen, 1911; 4th ed., 1928.

Weiss, B. *Lehrbuch der Biblischen Theologie des Neuen Testaments*. Berlin, 1868; 7th ed. Stuttgart/Berlin, 1903.

Weiss, J. *Die Predigt Jesu vom Reich Gottes*. Göttingen, 1892; 2nd ed., 1900.

Wenham, J. *Christ and the Bible*. Chicago, 1972.

Westermann, C. *The OT and Jesus Christ*. Minneapolis, 1970.

———. "The Way of Promise through the OT," *OTCF*, 200-224.

Wilckens, U. "Über die Bedeutung historischer Kritik in der Bibelexegese," *Was heisst Auslegung der Heiligen Schrift?* (Regensburg, 1966), 85ff.

Wildberger, H. "Auf dem Wege zu einer biblischen Theologie," *EvTh* 19 (1959), 70-90.

Wilder, A. N. "New Testament Theology in Transition," *The Study of the Bible Today and Tomorrow,* ed. H. R. Willoughby (Chicago, 1947), 419-436.

Wink, W. *The Bible in Human Transformation: Toward a New Paradigm for Biblical Study.* Philadelphia, 1973.

Wolff, Hans Walter, ed. *Probleme biblischer Theologie. Gerhard von Rad zum 70. Geburtstag.* Munich, 1971.

Wood, H. "The Present Position of New Testament Theology: Retrospect and Prospect," *NTS* 4 (1957/58), 169-182.

Wrede, W. "Über Aufgabe und Methode der sogenannten Neutestamentlichen Theologie" (1897), *PTNT,* 81-154. Trans. "The Task and Methods of New Testament Theology," by R. Morgan, *The Nature of New Testament Theology* (SBT II/25; London, 1973), 68-116.

———. *Paulus.* Tübingen, 1904. Trans. *Paul.* London, 1908.

Wright, G. E. "Interpreting the New Testament," *Theology Today* 3 (1947), 176-191.

Zahn, T. *Grundriss der Neutestamentlichen Theologie.* Leipzig, 1928.

Zyl, A. H. van. "The Relation Between Old Testament and New Testament," *Hermeneutica* (1970), 9-22.

Index of Names

Index of Subjects